Marilyn

Marilyn

The Classic by

Norman Mailer

pictures by
the world's foremost
photographers

the photographers

Eve Arnold

Richard Avedon

George Barris

Cecil Beaton

John Bryson

Cornell Capa

Bruce Davidson

André de Dienes

Elliott Erwitt

Milton H. Greene

Ernst Haas

Philippe Halsman

Bob Henriques

Tom Kelley

Douglas Kirkland

Lee Lockwood

Inge Morath

Arnold Newman

Lawrence Schiller

Sam Shaw

Bert Stern

John Vachon

Bob Willoughby

William Read Woodfield

PRODUCED BY Lawrence Schiller

DESIGNED BY Allen Hurlburt

PUBLISHED BY **Galahad Books**

Text by Norman Mailer

Photographs previously copyrighted by: Eve Arnold, Richard
Avedon, George Barris, Cecil Beaton, John Bryson, Cornell
Capa, Bruce Davidson, André de Dienes, Elliott Erwitt, Milton H.
Greene, Ernst Haas, Philippe Halsman, Bob Henriques, Tom Kelley,
Douglas Kirkland, Lee Lockwood, Inge Morath, Arnold Newman,
Lawrence Schiller, Sam Shaw, Bert Stern, John Vachon, Bob
Willoughby, William Read Woodfield, and Alskog, Inc. All
rights reserved.

The facts in this book have been based in the main on the book
Norma Jean: The Life of Marilyn Monroe by Fred Lawrence Guiles
copyright © 1967, 1972, 1973 by Norman Rosten and reprinted
by permission of Harold Ober Associates, Inc., and Norman Rosten.

"The Legend and the Truth" copyright © 1972 by Alskog, Inc.

Copyright © 1973 by Alskog, Inc. and Norman Mailer.

Published in 1988 by
Galahad Books
A division of LDAP, Inc.
166 Fifth Avenue
New York, NY 10010

By arrangement with The Putnam Publishing Group.

Library of Congress Catalog Card Number: 73-6899

ISBN: 0-88365-731-7

Printed in Italy.

A Note on the Photographs

This work was conceived by Larry Schiller, who became involved in curious fashion with the life of Marilyn Monroe, since he was one of three photographers present (not two months before her death) on the day she did her nude swimming scene in *Something's Got to Give*. In the weeks that followed, he was to oversee the release of those nude pictures to the world. Indeed, he even saw Marilyn on the morning of her last day. Years later, still convinced she was the most exciting film personality ever to pose for a still camera, it occurred to him that there had been no retrospective presentation of her superb if less heralded skill as a photographer's model, no compendium of her performance before fashion photographers, news photographers, portraitists, photo journalists, and illustrators, and therefore no revelation of the facets of her shifting personality which (like that diamond who proved to be a girl's best friend) was never about to reflect the same light twice.

So he set out to arrange a collaboration of the talents of twenty-four major photographers who had worked with Marilyn Monroe. Out of a study of some sixteen thousand photographs, an exhibition was put together called "MARILYN MONROE—The Legend and the Truth," and proved so successful that a book was planned. In the course of such arrangements, an author was invited, myself. At the end of this book, there are a series of acknowledgments and a passing description of how my share of the project managed to expand from twenty-five thousand words to ninety, but here what may be emphasized is that the collaboration between Schiller and myself is not intended to be directly chronological or even particularly hand in glove. Indeed, some photographs, in order to contribute to the visual flow of the book, will even appear out of chronological sequence. To aid the reader, therefore, pictures are dated unless they fit closely in period to the prose beside them. While on many a page a portrait has then been placed to illumine some remarks on the accompanying page, others will contrast in time or in mood. For Marilyn, so soon as one attempts to classify her too neatly, goes to phosphorescence and dust. She is an actress, and her experiences can reappear at odd moments across the years. A particular photo can portray a mood she may have felt a decade earlier. Another will reveal anticipation of pleasures or sorrows yet to come. Let us leave it that we have two chronologies here, one in photography, another in words. If successful, they will come together in the shape of an elusive search for that most mercurial charm— the identity of a lovely if seldom simple woman.

Contents

I. A NOVEL BIOGRAPHY

So we think of Marilyn who was every man's love affair with America, Marilyn Monroe who was blonde and beautiful and had a sweet little rinky-dink of a voice and all the cleanliness of all the clean American backyards. She was our angel, the sweet angel of sex, and the sugar of sex came up from her like a resonance of sound in the clearest grain of a violin. Across five continents the men who knew the most about love would covet her, and the classical pimples of the adolescent working his first gas pump would also pump for her, since Marilyn was deliverance, a very Stradivarius of sex, so gorgeous, forgiving, humorous, compliant and tender that even the most mediocre musician would relax his lack of art in the dissolving magic of her violin. "Divine love always has met and always will meet every human need," was the sentiment she offered from the works of Mary Baker Eddy as "my prayer for you always" (to the man who may have been her first illicit lover), and if we change *love* to *sex*, we have the subtext in the promise. "Marilyn Monroe's sex," said the smile of the young star, "will meet every human need." She gave the feeling that if you made love to her, why then how could you not move more easily into sweets and the purchase of the full promise of future sweets, move into tender heavens where your flesh would be restored. She would ask no price. She was not the dark contract of those passionate brunette depths that speak of blood, vows taken for life, and the furies of vengeance if you are untrue to the depth of passion, no, Marilyn suggested sex might be difficult and dangerous with others, but ice cream with her. If your taste combined with her taste, how nice, how sweet would be that tender dream of flesh there to share.

In her early career, in the time of *Asphalt Jun-gle* when the sexual immanence of her face came up on the screen like a sweet peach bursting before one's eyes, she looked then like a new love ready and waiting between the sheets in the unexpected clean breath of a rare sexy morning, looked like she'd stepped fully clothed out of a chocolate box for Valentine's Day, so desirable as to fulfill each of the letters in that favorite word of the publicity flack, *curvaceous*, so curvaceous and yet without menace as to turn one's fingertips into ten happy prowlers. Sex was, yes, ice cream to her. "Take me," said her smile. "I'm easy. I'm happy. I'm an angel of sex, you bet."

What a jolt to the dream life of the nation that the angel died of an overdose. Whether calculated suicide by barbiturates or accidental suicide by losing count of how many barbiturates she had already taken, or an end even more sinister, no one was able to say. Her death was covered over with ambiguity even as Hemingway's was exploded into horror, and as the deaths and spiritual disasters of the decade of the Sixties came one by one to American Kings and Queens, as Jack Kennedy was killed, and Bobby, and Martin Luther King, as Jackie Kennedy married Aristotle Onassis and Teddy Kennedy went off the bridge at Chappaquiddick, so the decade that began with Hemingway as the monarch of American arts ended with Andy Warhol as its regent, and the ghost of Marilyn's death gave a lavender edge to that dramatic American design of the Sixties which seemed in retrospect to have done nothing so much as to bring Richard Nixon to the threshold of imperial power. "Romance is a nonsense bet," said the jolt in the electric shock, and so began that long decade of the Sixties which ended with television living like an inchworm on the aesthetic gut of the drug-deadened American belly.

In what a light does that leave the last angel of the cinema! She was never for TV. She preferred a theatre and those hundreds of bodies in the dark, those wandering lights on the screen when the luminous life of her face grew ten feet tall. It was possible she knew better than anyone that she was the last of the myths to thrive in the long evening of the American dream—she had been born, after all, in the year Valentino died, and his footprints in the forecourt at Grauman's Chinese Theatre were the only ones that fit her feet. She was one of the last of cinema's aristocrats and may not have wanted to be examined, then *ingested*, in the neighborly reductive dimensions of America's living room. No, she belonged to the occult church of the film, and the last covens of Hollywood. She might be as modest in her voice and as soft in her flesh as the girl next door, but she was nonetheless larger than life up on the screen. Even down in the Eisenhower shank of the early Fifties she was already promising that a time was coming when sex would be easy and sweet, democratic provender for all. Her stomach, untrammeled by girdles or sheaths, popped forward in a full woman's belly, inelegant as hell, an avowal of a womb fairly salivating in seed—that belly which was never to have a child —and her breasts popped buds and burgeons of flesh over many a questing sweating moviegoer's face. She was a cornucopia. She excited dreams of honey for the horn.

Yet she was more. She was a presence. She was ambiguous. She was the angel of sex, and the angel was in her detachment. For she was separated from what she offered. "None but Marilyn Monroe," wrote Diana Trilling,

> could suggest such a purity of sexual delight. The boldness with which she could parade herself and yet never be gross, her sexual flamboyance and bravado which yet breathed an air of mystery and even reticence, her voice which carried such ripe overtones of erotic excitement and yet was the voice of a shy child—these complications were integral to her gift. And they described a young woman trapped in some never-never land of unawareness.

Or is it that behind the gift is the tender wistful hint of another mood? For she also seems to say, "When an absurd presence is perfect, some little god must have made it." At its best, the echo of her small and perfect creation reached to the horizon of our mind. We heard her speak in that tiny tinkly voice so much like a little dinner bell, and it tolled when she was dead across all that decade of the Sixties she had helped to create, across its promise, its excitement, its ghosts and its center of tragedy.

Since she was also a movie star of the most stubborn secretiveness and flamboyant candor, most conflicting arrogance and on-rushing inferiority; great populist of philosophers—she loved the working man—and most tyrannical of mates, a queen of a castrator who was ready to weep for a dying minnow; a lover of books who did not read, and a proud, inviolate artist who could haunch over to publicity when the heat was upon her faster than a whore could lust over a hot buck; a female spurt of wit and sensitive energy who could hang like a sloth for days in a muddy-mooded coma; a child-girl, yet an actress to loose a riot by dropping her glove at a premiere; a fountain of charm and a dreary bore; an ambulating cyclone of beauty when dressed to show, a dank hunched-up drab at her worst—with a bad smell!—a giant and an emotional pygmy; a lover of life and a cowardly hyena of death who drenched herself in chemical stupors; a sexual oven whose fire may rarely have been lit—she would go to bed with her brassiere on—she was certainly more and less than the silver witch of us all. In her ambition, so Faustian, and in her ignorance of culture's dimensions, in her liberation and her tyrannical desires, her noble democratic longings intimately contradicted by the widening pool of her narcissism (where every friend and slave must bathe), we can see the magnified mirror of ourselves, our exaggerated and now all but defeated generation, yes, she ran a reconnaissance through the Fifties, and left a message for us in her death, "Baby go boom." Now she is the ghost of the Sixties. The sorrow of her loss is in this passage her friend Norman Rosten would write in *Marilyn—An Untold Story:*

> She was proud of her dishwashing and held up the glasses for inspection. She played badminton with a real flair, occasionally banging someone on the head (no damage). She was just herself, and herself was gay, noisy, giggling, tender. Seven summers before her death. . . . She liked her guest room; she'd say, "Make it dark, and give me air." She slept late, got her own breakfast and went off for a walk in the woods with only the cat for company.
>
> Marilyn loved animals; she was drawn to all living things. She would spend hundreds of dollars to try to save a storm-damaged tree and would mourn its death. She welcomed birds, providing tree houses and food for the many species that visited her lawn, she worried about them in bad weather. She worried about dogs and cats. She once had a dog that was by nature contemplative, but she was convinced he was depressed. She did her best to make him play, and that depressed him even more; on the rare occasions when he did an antic pirouette, Marilyn would hug and kiss him, delirious with joy.

They are loving lines. Rosten's book must offer the tenderest portrait available of Monroe, but those who suspect such tender beauty can find other anecdotes in Maurice Zolotow's biography:

> One evening, some of the cast—though not Monroe —were watching the rushes of the yacht sequence.

. . . [Tony Curtis] is posing as a rich man's son who suffers from a frigid libido. Girls cannot excite him. Monroe decides to cure him of his ailment by kissing him and making love to him. On the fifth kiss, the treatment succeeds admirably.

In the darkness, someone said to Curtis, "You seemed to enjoy kissing Marilyn." And he said loudly, "It's like kissing Hitler."

When the lights came on, Paula Strasberg was crying. "How could you say a terrible thing like that, Tony?" she said. "You try acting with her, Paula," he snapped, "and see how you feel."

During much of the shooting, Monroe was reading Paine's *Rights of Man.* One day, the second assistant director, Hal Polaire, went to her dressing room. He knocked on the door. He called out, "We're ready for you, Miss Monroe."

She replied with a simple obliterative. "Go fuck yourself," she said. Did she anticipate how a future generation of women would evaluate the rights of men? Even so consummate a wit as Billy Wilder would yet describe her as the meanest woman in Hollywood, a remark of no spectacular humor that was offered nonetheless in an interview four years after her death, as though to suggest that even remembering Marilyn across the void was still sufficiently irritating to strip his wit. Yet during the filming of *Let's Make Love* she was to write in her dressing room notebook, "What am I afraid of? Why am I so afraid? Do I think I can't act? I know I can act but I am afraid. I am afraid and I should not be and I must not be." It is in fear and trembling that she writes. In dread. Nothing less than some intimation of the death of her soul may be in her fear. But then is it not hopeless to comprehend her without some concept of a soul? One might literally have to invent the idea of a soul in order to approach her. "What am I afraid of?"

It may be fair to quote another woman whose

life ended in suicide: "A biography is considered complete if it merely accounts for six or seven selves, whereas a person may well have as many as one thousand." The words are by Virginia Woolf. In its wake, the materials of any biographer come begging with his credentials.

But why not assume Marilyn Monroe opens the entire problem of biography? The question is whether a person can be comprehended by the facts of the life, and this does not even begin to take into account that abominable magnetism of facts. They always attract polar facts. Rare is the piece of special evidence in any life that is not quickly contradicted by other witnesses. In a career like Monroe's, where no one can be certain whether she was playing an old role, experimenting with a new one, or even being nothing less than the *true* self (which she had spent her life trying to discover), the establishing of facts dissolves into the deeper enigma of how reality may appear to a truly talented actor. Since the psychological heft of a role has more existential presence than daily life (and in fact the role creates *real* reactions in everyone who sees it), so the twilight between reality and fantasy is obliged to become more predominant for a great actor than for others. Even if a few of the *facts* of Monroe's life can be verified, therefore, or, equally, if we learn the sad fact that Monroe reminiscing about her past at a given moment is not being accurate—to say the least!—how little is established. For an actor lives with the lie as if it were truth. A false truth can offer more reality than the truth that was altered.

Since this is a poor way to establish history, the next question is whether a life like hers is not antipathetic to biographical tools. Certainly the two histories already published show the limitations of a conventional approach. The first, by Maurice Zolotow, *Marilyn Monroe*, written while she was still alive, is filled with interesting psychoanalytical insights of the sort one can hear at a New York coffee table when two intelligent people are analyzing a third, but much of the conversation is reamed with overstressed anecdotes. For here is a feature writer who has included in his source material the work of other feature writers and so develops a book with facts embellished by factoids (to join the hungry ranks of those who coin a word), that is, facts which have no existence before appearing in a magazine or newspaper, creations which are not so much lies as a product to manipulate emotion in the Silent Majority. (It is possible, for example, that Richard Nixon has spoken in nothing but factoids during his public life.)

So Zolotow's book is able to make another biographer wistful. If a few of his best stories were true, how nice they might be for one's own use; but one cannot depend on them entirely. Some of them were written by Marilyn, which is to say, by Marilyn as told to Ben Hecht, a prodigiously factoidal enterprise printed as Sunday supplement pieces in 1954. Hecht was never a writer to tell the truth when a concoction could put life in his prose, and Marilyn had been polishing her fables for years. No team of authors contributes more to the literary smog that hangs over legend than Marilyn ben Hecht.

The other book, *Norma Jean*, by Fred Lawrence Guiles, seems more accurate, and is certainly more scrupulous, as close to the facts of its subject as Carlos Baker's book may have been for Hemingway, a work of sources and careful chronology, a reporter's job of love since in journalism the labor of cross-checking is equal to love. Therefore it is a biography of much estimable value for verifying the events of her life. Yet her personality remains mysterious. The facts live, but Marilyn is elusive. So the final virtue of *Norma Jean* is that a great biography might be constructed some day upon its foundations, although it might have to contend with the notion that exceptional people (often the most patriotic, artistic, heroic, or prodigious) had a way of living with opposites in themselves that could only be called schizophrenic when it failed. That was a theory developed while studying astronauts, and it seemed suitable for Marilyn, and so most interesting, for what had a movie star like Monroe in common with an astronaut? One has to speak of transcendence. But transcendence was precisely the enigma which faced every psychohistorian, for it was a habit as much as a miracle, yet a mystical habit, not amenable to reason—it assumed that something in the shape of things respected any human who would force an impossible solution up out of the soup, as if the soup itself were sympathetic to the effort. By the logic of transcendence, it was exactly in the secret scheme of things that a man should be able to write about a beautiful woman, or a woman to write about a great novelist—that would be transcendence, indeed! The new candidate for biographer now bought a bottle of Chanel No. 5—Monroe was famous for having worn it—and thought it was the operative definition of a dime-store stink. But he would never have a real clue to how it smelled on her skin. Not having known her was going to prove, he knew, a recurrent wound in the writing, analogous to the regret, let us say, of not having been alone and in love

in Paris when one was young. No matter how much he could learn about her, he could never have the simple invaluable knowledge of knowing that he liked her a little, or did not like her, and so could have a sense that they were working for the same god, or at odds.

If the temptation, then, to undertake such a work of psychohistory was present, he still knew he was not serious. It would consume years, and he was not the type to bed down into the curious hollow of writing about a strange woman whose career had so often passed through places where he had lived at the same time. One of the frustrations of his life was that he had never met her, especially since a few people he knew had been so near to her. Once in Brooklyn, long before anyone had heard of Marilyn Monroe—she had been alive for twenty years but not yet named!—he had lived in the same brownstone house in which Arthur Miller was working on *Death of a Salesman* and this at just the time he was himself doing *The Naked and the Dead*. The authors, meeting occasionally on the stairs, or at the mail box in the hall, would chat with diffidence as they looked for a bit of politics or literary business to mouth upon—each certainly convinced on parting that the other's modest personality would never amount to much. In later years, when Miller was married to Monroe, the playwright and the movie star lived in a farmhouse in Connecticut not five miles away from the younger author, who, not yet aware of what his final relation to Marilyn Monroe would be, waited for the call to visit, which of course never came. The playwright and the novelist had never been close. Nor could the novelist in conscience condemn the playwright for such avoidance of drama. The secret ambition, after all, had been to steal Marilyn; in all his vanity he thought no one was so well suited to bring out the best in her as himself, a conceit which fifty million other men may also have held—he was still too untested to recognize that the foundation of her art might be to speak to each man as if he were all of male existence available to her. It was only a few marriages (which is to say a few failures) later that he could recognize how he would have done no better than Miller and probably have been damaged further in the process. In retrospect, it might be conceded that Miller had been made of the toughest middle-class stuff—which, existentially speaking, is tough as hard synthetic material.

So there would be then no immense job on Monroe by himself, no, rather a study like this, bound to stray toward the borders of magic. For a man with a cabalistic turn of mind, it was fair and engraved coincidence that the letters in Marilyn Monroe (if the "a" were used twice and the "o" but once) would spell his own name leaving only the "y" for excess, a trifling discrepancy, no more calculated to upset the heavens than the most minuscule diffraction of the red shift.

Of course, if he wished to play anagrams, she was also Marlon Y. Normie, and an unlimited use of the letters in *el amor* gave Marolem Mamroe, a forthright Latin sound (considerably better than Mormam Maeler). But let us back off such pleasures. It is possible there is no instrument more ready to capture the elusive quality of her nature than a novel. Set a thief to catch a thief, and put an artist on an artist. Could the solution be nothing less vainglorious than a novel of Marilyn Monroe? Written in the form of biography? Since it would rely in the main on other sources, it could hardly be more than a long biographical article—nonetheless, a *species* of novel ready to play by the rules of biography.

No items could be made up and evidence would be provided when facts were moot. Speculation *had* to be underlined. Yet he would never delude himself that he might be telling a story which could possibly be more accurate than a fiction since he would often be quick to imagine the interior of many a closed and silent life, and with the sanction of a novelist was going to look into the unspoken impulses of some of his real characters. At the end, if successful, he would have offered a literary hypothesis of a *possible* Marilyn Monroe who might actually have lived and fit most of the facts available. If his instincts were good, then future facts discovered about her would not have to war with the character he created. A reasonable venture! It satisfied his fundamental idea that acquisition of knowledge for a literary man was best achieved in those imaginative acts of appropriation picked up by the disciplined exercise of one's skill. Let us hasten, then, to the story of her life. Magic is worked by the working.

She was born on June 1, 1926 at 9:30 in the morning, an easy birth, easiest of her mother's three deliveries. As the world knows, it was out of wedlock. At the time of Marilyn's first marriage to James Dougherty, the name of Norma Jean Baker was put on the marriage license (Baker by way of her mother's first husband). On the second marriage to Joe DiMaggio, the last name became Mortenson, taken from the second husband. (Even the middle name, Jean, was originally written as Jeane—a quintessentially prairie spelling like Choreanne for Corinne.) There is no need to look for any purpose behind the use of the names. Uneducated (that familiar woe of a beautiful blonde), she was also cultureless—can we guess she would not care to say whether Rococo was three hundred years before the Renaissance, any more than she would be ready to swear the retreat of Napoleon from Moscow didn't come about because his railroad trains couldn't run in the cold. Historically empty, she was nonetheless sensitive—as sensitive as she was historically empty—and her normal state when not under too much sedation was, by many an account, vibrant to new perception. It is as if she was ready when exhilarated to reach out to the washes of a psychedelic tide. So, talking to one publicity man, it would seem natural in the scheme of things that her last name was Baker—maybe that sounded better as she looked at the man's nose. Another flack with something flaccid in the look of his muscles from the solar plexus to the gut would inspire Mortenson. Since it was all movie publicity, nobody bothered to check. To what end? Who knew the real legal situation? If the mother, Gladys Monroe Baker, had been married to Edward Mortenson, "an itinerant lover," he had already disappeared by the time Marilyn was born; some reports even had him dead of a motorcycle accident before Norma Jean was conceived. There may also have been some question whether Gladys Monroe was ever divorced from the first husband, Baker, or merely separated. And the real father, according to Fred Guiles, was C. Stanley Gifford, an employee of Consolidated Film Industries, where Gladys Baker worked. A handsome man. Shown a picture of him by her mother when still a child, Marilyn described him later "wearing a slouch hat cocked on one side of his head. He had a little mustache and a smile. He looked kind of like Clark Gable, you know, strong and manly." In her early teens, she kept a picture of Gable on her wall and lied to high school friends that Gable was her secret father. Not too long out of the orphanage where she had just spent twenty-one months, then veteran of numerous foster homes, it is obvious she was looking for a sense of self-importance, but we may as well assume something more extravagant: the demand upon a biographer is to explain why she is exceptional. So, in that part of her adolescent mind where fantasy washes reality as the ego begins to emerge, it is possible she is already (like Richard Nixon) searching for an imperial sense of self-justification. Illegitimate she might be, but still selected for a high destiny—Clark Gable was her secret father. That she would yet come to know Gable while making *The Misfits* (know him toward the end of her life down in the infernal wastes of that psychic state where the brimstone of insomnia and barbiturates is boiled, her marriage to Miller already lost, her lateness a disease more debilitating than palsy), what portents she must have sensed playing love scenes at last with the secret father, what a cacophony of cries in the silence of her head when Gable was dead eleven days after finishing the film. But then omens surrounded her like the relatives she never had at a family dinner. If her footprints fit Valentino's about the time she became a star, so too was a bowl of tomato sauce dropped on her groom's white jacket the day of her first wedding, and down she was turned, down a hall with no exit in City Hall in San Francisco just before she married Joe DiMaggio, little fish of intimation too small for a biographer to fry, but remembered perhaps when a woman reporter was killed chasing after her in a sports car the day she was getting married to Miller. (And Marilyn was having her period that day.) What a vision of blood!—a woman smashed and dead on the day she is joining herself to the one man she may be convinced she does love. It is not sedative for a young woman whose sense of her own sanity can never be secure: she has no roots but illegitimacy on one side and a full pedigree of insanity on the other. Her grandfather Monroe (who would naturally claim to be descended from President Monroe) had spent the last part of his life committed to a state asylum. Monroe's wife, Marilyn's grandmother, Della Monroe Grainger, a beauty with red hair and green-blue eyes, had insane rages on quiet surburban semi-slum streets in environs of Los Angeles like Hawthorne, and was also committed to a mental hospital before she died. So was Marilyn's mother in an asylum for most of Marilyn's life. And the brother of the mother killed himself. When the wings of insanity beat thus near, one pays attention to a feather. The most casual coincidence is obliged to seem another warning from the deep. So must it have been like opening the door to a secret room (and finding that it looks exactly as envisioned) to know that the director of her first starring movie, *Don't Bother to Knock* (about a girl who was mad), should have the name of Baker.

Still, these reinforced roots of insanity, and this absence of clear identity, are not only a weakness but an intense motive to become an actor. In the logic of transcendence, every weakness presupposes the possibility of a future strength. Great actors usually discover they have a talent by first searching in desperation for an identity. It is no ordinary identity that will suit them, and no ordinary desperation can drive them. The force that propels a great actor in his youth is insane ambition. Illegitimacy and insanity are the godparents of the great actor. A child who is missing

either parent is a study in the search for identity and quickly becomes a candidate for actor (since the most creative way to discover a new and possible identity is through the close fit of a role). But then the origins of insanity can also be glimpsed in wild and unmanageable ambition. While the appearance of insanity is not ever simple, and two insane people are rarely alike (except when in depression), still the root of insanity is easier to locate than sanity, for it is more single-minded. The root is to be found in frustrated ambition, no more, provided we conceive the true pain of such a state—an undying will existing in conditions of hopeless entombment. To be buried alive is insanity. What creates such complexity in the mad—that labyrinth of interlocking selves with every knotted incapacity to act on simple lines—is the reaction of thwarted will upon every structure of the character. While the cause of insanity is therefore as simple as the process that makes an enlargement (where a focus of light burns in, distorts, dodges, or solarizes the original negative), still the content of the insanity is not simple, for it must remain at least as complex as the content of the negative itself, that is, the complexity of the original character.

While formal psychiatry is a maze of medical disciplines that seek to cure, stupefy, or *pulverize* madness, it is another kind of inquiry to search into the uncontrollable ambition to dominate one's own life, the life of others, or the life of communities not yet conceived, that simple rage to put one's signature upon existence. Let us bow our heads. If we want to comprehend the insane, then we must question the fundamental notion of modern psychiatry—that we have but one life and one death. The concept that no human being has ever existed before or will be reincarnated again is a philosophical rule of thumb which dominates psychiatry; yet all theory built upon this concept has failed—one is tempted to say *systematically*—in every effort to find a consistent method of cure for psychotics. Even the least spectacular processes of reasoning may therefore suggest that to comprehend psychosis, and the psychology of those who are exceptional (like our heroine), it could be time to look upon human behavior as possessed of a double root. While the dominant trunk of our actions has to be influenced by the foreground of our one life here and now and living, the other root may be attached to some karmic virtue or debt some of us (or all of us) acquired by our courage or failure in lives we have already lived. If such theory is certainly supported by no foundation, nonetheless it offers some immediate assistance for comprehending the insane, since it would suggest we are not all conceived in equal happiness or desperation. Any human who begins life with the debt of owing existence somewhat more than others is thereby more likely to generate an ambition huge enough to swallow old debts. (And be less content with modest success.) Of course, the failure of such ambition must double all desperation.

Double-entry bookkeeping on a celestial level! I stub my toe because of a leap taken in another life! Then I fight with my wife because once I disputed in similar circumstances with my fourteenth-century mother. Absurdities eat into the argument with the ferocity of ants. Yet if we are to understand Monroe, and no one has—we have only seen her limned as an angelic and sensitive victim or a murderous emotional cripple—why

not assume that in a family of such concentrated insanity as her own, the illegitimate daughter of Gladys Monroe Baker may have been born with a desperate imperative formed out of all those previous debts and failures of her whole family of souls. And the imperative may have been to display herself as a presence to the world, there to leaven the thickening air with the tender, wise and witty flesh of an angel of sex. Conscious of how this presence may have been managed and directed and advanced its insufferably difficult way forward by a harsh and near to maniacal voice of the most inward, concealed and secretive desperation, since the failure of her project was insanity, or some further variety of doom.

We draw back from such a projection. It is too much, and much too soon. She was a dumb and sexy broad, a voice of outraged bitterness is bound to say, a dizzy dish with a flair and a miserable childhood and much good and bad luck, and she took a little talent a long way. You could go to any southern town and find twelve of her. A familiar voice. It is comfortable. Yet facing the phenomenon of her huge appeal to the world—Napoleonic was her capture of the attention of the world—let us at least recognize that the reductive voice speaks with no more authority than the romantic, that it is also an unproved thesis, and does no more than scorn the first thesis, indeed, it fails to explain her altogether. There are a million dumb and dizzy broads with luck and none come near to Monroe, no. To explain her at all, let us hold to that karmic notion as one more idea to support in our mind while trying to follow the involuted pathways of her life.

II. BURIED ALIVE

While Gladys Baker, the mother, worked as a film technician, that was probably no more of a co-incidence than if we were to read that the father of a brilliant automotive engineer had been a foreman on a Detroit assembly line. For that matter, Gladys Baker was a foreman, a section head with five girls under her; their job at Consolidated Film Industries was to splice together processed negatives. The father (at least the man considered to be the father by the reckoning of most of Gladys' fellow workers) was also employed at Consolidated. He had a romance with Gladys that lasted for several months, a fair period for C. Stanley Gifford, since he was known in the company as a lover and therefore did not usually take long to move on. Hollywood, in 1926, being more tolerant of broken sex mores than other places, a collection was taken up among Gladys' co-workers to help with the expenses of the delivery. The sum came to $140, which in those days may have paid most of the bills at Los Angeles General Hospital. Gifford did not contribute. The psychology of the stud speaks in his silence: "Considering the sweat that bitch cost me. . . ." Of course, Gladys Baker, known as a slavedriver of a foreman, was sharp-tongued. Twenty-five years later, Marilyn discovered her father was a successful dairyman living in Hemet, California, and put in a call to visit, for she had never seen him. He would not come to the phone. "He suggests," said his wife, "you see his lawyer in Los Angeles if you have some complaint. Do you have a pencil?"

Is Gifford a small-town monument to bad conscience, afraid of his wife, or profoundly suspicious of the financial intentions of long-lost bastards? Perhaps he is the holder of an enduring grudge—we can as easily assume some evaluation of his manhood was left in the flesh by Gladys Baker. In any case, two and a half decades later, he was small prize to a young woman looking for her identity. Probably his greatest gift to the illegitimate daughter had been libido. It is no accident that studs are usually heartless about the aftermath. By their logic they have already treated the mother well and given the baby a good beginning. If his abandoned daughter would be obliged to look harder for a father than anyone in American life since Thomas Wolfe, well, that by his logic was the balance of justice: the mother, after all, *had* looked for a stud.

If it is the acme of the facetious to speculate about the character of her father, we cannot remind ourselves often enough that little as we know about C. Stanley Gifford, we know less about Mr. Monroe, the grandfather, not even his first name. We can be told that Della Monroe Grainger, Marilyn's grandmother, was born Hogan, from a lower-middle-class family of Hogans in the state of Missouri, and came West when adolescent, later traveled to India after her second husband Grainger had been sent there by the oil company for which he worked. We also know she was a follower of Aimee Semple Mc-Pherson and went to prayer service regularly at Angelus Temple, even had Norma Jean baptized by Aimee in the Foursquare Gospel Church when Della came back to Hawthorne from India, alone, her marriage with Grainger terminated. The baby, Norma Jean, now six months old, was living across the street with a family named Bolender who were foster parents (for the reasonable sum of five dollars a week), and on Saturdays Gladys Baker took the long trolley ride from her furnished room in Hollywood (where she was working once more at Consolidated) out to Hawthorne. The supposition was that she could stay overnight and thereby be with the baby again on Sunday, but usually she had a date for Saturday night in Hollywood and took the trolley back. The date was necessary if she thought to find a husband and make a home for her daughter, but it is not difficult to conceive of lonely, arid, afternoon hours spent in the Bolender home with an infant that was hers and yet strange to her, this small handsome mother (with a resemblance to the young Gloria Swanson), whose face stares out of a photograph with clear and elegant features. There she is, again, unphotographed, in the Bolender living room holding her infant, a love child. We have to recognize the measure of the decision. If abortions were not routine in 1926, still they were available in Hollywood. Some inner imperative may have told her this child was too special to abort, for it was clear she was not sentimental about babies. Her first husband Baker had permanent possession of her other two children. Gladys even listed them as "dead" when admitted to the hospital for Norma Jean's birth, and they may have been as dead to her as the dead love of that past which married her to Baker in Mexico at the age of fifteen—what a life had Gladys Monroe Baker before she was even twenty-five! Now the child who had disrupted her chance for a career or an advantageous marriage was in her arms and, specter of family insanity, was boring her, was remote from her, strange infant, strange project to which she had committed herself for a purpose she could not now name, not as she sits on Saturday afternoon in a home so religious a colored poster of Christ is on the living room wall. (Mr. Bolender, a mail carrier, prints up religious pamphlets on a press he has in a workshop at the end of the house.)

Across the street from the Bolenders is the house of her mother, another one-story stucco bungalow with a veranda and a scraggly palm tree in the front yard, and to spend time with Della Grainger is worse than to spend time with the Bolenders. Her mother's rages are even more unpredictable than her own (although probably no worse than her father's). The one memory of Gladys' father which comes down to us is how Mr. Monroe once pulled a pet kitten out of his daughter's hands and threw it against a wall. We can see that near-insane man with his profound vision of darkest dalliances between women and cats as he stands in the presence of his wife, a most violent-tempered red-haired witch, and of his daughter, showing every sign of soon growing into a witch as she plays with the kitten, while he, descendant of President Monroe and now married all the way down to a green-eyed red-headed Hogan with airs, will not yet be dominated in his own home—death to cats. He believes God will applaud him.

Yes, the baby means incarceration for a weekend with the timid sanctity of the Bolenders or the on–off rages of her screaming, deserted and ladylike mother, while back in Hollywood, trolley-ride to the other end of endless Los Angeles, they have just been making *The Jazz Singer* with Al Jolson. Greta Garbo and Joan Crawford, Gloria Swanson and Clara Bow, Constance Bennett and Norma Talmadge are stars. Norma Jean has—we may as well guess—even been named after Norma Talmadge. But then Gladys also has a resemblance to her. John Barrymore, a very handsome version of Gifford, is a leading man, and John Gilbert, and Adolphe

26

Menjou. Valentino, in whose footprints Gladys' daughter will stand, has just died. He is the only one of these "strong and manly" lovers without a mustache.

Of course, Gladys will stay overnight in Hawthorne now and again and go to Sunday sermon with the Bolenders, carrying Norma Jean in her arms. The baby will rarely cry. Indeed, later, when Norma Jean can walk, Gladys will occasionally take her to the film lab and let her sit there quietly while she works. Workers congratulate the mother for her good child. But it is as likely a first sign of the spiritual orphan who does not expect attention, and in later years the comments on such calm behavior will be less adulatory. Natasha Lytess, once her dramatic coach, later ignominiously dismissed, was to say, "I often felt like she was a somnambulist walking around," and Nunnally Johnson, the scriptwriter, described her as "ten feet under water . . . a wall of thick cotton . . . she reminds me of a sloth. You stick a pin in her and eight days later it says 'Ouch.' " Already in infancy it is possible her thoughts are turning circular and bear the same relation to purposeful inquiry that the steps of a prisoner pacing a cell offer to a journey.

On most Sundays, however, the well-behaved baby did not see the inside of church with her mother. The mother was in Hollywood awakening after a Saturday night without her. Is it safe to assume Gladys never felt closer to the baby than when she was without her? But the emotional impost of going to Hawthorne was steadily on the increase. Della was each week less stable. If she were always capable of shrieking at delivery boys one day, then being gracious the next, one newsboy was now so terrified of her that he asked his supervisor to send the weekly bill by mail; and Ida Bolender, caught in the act of spanking Norma Jean for upsetting a bowl of food, heard Della scream, "Don't ever let me catch you doing that again!" Her voice must have had that recognizable tone which speaks of the blood-of-my-blood, for Ida Bolender, never a bold woman, was thereafter in fear of Della, and forever worried when Della, rising at last to a grandmotherly function, would take Norma Jean across the street for a visit. Ida dares not interfere, and yet is resentful, one might as well assume, since Della, if just turned fifty, is still sufficiently beautiful to play the dilettante even as a grandmother.

It is the classic American small town comedy. People are going mad on quiet shabby end-of-town streets while envy is generated, proprieties are abused, and proprieties are maintained. Yet the fundamental sense of the American madness, that violence which lives like an electronic hum behind the silence of even the sleepiest Sunday afternoon, is incubating in the balmy smog-free subtropical evenings of Hollywood: the vision of the American frontier has gone into a light-box and come out as ten-foot ghosts upon a screen.

If a void in one's sense of identity is equal to a mental swamp where insane growths begin, then America is an insane swamp more than other lands. With the exception of the Indians, we are a nation of rejects already once transplanted by the measure of every immigration of the last three hundred and fifty years. And the Indians, having originally possessed a relation to land and sky more sensitive than the telepathies of the TV set, have been driven mad by our disruption of their balance, so we are, yes, twice an insane land, Indians and others—it is, at the least, a working hypothesis. Los Angeles had to be the focus within such focus, the deepest swamp of the national swamp, the weed of weeds, for in the period which began after World War I some of that same intimation of oncoming insanity if one failed to move (which had already moved tens of millions over here from Europe) now picked up many a soul who felt himself a weed in his surroundings and transplanted him still again to the West Coast. And there in Hawthorne in 1927, the weed Della Hogan Monroe Grainger, festering in the psychic swamp life of quiet Hawthorne, is believed to have crossed the street one afternoon, picked up the baby, taken her to her home, and there begun to suffocate her with a pillow. No witnesses are present and no evidence is with us other than Marilyn Monroe's own recollection. She would prove more than once a confirmed source of inaccuracy, but still it is her first recollected image, accurate or no—"I remember waking up from my nap fighting for my life. Something was pressed against my face. It could have been a pillow. I fought with all my strength." So it is recorded by Guiles as told to Arthur Miller by Marilyn, and she was to tell it to others. It is one of the stories she always told. While other such dramatic items are usually false —she was, for example, probably not raped at the age of seven or eight although she told the tale to reporters for years—still Della was committed about this time to the Norwalk asylum after a series of accelerating attacks. Ida Bolender would claim no knowledge of an assault on the baby, but it is agreed Della stopped seeing Norma Jean almost completely a few weeks before she was committed. Besides, there is something in the prodigious tortures of Monroe's later insomnia that all but insists on traumatic origin. "Sleep was her

demon," Miller was to say, "the fundamental preoccupation of her life," and no one was in a better position to know.

For what it helps to explain, let us assume some sort of partial suffocation probably occurred. Obviously a thirteen-month-old baby does not push away a pillow pressed down upon her by a grown woman, not unless we assume the baby has as much sudden strength and agility—in such a crisis—as a kitten fighting for its life. But then there is no need to envisage a struggle. The grandmother may have played too vigorously until the baby was caught beneath blankets and in a panic for fresh air, or as easily laid a pillow for an instant upon the child's face, and held it there an instant more, then held it longer, as though hearing the first note of a far-off spell— and time began to pass—was there time enough for both to travel that long aisle which leads from the pounding heart of consciousness down into death, long enough for the grandmother to know that the spell she had entered spoke of murder; and for the baby to have been forced into suffocation long enough to take a fix on the onset of death, and be in part attracted to its dimensions, attracted enough so that the fall into sleep in later years would ring every alarm, for death was not unseductive. If this is Marilyn's first memory, oncoming sleep may suggest death is near—so, adrenaline may electrify her limbs.

We have now transgressed every border of history. But then it is hardly possible to conceive of grandmothers attacking grandchildren unless we also accept the first logic of insanity: "I am a soul of the most mighty dimensions engaged in a dialogue with eternity." Should someone like Della decide that her relation to eternity is evil, then so are her offspring: the duty is to kill off-

28

spring. It is a logic considered insane only when grandmothers set out to suffocate one-year-olds; it is not nearly so insane when one-year-olds are ignited from one mile or more up in the sky by young men who are not related—no, it must be that all acts of violence, love, and war presuppose some unconscious dialogue with eternity. A clean-cut twenty-two-year-old American pilot does not drop firebombs on hamlets, nor do the citizens of a great nation support the act by re-electing his Godfather, unless our unconscious dialogue with eternity assumes that America is closer to God's will than other lands. It is the pride of the weed that knows it is the true flower of the garden. By this logic, Della Monroe Grainger was as American as most.

Of course, short of Marilyn's dubious witness, we do not know that Della ever touched the child. Perhaps the memory was no more than a recollected sense of terror the baby used to experience when alone with Della; and the grandmother, poor woman, could have been innocent, and Norma Jean merely tangled in her own blanket and then rescued by Della. It is even conceivable Marilyn made it all up as still one more exercise of the skill with which she would later invent particular histories to attract pity. On the other hand, if there is nothing to the story, then there is also no dramatic explanation for her acute insomnia. Let us leave it there. Easier evidence on the shaping of her character can be found in the atmosphere of the first year of her life, spent living in the Bolenders' house of piety. Certainly when Norma Jean would call Ida "Mama," she was rebuked. "The lady with the red hair is your mama," would be the answer. One of Norma Jean's first sentences on seeing a woman walk by holding a child's hand was, "There goes a mama." It is a touching tale, told by Ida Bolender, but one can sense her fear of Gladys' wrath if the baby should think to call the wrong woman mama in front of the actual red-headed mother. But it is of Della, however, that Ida is truly afraid, Della who does not go to church any longer, Della who scorches the most casual conversation with a flare of anger hot as burning gasoline, Della building to a riot of the cataclysmic for a Hawthorne street.

But we may as well give the description to Fred Guiles to tell, since it is his biography we have been using up to here.

> Early that critical Saturday, Albert Wayne Bolender heard a commotion in his front yard. (He could remember the details vividly even forty years later.) Della, in a rage, was hurrying up the walk toward their porch. Seeing her approach he slammed the front door and bolted it.
>
> No one could make out a word she was saying. It was clear, however, that the subject was Norma Jean; she had no other reason to be there. Ida came into the living room from the kitchen and peered out at the woman, who was now pounding on their door. "Call the police, Wayne," she said. "Hurry!"
>
> Within minutes, a black patrol car pulled up in front of the Bolender home. By this time, Della had succeeded in breaking a panel of the door, injuring her hand. Two policemen subdued her and dragged her to the car. Her head was thrown back as though seeking God's help.
>
> A few weeks after her entrance into the asylum at Norwalk, mercifully Della died of a heart attack during her last seizure on August 23, 1927.

Of course, we do not know if the heart attack was merciful. It could have been created by still another excess of rage at having failed in her mission to extinguish Norma Jean.

ella's death takes place in the summer of 1927, and in Whittier on the other side of Los Angeles, out past Pasadena, maybe twenty miles away, another American, Richard Milhous Nixon, is fourteen years old and growing up to form his ideas of the Silent Majority. If we are certain of anything in the childhood of Marilyn Monroe it is that she spent her first seven years in a home which was hymn and fundament, flesh and spine, thesis and axis of the world-view of the Silent Majority. For "Aunt" Ida and "Uncle" Wayne Bolender were poor, pious, stern, kindly, decent, hardworking, and absolutely terrified of the lividity of the American air in the street outside. Indeed we do not require much more than the description of their rush to bolt the door to understand how much the Silent Majority lives in dread of the danger which lies beneath appearances. It is the home in which Norma Jean grew up, and most certainly it must have helped to establish that pleasant middle of her personality—at least as it appeared on screen—that clean scrubbed girl who lived next door. There is ice cream on her tongue, and the Church Visible in the bland expression of the spaced-out eyes. If that is a fair and cruel description of many a good American cheerleader, and will yet fit Marilyn on occasion, it is not accurate to speak of her as spaced out so early. She is a vigorous-looking baby with keen eyes and good tough little features; nothing of her future beauty is particularly indicated—rather it is her good health. In later years on those occasions when she was relatively free of sleeping pills, friends will speak of her extraordinary vitality and Miller will attribute part of her readiness for pill-taking to her powers of recuperation, which left her willing to take greater chances with her health—a confidence found in many a junkie.

In fact, as we look at those early photographs, it is a rugged little boy-girl who grins back, an early record of a child who seems more likely to turn out an athlete than an actress. And although she will not become the world's greatest dancer, it is impossible to study her films without being obliged to recognize how well she has trained herself to move—she has easily enough coordination to be on a girl's softball team or in a roller derby. Even a snapshot taken at the age of four with foster-brother Lester, two months younger than herself, shows Norma Jean preempting the leadership of their two bodies, while her face has the rugged bulldog solidity, the wide jaws and wide nose of her father's features. She grew up with Lester in these first years, played with him, ate with him, and was even set next to him for sunning in the same baby carriage. Since girl and boy were referred to as "the twins" by the Bolenders, Lester is Norma Jean's first mate, or at any rate the first of future habits she formed for living with a mate are with Lester. Since she was stronger and "got into more trouble than the other kids" it suggests her first relation with men was to dominate. Early relations do not engrave one's sexual possibilities for life so much as set up a school of habits to call upon. So her years with Lester can explain some of the difficulty she found with men who had independence of her (such as her three husbands).

It should be added that the Bolenders adopted Lester legally, which they did not care to do for Norma Jean or could not afford to do. Besides, Gladys still wanted her child. The adoption of Lester, however, had to establish a difference in

treatment. Ida Bolender claims she loved Norma Jean "just like my own," and there is evidence in the photographs. Norma Jean even looks pampered in one snapshot where she is wearing a ruffled dress and scalloped bonnet. When we learn the outfit was put together by Ida Bolender on her sewing machine, the idea of a child who was utterly ignored in her first years has nothing to sustain it. Too much craft has gone into the making of the dress.

Still, there is a difference. Lester could address Ida as his mama, Norma Jean could not; both could undress (at least once) in the front yard to examine each other, but Norma Jean was the one who would catch the blame—it is part of the scenario of dread in the mind of the Silent Majority that a boy's penis is, on occasion, exhibitable, but murder draws a rifle sight on open vagina. Ida Bolender may well have been scolding Norma Jean to protect her from the future wrath of neighbors—a fear not altogether out of contact with real ground, as we will yet discover. Quiet Hawthorne streets. Norma Jean's first song learned at Sunday school was "Jesus Loves Me, This I Know," and she sings it to the world at large, once even in a crowded cafeteria.

If, however, she was giving signs of vivacity and eagerness to perform, a subtle envy had to be created again in Ida—it is no joy to have adopted the less interesting child. While equality was the order of treatment, and a tricycle was bought for the use of both children as a Christmas present, it is not beside the point that Lester was riding it when Norma Jean pushed him over, and thereby excited Ida to give her a whipping with a razor strop. Gladys comes to visit, and agrees with Ida's explanation of the punishment when Norma Jean complains to her.

But then, Gladys was trapped in embarrassments. Just previously, she had come to visit with dark glasses—she was hiding a black eye! Under Ida's shocked scrutiny, she lit a cigarette —it is 1929!—then asked if Ida minded.

"It's not a thing I would do," said Mrs. Bolender, "but this is your house when you are here."

Of course, Norma Jean can hardly be too afraid of Ida if she dares to protest so visibly to Gladys, but on the other hand, Gladys has accepted Ida's version of the accident. It must reach the child with shock—is the guard of forces being altered? Norma Jean comes down with whooping cough. She has caught it from Lester— a sibling transaction. His twin can knock him off his bike, but he will infect her back—the relations between strong and weak nations are in capsule here!

Gladys now gets some days off from work to take care of her child and before the illness is over has spent three weeks in Ida's guest room with Norma Jean, the longest period she has been with the child since the birth. Since she is now a film cutter at Columbia, and making better money, the desire to afford a place for her daughter and herself begins to assert itself again. Glimpses of Gladys are few indeed, and Marilyn will speak coldly of her later, but the mother's motivation remains something of a moral enigma. It may be worth assuming once more that she has some premonition of the value of the child she is bearing. While little in Gladys' life suggests anything other than egocentric preoccupations, and she does not seem superstitious if she can list her first two children as dead— one wonders if they expressed a clear enough preference for the father to leave her vindictive—

still, she *chooses* to have Norma Jean, does not give her up for adoption, and works seven long years to scrape together a situation where she can bring her child to live with her. That is a project of the sort to hold a mind together.

Let us dare the argument that Gladys had early intimations of an exceptional baby who would carry out the balked ambitions of her own career. If it is said of a child who looks exactly like the father that there is no need for wonder since the woman never took her eyes off the man while carrying, what has to be said of Marilyn, whose working mother never took her eyes off movie film?

At the time of the whooping cough, however, Gladys is still several years away from taking Norma Jean to live with her, and a new event is about to occur at the Bolenders' that will yet create caverns of fright in the child, although it first produces real happiness. Since it comes at the end of the whooping cough, it may even seem a species of compensation for her illness—a black and white dog follows Mr. Bolender home from the trolley one evening, and the child plays with this pet through her convalescence. When kindergarten begins in the fall, Lester and Norma Jean walk the four blocks to school together; the dog, Tippy, will follow and wait around the school yard until recess. Norma Jean is in cotton dresses, starched and changed every day, a big bow in her hair—she and Lester are given roller skates and race together; the dog chases them. Contrast with the picture given by Zolotow:

> She dreamed of becoming "so beautiful that people would turn to look at me as I passed." When she was six she imagined herself going naked in the world. This fantasy often possessed her in church.

As the organ thundered out hymns, she quivered with a desire to throw off her clothes and stand naked "for God and everyone else to see. My impulses to appear naked had no shame or sense of sin in them. I think I wanted people to see me naked because I was ashamed of the clothes I wore. Naked, I was like other girls and not someone in an orphan's uniform."

We have just been bombarded with factoids—whether Marilyn's or Ben Hecht's is hard to say—but we know she was in no orphan's uniform at the age of six. The passage is all the more worth quoting as an example of the kind of systematic misrepresentation of her childhood Marilyn would usually collaborate upon with any near reporter and suggests that she either did not have the literary instinct to present the quieter facts with their own pain, or, on the contrary, had everything to teach us about the American addiction to factoids. In actuality, the horrors of her childhood were not so much apocalyptic—"naked for God and everyone else to see"—or Chaplinesque—"someone in an orphan's uniform" —as they would be, on occasion, deadening. Whatever her fear of the world, and we can hear the last echo of that fear in the tininess of her voice, we can recognize her fear was justified. The end of the love affair with Tippy proved traumatic. In 1932, when Norma Jean was almost six, Tippy began to get out of the house on spring evenings and make his run in the dark. One night a blast rolled down the street, and the milkman found the dog's body in the dawn and told the postman Bolender. A neighbor, sitting on his porch, had waited for Tippy with a shotgun. For three nights running Tippy had rolled in the neighbor's garden. On the third night, the neighbor shot him. We can sense that man. There is dog heat and dog body, dog funk leaving its odor on his new greens, rolling dog lusts on the garden crop. That's one night for you, dog, he counts to himself; two nights for you, dog; on the third night—with what backed-up intensity of the frontier jammed at last into a suburban veranda we can only hear in the big blast—the dog is dead. The fears of the Bolenders have stood on real ground. And their timidity also stands revealed. For there is no record of confronting the neighbor and his shotgun. So to the child, a catastrophic view of history must have begun. It is the view which assumes that at the end of every sweet and quiet passage of love, amputation or absurdity is waiting. Whole washes of the apathy that would sit upon her in later years, that intolerable dull and dead round she passed through in the year after her marriage to Miller was over, is probably sealed in the reflex of sorrowing for Tippy, as well as her descent in school from a bright child to an average child. We know that she was ordinary in class, and timid. It was only in the Bolender house that she was bold. But the institution of school must have seemed part of the *other* world outside the Bolender house, a reflection of powerful men with shotguns who sat on porches. Did her stammer begin then as well? If the first joy of speaking in her fifth year must have been to whistle for her dog, now the dog was obliterated, and the joy of speech was jammed.

Gladys put together the money for a down payment on a bungalow off Highland Avenue in Hollywood, bought some furniture at auction, and rented all but two rooms of the house to an English couple who worked in pictures, the husband as a stand-in for George Arliss and the wife as a "dress" extra, which is to say an extra who could look convincing in chic party gowns. (Since their daughter was a stand-in for Madeleine Carroll, the moral has been pointed—when it comes to work, the British know how to locate a niche!)

Her economics thus assured, Gladys moved into the two rooms with her child. Life with Ida was over. For Norma Jean, up from Hawthorne and now in Hollywood thirteen years before she would begin her career, the shift must have been equal to moving from gravity into weightlessness. Or is it the other way? The English couple were neither wild nor cruel—they merely drank and smoked, talked shop and played records, and were bored, and, of course, appalled, when Norma Jean sang "Jesus Loves Me." Their daughter gave parties, that was all, but it must have been not without oppression to the child, for in addition to the shock of moving from the Bolenders' home, where prohibition liquor was the essence of sin, into a house of polite and elegant people who showed no concern at being damned and probably asked her upon occasion to fetch them the bottle, she entered as well into the environs of an English accent, and this could have had its effect. While Marilyn would never sound English, there is something analogous to an English accent in her voice—perhaps it is the knowledge (which also resides in a good southern accent) that language says more when savored. Most Americans speak to communicate an idea, but a good English accent puts emphasis on those words which carry the personality. So Marilyn may have learned from the English couple how to communicate more than a single thought with one speech. In films, she was usually saying two things at once. When she will fall off the piano bench in *The Seven-Year Itch* and as quickly says to Tom Ewell that he must not feel bad because men always made passes at her, she is blonde, full-blown, and altogether nurturing to the thin quivering banjo-string repressions of thin Tom Ewell, she is all of that, but she is also the mistress of that great remote female void where wonder at the comedy of men's urgencies resides. "What is it I got that makes them twitch?" is what she is also saying. It is why we laugh. When we perceive a paradoxical truth just long enough to be warmed by the novelty, but not so long that we must pay by altering our ideas, we laugh. The truth she is offering in the scene is that ubiquitous sex appeal, there for everyone! seems to depend on the existence of a void. But, already, her arch little voice, so much in control of its paradoxes, is moving on to some new artful and double expression of what had been hitherto a single thought. So we do not stop to think—we laugh. And maybe we enjoy the influence of that English accent she heard in her childhood.

We will hardly know for certain. One would have to go through the payrolls of old George Arliss movies to discover the couple's name, and they would be dead. Sixty years old then, they would be a hundred now. Besides, it is the least of the mysteries in this period of Norma Jean's life. For Gladys will not be with her long. In no more than three months the mother will go mad, will literally be carted away by force, and will end—now, we *are* looking at scenes from a Chaplin film—will end in the state asylum at Norwalk where her own mother died. Gladys' sanity must have been maintained for years as an act of will, a species of discipline in the name of her grand project. Now the grand project was manifest in a little girl who wandered around the house, stared at people drinking, sang "Jesus Loves Me," disappeared into movies on Saturday, and had no relation to her mother other than an occasional numb embrace. It is worth supposing that this relatively undramatic condition, this increment of Gladys' long continuing depression, was finally enough to pull apart whatever fine membrane of sanity she had wrapped over all her isolated traps and fires. She woke up one morning in a depression too complete to go to work—the horrors were upon her. Then came a psychic explosion. The English couple were distraught. Attendants from the hospital, called in to subdue her, had to take her away lashed to a stretcher. The Englishman gives a gentle word to Norma Jean when she comes home from school. "Your mother," he tells her, "was taken ill today. She's gone to the hospital." She would not learn what was wrong with Gladys until she was a woman herself, nor would she live with her again for twelve years.

Her life is washing out of the last nets of social life. Norma Jean is on the edge of institutional life herself. The English couple still take care of her during this period (which lasts for almost a year), but are obliged to sell her mother's furniture to meet the taxes and mortgage payments. They are even obliged to sell the prize of the house, a white piano, reputedly owned once by Fredric March and bought by Gladys at auction for her daughter to play. (Norma Jean, when still with the Bolenders, had taken piano lessons with a teacher named Marion Miller; it is one arm of the coincidence that she will run across the white piano again when she is a star and buy it and keep it in her apartment in New York with Arthur Miller—at every step of her life, coincidences spring underfoot like toadstools.)

Since there are not too many other objects to sell, and work for the English couple has become insecure—the Depression is heavy over Hollywood in 1934—they decide at last to go back to England. Norma Jean is taken in by some neighbors, the Giffens, who are fond enough of her to think of adoption when they learn that Mr. Giffen's job will oblige him to move to Mississippi. Even from the asylum, however, Gladys says no.

The child goes instead to an orphanage. Her only connection to the past will be in the weekly visits of Grace McKee, her mother's best friend, a film librarian at Columbia, who is now her legal guardian. There is a moment when Norma Jean goes through the portals for the first time which tolls a bell as loudly as any sentimental event since Charles Dickens wrote, "Please, sir, can I have some more?" For a clue to how legions of publicity writers have gilded this historic moment, we can pick up a hint from Guiles' usually restrained account:

> Norma Jean could read the sign [Los Angeles Orphans' Home] on one of the columns clearly, and she knew she was not an orphan. Her mother was alive. Someone was making a terrible mistake.
>
> She refused to walk in and they had to drag her all the way into the central hall. "*I'm not an orphan!*" she screamed. Her cries could be heard by several of the children nearest the tall arched doorway at the rear . . .

The clue to the quieter reality of the situation is in the next few sentences: ". . . it was their dinner hour. Some children's faces turned; Norma Jean became embarrassed and fell silent." She would undergo her horrors while in the orphan asylum, but they would not be the dramatic exploitations of Fagin and Scrooge; rather the monotonous erosion of her ego. The Los Angeles Orphans' Home, to which she was taken by Grace McKee, was not a factory to sweat child labor—an impression she was to give in publicity stories—but rather an organized and flat environment. Her hatred at what that boredom did to her was cause enough to lie in later years about the experience. Besides, it is almost impossible for people who live in institutions not to tell lies, since an institution works best if none of the inmates tells the truth. Honesty creates bureaucratic snarls and opens questions—the end of a chain of open questions is the revolutionary question, "By what right does this institution stand and govern?" Lies, on the other hand, reflect the bureaucratic need for certain answers. "How do you feel today, Inmate?—I feel fine, sir." The interrogator is hearing the reply as he speaks; the bureaucratic need is to move on to the next question. Or to the next inmate and his lies. Besides, the inmate population feel a false happiness that they are successfully cheating the institution; in fact, their lies keep the population in a state of uneasiness where they are more vulnerable to discipline. So if one is going to blame the orphanage for anything, it is probably for confirming her into a liar, and reinforcing everything in her character that was secretive. Let us assume it was even worse. If she was bound to be somewhat unstable considering the concentrated insanity of her inheritance, and had possibly been given a future of insomnia by Della, and certainly known trauma in the murder of her dog, it was probably her future capacity for happiness that was most injured by the twenty-one months she spent in the orphanage. But this was not because she had to "wash 100 plates, 100 cups, 100 knives, forks and spoons, three times a day, seven days a week . . . scrub toilets and clean bathubs," and for this receive ten cents a month for working in the kitchen. Zolotow quotes the superintendent, Mrs. Ingraham, speaking more than twenty years later.

> "I really don't know why Miss Monroe tells these terrible stories about us. And people print them, whatever she says. We don't *have* to give the children any work assignments. We have a staff of twenty-one here, including a housemother for every ten children. We have a staff in the kitchen fully capable of attending to the dishes. But we do give the children small jobs and pay them for it. We do this deliberately to give the child a feeling of being useful, of her own importance, and to give her money to spend as she wants to spend it. Now this story of Marilyn's that we made her wash dishes three times a day is just plain silly. It would take a child four hours to wash that many dishes. How would Marilyn have had time to go to school and do homework and be in bed by nine, which is lights-out time, if she was washing that many dishes three times a day?"
>
> "How many dishes did she wash?"
>
> "Oh, she never washed any dishes and she never scrubbed toilets. The most she did was to help dry the dishes an hour a week, one hour. That's all. She had to make her own bed and keep her section of the girls' cottage tidied up, is all."
>
> "How much did you pay her?"
>
> "It wasn't really payment. It would be much easier for us just to give the children a dime a week and let it go at that, because it actually makes it harder for us in the kitchen when we have them helping out. They get in the way. But it's our theory that giving the child five cents a week, which was what Marilyn received, is good for a child's morale. She feels she has a place in the world. No institution can ever take the place of a family or a good foster home. We know that. We know the children here do suffer from feelings of rejection. The idea of having them do little tasks and giving them money is to make them feel proud of themselves. We do it even now."

While the children did have to go to public school together and return together and were thereby marked by other children as from the Home, still they wore no uniforms—Norma Jean had a plaid skirt and a sweater. And if they were obliged to live in a dormitory, there were large windows for air and sunlight. They all had their own beds and chests of drawers. There were five acres to play on, swings, seesaws, exercise bars, a sandbox. Zolotow even mentions a swimming pool! Inside were toys and games, a radio and phonograph, an auditorium and stage. The sense of plastic surfaces, communal living, and indifferent mass food is probably worse in any student union in any American university today—at least any union that has recently been built. (In fact, Norma Jean's orphanage consisted of several buildings that were not without a little bit of architectural distinction.) If there was cruel and unusual punishment, it was in the brute fact of the orphanage itself—the emptiness at the core of every tender sensation. One housemother for ten orphans—how can an institution afford more?—and yet what competition to get the fragment of good feeling available in a woman who must divide that small pie of her working heart into ten slices. How little can be there, yet for the children what huge and ruthless elbowing to get up under her nose for award, often by telling the most skillful lies, all the while knowing the most complete loneliness if one is to the rear. The real horror is that slowly, progressively, the child loses all sense of inhabiting even the fair volume of its own body. Since it is existing on the lowest levels of social significance, supervisors tend to look through the child as if it is to a degree invisible. *The volume it inhabits is without importance.* Indeed, one of Monroe's wittier remarks concerned people being rude: "I guess they think it's happening to your clothing." At its worst, in the orphanage one was nothing but an item recognizable by its garments. Given this diminution of the ego, the hours of play have to turn vacuous. To whom does one refer a triumph? It is like conceiving of an orgy where everyone is finally spent. Who is left to offer a compliment? Silences work at the void in oneself and enlarge it. We need look no longer for an explanation to any void in her portrayal of sex (which void paradoxically has made her more sexual, since it suggested she is available to all), no, that hollow was shaping in all the tolerance for apathy and torpor she would develop during the twenty-one months when she was nine, then ten and now eleven and still in the orphanage—the dreadful spread of the habit to be bored, which is equal to saying that a rootless resentment would occupy central positions of power in her psyche. The explanation for her future inability to be on time, memorize lines, or bring her concentration to focus quickly—all these professional vices which will bring her into murderous wars with the studios—all have their beginnings in the drabness of these orphanage hours over twenty-one months. The itch to kill love in many a life around her will form in these years, and all the future wastes of her life, all collecting. Yet it is even worse than that. If we are indeed born with a double psyche and so are analogous in our mental life to twin trees, possessed of one personality which is plunged into the life before us, and of another karmic root that retains some unconscious recollection of another existence from which we derive, it is not the same as saying that because each of us builds a mental life on two fundamentally separate personalities, that we are all therefore, in the old-fashioned sense, schizophrenic. Two personalities within one human being may be better able to evaluate experience (even as two eyes gauge depth), provided the personalities are looking more or less in the same direction. A fragmented identity is the refusal of one personality within oneself to have any relations with the other. If such a notion has value, let us assume that the conditions of an orphanage are suited to creating too wan a psyche and too glamorous a one. Since the orphan's presence in the world is obliged to turn drab, the life of fantasy, in compensation, can become extreme. We are all steeped in the notion that lonely withdrawn people have a life of large inner fantasy. What may be ignored is the tendency to become locked into a lifelong rapture with one's fantasy, to become a narcissist. The word, however, fails to suggest the hermetic imprisonment of such a love affair, or the depth of the incapacity to love anyone else, except as a servant to one's dream of glamour. Since there is also a great tendency for every bastard to become a narcissist—the absence of one parent creating a sense of romantic mystery *within oneself*, within one of the two governing senses of self, the future Marilyn Monroe was by illegitimate birth already in a royal line of narcissists. The orphanage would confirm it. She would come out an orphan—which is to say a survivor—which is to say her love affair would be of necessity with herself. It could be said that if it is the tendency of families, happy families at any rate, to give personalities to their children which are more comfortable and expansive at home than in the world—because the home obviously is safer and more encouraging than the world—so in the psychology of the survivor, the opposite is true. One is drab and quiet at home, there in the deadening lack of amplitude of home, and one is glorious in the world, or possessed at least of the potential for moments of high glory in the world. Combat heroes are such survivors.

We are ready to leave the orphanage, but a few facts are worth recording plus one coincidence. There is reference by all authors to the lot across the field from the Home. There a movie company's sound stages are visible from the window by her bed. At night, a repeating flash of forked neon lightning shows "RKO" through the window. Sixteen years later she will make *Clash by Night* for RKO release.

Otherwise, she makes no friends for the future, and leaves little record of herself. Her reports said she was "normal," "bright and sunshiny"— even here!—"well-behaved," "cooperative." If she lied by offering a face more alive than the deadening pool of her feelings, the asylum lied back with the fiction of pleasant adjectives and good reports. They have to be false. Otherwise, how can one explain her desire to tell such lies about the orphanage later? Or account for her attempt to escape?

One new habit is of significance. She gets her first taste of makeup. Grace McKee, Gladys' friend, who comes to visit on Saturdays, will buy her a soda, take her into a clothing shop, treat her to a movie—she loves movies the way invalids cling to life for a good day—and, ecstasy of stolen sweets, will "permit Norma Jean to try on her lipstick." What a leap! As she looks in the mirror, does she see the face with which she will fall in love? Grace will even take her for a marcel. The beloved is having its hair done. Guiles gives us a glimpse of a moment of sexual beauty, altogether pristine, with the Directress of the Home:

That lady—whose sensibilities were more easily touched than the matrons'—called Norma Jean into her office one Saturday. She sat behind a highly waxed walnut desk in a corner office at the front of the main building, a Pekinese dog near her feet. Norma Jean feared one of the matrons had reported her for some misdemeanor and she tried to recall just what might have provoked this confrontation.

"You have such a lovely skin, dear," the Directress said. Norma Jean, embarrassed by the compliment, went crimson and stooped to pet the dog.

"Stay that way for a minute," the lady told her, and she took out a powder puff and began applying a delicately fragrant powder to her face. "Now look in the mirror," she said. Norma Jean got up and walked to an antique mirror on the wall. Her face was soft, alabaster smooth as her mother's had been.

"Since it's Saturday, you may wear it all day, Norma Jean."

Zolotow, telling the same story in the years when Marilyn was working like a pearl diver for her legend, relates it this way:

About four or five months after she moved into the orphanage, she fell into a depressed mood. It came on during a rainy day. Rain always made her think of her father and set up a desire to wander. On the way back from school, she slipped away from the line and fled. She didn't know where she was running to and wandered aimlessly in the slashing rainstorm. A policeman found her and took her to a police station. She was brought back to Mrs. Dewey's office. She was changed into dry clothes. She expected to be beaten. Instead, Mrs. Dewey took her in her arms and told her she was pretty. Then she powdered Norma Jean's nose and chin with a powder puff.

In 1950, Marilyn told the story of the powder puff to Sonia Wolfson, a publicity woman at 20th Century-Fox and then confided, "This was the first time in my life I felt loved—no one had ever noticed my face or hair or me before."

Let us assume it even happened in some fashion. For it gives a glimpse as the powder goes on and the mirror comes up of a future artist conceiving a grand scheme in the illumination of an instant—one could paint oneself into an instrument of one's will! ". . . Noticed my face or hair"—her properties—"or me . . ."

III. NORMA JEAN

Of the foster homes she entered after the orphanage there is not too much to tell. Zolotow places her altogether in seven or eight and has her raped before the age of nine, but he has been reading Marilyn ben Hecht's childhood, and that is a rainbow of tear-washed factoids. We are told of the scrubbing of floors, nights on knees for prayer, revival meetings with religious fanatics, beatings with a hairbrush, even the accusation she stole a pearl necklace, to which she refers: "I have never forgotten the shame, humiliation, and the deep, deep hurt." On Saturday night, living with a factoidal family, she was obliged to take her bath last in the dirty bath water of the others! What an imagination she possessed: of clean America forgiving her any sin after that fearsome immersion! Only Richard Nixon thinks as well! Once Grace McKee left her a factoidal fifty-cent piece, and it was taken away because she dirtied her clothes. At one foster home she sleeps in a closet without windows and is raped by the wealthiest boarder in the house, who invites her into his room. Yes, it is all in Zolotow (out of Hecht), and it is all untrue. According to Dougherty, her first husband, who is now a cop, she was a virgin when they married. Of course we have only his word for it, and we need never depend on the word of a policeman, but then where is the wealthy boarder to be found if she spent the first seven and a half years of her life with the Bolenders, and close to the next two with the English couple? It is more likely that her rape comes exactly out of Marilyn's knowledge of the limits to good copy about Ida Bolender's sewing machine, or the English couple who thought to improve her grammar. That would make one good grammatical sentence in a feature story.

No, the less extraordinary truth, if we are to rely on Guiles, is that Norma Jean was in three foster homes before the orphanage—with the Bolenders, the English couple, and the well-to-do Giffens who wished to adopt her but went to Mississippi; then she was in only two more after she left the orphanage at the age of eleven. Here is Guiles' account of the first, which was "the home of a couple in Compton, California, who sold furniture polish made by the husband":

> The wife spent most of each day with Norma Jean by her side in a battered old Chevrolet. It was summer, and the girl was to remember that vacation as one spent mostly rocking back and forth over back roads seeking out small hardware stores. . . . There was no escape. While she dawdled over her breakfast, the woman was in the garage loading up the back seat of the car with white bottles. Later, Marilyn recalled, she would hear the offensive sound of the old engine revving up and the woman's voice crying out the same words every morning, "Norma Jean! Let's go! Lock the door as you come out." In less than a month Norma Jean knew the name of every village in Los Angeles County.

Finally she complained to Grace McKee, who got her into a second foster home. Norma Jean disliked this place even more and asked to be sent back to the orphanage. In what could not have been an easy choice, Grace took Norma Jean to live with her in Van Nuys. The difficulty was that she had just gotten married to a man ten years younger than herself, who had three children of his own, Erwin "Doc" Goddard, a research engineer, an inventor with dreams. He drank. In later years he might not only drink, but cast an eye at Norma Jean.

Still, the girl was established at last at Grace's house. She went to Emerson Junior High School, then to Van Nuys High School, a C student except for English, and very weak in arithmetic. (She would never have any sense of money, or time.) Writing poetry appealed to her, and essays. She won a fountain pen for "Dog, Man's Best Friend"—homage to Tippy—and claims to have been interested in Abraham Lincoln. At Van Nuys High was a well-established Dramatic Society, and Norma Jean tried out for *Art and Mrs. Bottle* by Benn W. Levy, but was not chosen. Her acting life was more intense at home. She was ready to do all the parts of films she saw, playing Marie Antoinette (*Norma* Shearer) and Jezebel (Bette Davis) in her bedroom over and over. Mrs. Esther Matthews, secretary to the principal, would tell Zolotow eighteen years later, "We are proud to claim Jane Russell, but we do not claim Marilyn Monroe. She didn't learn anything about acting while she was at Van Nuys High." No, she was not forward. A year or two earlier, when she first came to live with them, Grace and Doc had called her "The Mouse," for she would sit and listen, too timid to make a sound. Her laughter was hardly more than a squeak, not so different from the high-pitched whimper a mouse will make when it bursts for liberty and a cat is on it. In later years, she would continue to laugh in that squeak—it was the least impressive sound she could make, and there are no scenes of her laughing at length in her films.

During these years, however, her relation with Grace Goddard's aunt, Ana Lower, was begun, and it was probably the happiest association of her life, and the longest—it lasted from 1938 until Aunt Ana died in 1948. It was certainly her first relation with someone who was not only concerned about her, but adored her. Even in the factoid which follows is some sense of feeling. Marilyn is speaking.

> "She changed my whole life. She was the first person in the world I ever really loved and she loved me. She was a wonderful human being. I once wrote a poem about her and I showed it to somebody once and they cried when I read it to them. It was called, 'I Love Her.' It was written about how I felt when she died. She was the only one who loved me and understood me. She showed me the path to the higher things of life and she gave me more confidence in myself. She never hurt me, not once. She couldn't. She was all kindness and all love. She was good to me."

The quality of Ana Lower can be seen in the inscription she wrote in the book she gave to Norma Jean before she died in her early seventies. "Norma dear, read this book. I do not leave you much except my love, but not even death can diminish that; nor will death ever take me far away from you." The book is Mary Baker Eddy's *Science and Health with Key to the Scriptures*. Ana made her living as a working practitioner of Christian Science, and even produced a bit of religious dedication in Norma Jean, who would spend every Sunday with Aunt Ana and go with her to a Christian Science church. Later, in 1941, after Doc Goddard came once when drunk into Norma Jean's room and embraced her, she moved over to live in Aunt Ana's house, and thereby began the most secure year of her life. Before it was over she would be in her first sexual bloom, and this for a variety of reasons, of which the least was not necessarily Ana Lower's Christian Science. If that was a religion which every sophisticated taste had always found unendurable (since the language is of an unrelenting fulsomeness: "imbibe the spirit," and "cast out evil as unreal" for "the full diapason of secret

42

tones" will reveal "the power of Truth demonstrated"), and if the brain of Mary Baker Eddy is livid, a fever of sugars and strictures, still, back of the language is the same American passion to slash a way through the great spaces and overwhelming tangle of American life so that the working of one's own individual Mind can *prevail*. That same passion would yet produce a thousand LSD guides through the Himalayas of psychosis. So Marilyn would respond to Christian Science. Her mind, muddy, drifting, fevered, possessed of unconnected desires and extraordinary fillips of vision, could of course not help but respond to the thought that "Divine Love always has met and always will meet every human need." That offered the possibility of a future success that was not to be measured by aptitude but by need. The more she needed, the more she would get, if only she could trust the voice of her instinct which was the manifestation of Mind. So she was close to an early Hippie, there in Van Nuys and West Los Angeles in 1940 and 1941, almost saintly in her newfound Christian Science, and yet the sex object of every neighborhood through which she passed. For the metamorphosis had come. She lived in a sudden coronation of sex, a sainthood of sex. If there was a Goddess of Sex, Norma Jean might as well have been anointed by her.

We have to reflect back on the boredom of the orphanage. That torpor was not unlike a storage cell in which resentment could build up potential, that nihilistic potential of the highest human voltage. Deep inside her must have developed a blank eye for power unattached to any notion of the moral. A manifest of Yeats' beast slinking to the marketplace, the unconscious pressure toward finding power was so great that of course

she could not speak with ease and squeaked when she laughed—other orphans, survivors, psychopaths, and delinquents have taken up rifles on rooftops to shoot down on the streets. It is in fact the "blank and pitiless gaze" of twentieth-century power that sits in their eyes.

But she encountered Ana Lower, and somewhere in the mills of her psyche, libido was commenced. Had a libido ever been concocted before out of such tender love mixed into the high voltage of such blank hate? A product issued forth from her pores. She emanated sex, a simple sweet girl on still another back street, emanated sex like few girls ever did. It was as if her adolescence had come forth out of so many broken starts and fragmented pieces of personality forcibly begun and more quickly interrupted that libido seemed to ooze through her, and ooze out of her like a dew through the cracks in a vase. Long before other adolescents could even begin to comprehend what relation might exist between this first rush of sex to their parts and the still unflexed structure of their young character, she was already without character. So she gave off a skin-glow of sex while others her age were still cramped and passionate and private; she had learned by Mind to move sex forward—sex was not unlike an advance of little infantrymen of libido sent up to the surface of her skin. She was a general of sex before she knew anything of sexual war.

And in this time she also began her exploration of the arts of makeup, a skill at which she would become sufficiently superb to be respected by the best makeup men in Hollywood. When girls were jealous and gossiped about her, she looked to wear her bathing suits smaller and was delighted at the result. She was a center of attention. If libido was always flowing out to her surfaces, then she would require that it also pour in, and whenever she was the center of attention, energy would come back to her from others. So her sex appeal is always a reflection of her surroundings. She is a mirror of the pleasures of those who stare at her. Like an animal, she is never in a photograph just as herself—rather, is herself plus the sum of her surroundings. In her high school yearbook, they do not place her under A for Ability, or B for Beauty. She has the M's all to herself. MMMMMMMMMM —Norma Jean Baker. MMMMM. The initials of Marilyn Monroe are on their way.

There is not a tight sweater she does not employ nor a beauty aid she would ignore. She will wash her face as often as fifteen times a day, and Grace or Ana give her permanents to curl her straight hair. Horns will honk as she walks to school. "Even the girls," she says, "paid a little attention. Hmm! *She's* to be dealt with." And this will be told with a laugh to Dick Meryman of *Life* not two months before her death. "The world became friendly . . . it opened up to me." Boys would come visiting like a swarm over the honey. Suddenly there are twelve or fifteen boys on a quiet street all milling around her yard, hanging upside down from tree limbs to catch up her attention. MMMMMM. Yet . . . "the truth was that with all my lipstick and mascara and precocious curves I was as unresponsive as a fossil . . . I used to lie awake at night wondering why the boys came after me." She is the general of sex, but like other generals she does not feel the excitement and fear of the infantryman.

Only her periods are a clue to this early distortion of herself. They were unendurable then, and excruciating later. Zolotow gives a description of fourteen Schwab pharmacy prescription boxes on a shelf in her dressing room in 1954— they have all been ordered to relieve the pain of menstruation; she will yet make the poorest Christian Scientist in the history of the religion, for there was no pain she cared to bear if a drug could be found.

It is only if we conceive of the importance Ana Lower would be obliged to place upon menstrual pains that we can comprehend her acquiescence to a plan conceived by Grace Goddard to marry off Norma Jean, and marry her early. As a Christian Scientist, Ana might not only believe in the fundamental non-existence of pain but also have to recognize its significance when present—Norma Jean was in the grip of some most unchristian desires. Ana must have had a sense of an imbalance that could crack Norma Jean overnight, even as Gladys had cracked. Perhaps Ana Lower felt she could never offer what Norma Jean might need in a crisis. This seems the only explanation why Ana Lower does not offer to become her guardian once Doc has been offered a better job in West Virginia, which means—since Grace will move out of California—that Norma Jean will have to go back to the orphanage. Ana looks to marriage as the best solution to the problem. Or, at least, she does not resist Grace in her plan.

A most curious courtship is arranged. Some former neighbors of the Goddards named Dougherty have a son named Jim, pleasant, well-built, interested in sports, and already making good wages at Lockheed. He owns his own car, a blue Ford coupe. He is four years older than Norma Jean and is perfectly set up with girls to date—he is even going with the Queen of the Santa Barbara Festival. Yet Grace asks him, *as a favor to*

her, to take Norma Jean to the dance that Doc's company is giving for its employees. Already, at her request, he has been driving Norma Jean from Dougherty's house to the Goddards often enough to inspire his girl friend, the Santa Barbara queen, to ask him why he is "hauling a little sexpot like that around in his car." Now, maneuvered into a date with a fifteen-year-old, he feels "until the evening got started, I thought I was robbing the cradle."

The evening, however, turned out otherwise. Zolotow provides Dougherty's sensations:

> Staring up at him with liquescent blue-gray eyes, her lips tremulously parted, this girl made him feel, he has said, "like a big shot." When they danced he discovered a soft helplessness in her body. . . . By March they were going steady . . . by May they were engaged.

The process had been accelerated by Grace Goddard. With Ana Lower she paid a call on Mrs. Dougherty to suggest that her son and Norma Jean would do well to be married, for in the words of Christian Science, they could "happify existence." Now something contradictory begins to appear in all accounts. Marilyn will say in later years that she had no interest in her first husband and only got married at Grace's prodding in order to escape the orphanage. Doc Goddard will defend his wife by saying Norma Jean was in love and "sought Grace's aid in getting Jim to propose." Dougherty will claim it was a "loveless courtship" and an arranged marriage of convenience. If true, it can hardly be to *his* convenience—why would he want to accept?

Since all the motives for the marriage are so far on Marilyn's or Grace's side, we must look to the Dougherty family for a clue. At Malibu, in 1961,

Marilyn will run into a brother, Tom Dougherty, with whom she had been friendly during her marriage. Invited by him to come over for a visit, she bites him off with the remark, "How much is it going to cost?" The echo of having lived with an Irish family, hard, practical, and grudged to the bite on money is in the remark. So we may as well have the imaginary pleasure of putting ourselves into the early discussion between Mrs. Dougherty on one side and Grace and Ana on the other. Since the Doughertys are working class and Grace is a film librarian and presumably, by the measure of the early Forties, a stylish and educated woman, married to an engineer, the fundamental offer, which we may be certain was never suggested, is that Jim is going to marry up! If he is getting a fifteen-year-old who wears too much makeup, Ana Lower is there to suggest by way of her own good manners that this is a passing phase and Norma Jean will yet become more of a lady than any girl in the neighborhood.

We need no more than suppose Mrs. Dougherty is a determined woman anxious for her children to better themselves, and we see her soon placing the full weight of her opinion in favor of the marriage. To this we need only disbelieve that the future groom was simply what he later claimed to be—a good-looking *practical* adolescent who was playing the field. Perhaps he thought he was being forced to go along. We need only remember it is *Marilyn* we are talking about. So we know he has to be—more than he will ever admit—has to be secretly and hopelessly entangled in the insane sexual musk which comes off a fifteen-year-old who talks to him with eyes as soft and luminous as a deer's and then become eyes that have just gone dead in a pouted painted mouth, a presence that comes down upon his own mouth like velvet, then withdraws into a veil of mist and tears tender as a warm and rainy fog.

He has never been near such luxury of mood, such emoluments of future sex, and such longing in a girl for the strength he can offer. His relations with other girls have been more even. She, however, is hopeless and incommensurate. To kiss her is to drift in a canoe. She does not neck—she floats. He has passed unwittingly into the drug of female sex. What also attracts the good athlete in him is that no girl in the neighborhood is so desired; what frightens the good athlete in him is that there are better athletes in the world.

And she in turn has to be off on the initial exercise of star status. Jim Dougherty is her first leading man—he goes with the Santa Barbara beauty queen and owns a car; in her near field of high school sophomores, he is a luminary. So she is discovering the first laws of the actor's creation. Pumped high on the premise that she is in love, the premise has become more real than whatever reality is left once the premise is removed. Why not assume she is playing her role with such invention she is ready to enter an actor's arena where reality can be measured only by the intensity of emotion. That is all that is real. So she adventures out for the first time into that psychic territory where fantasy can reach into terrors never confessed before to anyone alive, and she confesses to him, her first actor, that she lives in terror of doing away with herself, yes, she knows she will kill herself some day.

There is no record of such a conversation, no particle of evidence to underwrite it, except that she is forever ready to tell him in their marriage that if he were to die or go away she would jump off the Santa Monica pier. It must have been said with enough seriousness to have brought forth the remark from Dougherty after her death that even if Norma Jean had remained with him she might have broken down.

So, at the least, we can guess she is more attracted to the idea of marriage than she will later confess. How to ignore that it will be her first thoroughgoing role? Already she must sense that the best route to her identity may be found by running simulations of experience through real situations. Dougherty, in turn, could easily have been overcome by the size of the mystery he was purchasing. While it is true he continues to date his other girl friends for weeks after the engagement is announced, there is no reason not to assume he is, like Norma Jean, experiencing the sensation of inhabiting two lives at once. In any case, they pass through their courtship, and are married in 1942, three weeks after her sixteenth birthday. She wears a white wedding gown, the gift of Ana Lower. Jim is in a rented tuxedo with a white jacket, the precise rental garment on which the Italian waiter at the Florentine Gardens will spill the bowl of tomato sauce. Norma Jean, shades of Marilyn to come, bursts out of the role of a demure bride when the floor show at the Florentine Gardens invites the drinking customers to come on stage and join the conga line. We can conceive of the future Monroe picking up a new role at her wedding party. We close our eyes, and see the movement of her hips—they are not floating. Her wedding peels off like a stripper kicking a gown—she is playing hoofer with real professionals.

Back to the table. The husband, brand-new husband, is livid. "You made a monkey of yourself," he tells her.

Being married to Jim, she would later remark, was like being retired to a zoo.

It is not, however, often that bad. (According to Dougherty, it is even a good marriage until the war comes along and takes him to sea.) It must be remembered that if the role she is playing is notoriously unhappy for an actress, since all emotional colors are obliged to run into the quiet gray of the housewife, Norma Jean is nonetheless ready for her first full assignment in acting—she throws herself into the part of the loving wife, and works at keeping an immaculate apartment in much the way Joseph Conrad must once have immersed himself in the study of English. It is as if she senses that it is the basic part out of which all the more interesting female roles react against. Besides, the condition of being a housewife may actually possess attraction for her. *Speaking as a human being* (the precise phrase actors employ when referring to that small part of themselves which is without a role), nothing in Norma Jean's previous life has ever been so centrally established. Naturally, "the human being" is looking for security, but then she will never have a relationship where such a motive is not present.

Soon, like ambitious newlyweds, they will move from a one-room studio apartment in Sherman Oaks to a furnished bungalow in Van Nuys, and in both places she will darn his socks, sew buttons, prove impeccably neat—which she most certainly will not be later—although the essential tinsel of such a performance stands out in her impulse to take into her living room a neighbor's cow who is shivering forlornly in the yard across the street on a rainy day. It is a tale by Zolotow, and one wants the story to be true. Only a particularly crazy young housewife will wish to take in a cow when she is also very neat. Of course, the habits and properties of animals are hardly clear to her. Once on a trip with Dougherty, who loves to camp out, they are riding along a trail at dusk. "How can this horse see in the dark?" she questions her husband, and he tells her to turn on the headlights. "Where are they?" she asks. No, the relations between man, animal and the machine are not clear to her. She is one dizzy and newly-wed dish. Her mind, at its worst, is in ways analogous to a basket-case who seethes with desires to move but has no limbs. Since she is also the kind of cook who could only have come out of a convent, it was allowed in an interview by Dougherty after her separation from Joe Di-Maggio that the reason for the split, in his opinion, was Marilyn's inability to give a man a good meal, and he recounted evenings when all Norma Jean served were peas and carrots. She liked the colors. She has that displacement of the senses which others take drugs to find. So she is like a lover of rock who sees vibrations when he hears sounds, and it is this displacement which will keep her innocent and intolerable to people who hold to schedule. It also provides her natural wit. Ten years later, when reporters will ask her about the nude calendar pictures, she will reply to the question, "Did you have anything on?" with the answer, "Oh, yes, the radio," a quip quickly telegraphed around the world, but just as likely she was not trying to be funny. To lie nude before a photographer in a state of silence was a different condition, and much more naked, than to be nude with the protection of sound. She did not have a skin like others.

Perhaps she was nearer to animals than most. She would not know about headlights on a horse because she would assume that after the barbarity of the saddle and the cinch, all other accessories were possible. Not only her libido but her intelligence lived on the surface of her skin. Like an animal, she was ready to collect any new omen in a shift of wind.

If she were animal, however, it did not mean that she was simple in her sex. The word from Hollywood over the years (where prowess in sex becomes as ticketed in men and women as batting averages) was that she was not to be celebrated as a fireball, and indeed was sometimes described—in the omnibus category of the disappointed male—as frigid. She was certainly, by more civilized report, pleasant in bed, but receptive rather than innovative, and somewhat ceremonious—like a geisha, as though the act was a tender turn in a longer passage, and food and conversation and easy laughter was also part of it, a tender description of her by a lover who had not been in love. "Of course, I cannot say how she was with other men," he remarked, "but she was always just a little remote with me. And very friendly. I liked her."

Descriptions by other men are similar. But we must not assume we know too much about her. She was secretive in the extreme, and if she had lovers in later life for which her body felt unruly desire we are not likely to find out easily. She was the measure of her surroundings. There is hardly a posed photograph in which she does not appropriate something of the background by the curve of her limbs—she is the mirror of the mood about her and may have had a tendency to return each man his own sexual goods, tenderness and detachment with a friend, but something else on a one-night stand for which she felt some blood. We will not ever know about the one-night stand.

So it is that when we make a supposition or two about her sexual nature in the time she was mar-ried to Dougherty it is not impossible to put together their wholly divergent versions of the marriage. She will call him in later years a "kind man" and a "brother." She will also state in the cold tone of a maiden aunt, "My marriage brought me neither happiness nor pain. My husband and I hardly spoke to each other. This wasn't because we were angry. We had nothing to say." Yet in Dougherty's account, her *only* flaw is the cooking. Years later, he would still be able to recite the text of typical notes she would put into his lunch pail for him to discover during coffee-break in the early morning hours of the night shift. "Dearest Daddy, when you read this," the note would say, "I'll be asleep and dreaming of you. Love and Kisses. Your baby." She is working twenty-four hours a day at the marriage.

Of course, these words are furnished by the memory of the abandoned husband years later, and his pride is hurt. She has been telling her side of it to the world for many a year and has left him measured as nugatory. So he will look to give every hint in his interviews that she enjoyed him. Unless he is a psychopathic liar, we may as well take some percentage of his word; the discrepancy can still be comprehended if we believe she was invariably the mirror of the man with whom she lived. Since he was young and athletic, and not without appetite, she was, in Dougherty's tell-it-all phrase, a "most responsive bride," and they could easily have made love in real coordination with his heart going over the hill in happiness and hers gone back to the numb center of that psychic ship she sailed without a rudder. Love they would make and love he would feel; but it was love in the middle of her role, and may have reached no further into her than an actor's simulation, a ride on a horse where finally she dismounts, the horse is gone, the ride is over. It is not a lack of grace that offers sexual problems when actors make love but the lack of an identity to give up to the act.

Meanwhile, her days as a housewife are descending into a long afternoon pall. Small surprise. She listens to the radio all day, goes on visits to Ana Lower, and serves Jim coffee once with salt, not a pinch but a spoonful, because she read somewhere that it brought out the taste. Highballs are offered to friends he invites in but appear on the table with five inches of whisky over the ice, and no water. Fish she tries to serve raw, from a picture of Japanese *sashimi;* of course they have a fight. Zolotow has it end by the husband throwing her into the shower, and because she is wearing a shrinkproof dress, they laugh. On Sunday they go to the Sherman Oaks Christian Science church. They do not smoke and not often do they drink. When they move to Van Nuys, there is a bath and she forms the habit of taking mind-meandering soaks in the tub—in later years she will keep newspapermen and studios waiting hours while she continues to soak.

> Sometimes on an oppressively hot day she would throw together an improvised picnic lunch—a couple of cold franks, a tomato, half a lettuce, and take a bus all the way to Santa Monica and "Muscle Beach." Jim had shown her where it was one Sunday. He believed in keeping fit and did some calisthenics every day, but told her "these muscle boys have gone around the bend." When one of the young men tried to make conversation, she raised her hand with her wedding band, then smiled, just to show there were no hard feelings.

Of course this has to be Dougherty's memory of what she told him after coming back from such a day, and it is perfectly possible she had a secret flirtation, or the idea of one. But we may as well accept her story as true, for it is likely she would have been transfixed by the narcissism of the weight lifters. Such shamelessness at slaving openly for one's own beauty had to suggest possibilities for herself.

Worried most likely about her restlessness, Dougherty bought a collie, Muggsie, the first dog she had dared to own since Tippy. When his parents moved into a bigger home, the young couple gave up their own bungalow and moved into the vacated apartment which was large enough to keep her cleaning all day. She was also taking funds of care of Muggsie. Two baths a week went to the dog, and it is not hard to picture her grooming him by the hour.

Uneasy at being out of uniform, however, Jim Dougherty joined the Maritime Service and they moved to a training base on Catalina Island where he became a physical instructor. It is like early adolescence all over again. She is one of the few women on the base. When she goes out for a walk, it is a theatrical happening. Men are on their knees along these service streets pretending to talk to Muggsie. The tight sweaters come back on her and the tight skirts, the shorts and the small bathing suits. She takes lessons once a week in weight lifting with little dumbbells. Her plumped breasts bounce like manifests of the great here! and now! and when she bends over, our view is into the Vale! She is still that classic American girl who will attract all men and yet have all her close relations with older women: Della, Ida, Gladys, Grace, the Directress of the Home, Ana Lower—it is the beginning of a long line. Dougherty does not begin to know where his real trouble exists. He is tempted to scold her—this dress too short, that lipstick too bright—but keeps silent. Of course, their sex, as he will hint later, is at its peak on Catalina—it could not fail to be when she comes back from every walk with the sexual waves of a hundred men still washing in on her, but Jim is feeling the natural discomfort of any man when his prize is capable of getting him into murderous fights if she persists in scattering moonlight every time she walks the midday streets. At the open-air training-base dances on Saturday night she is a sensation in a white dress as she does the lindy, her hips bobbing under each man's nose, and a hint of a hard look she does not often show (that hard look which doubles the ante of sex) is in her eyes and her mouth. She may not know it, but her unconscious is ready to take on the biggest bidder—a survivor triumphant is standing in that face.

"Come on," he says, "let's go home."

"Why?"

"I'm tired."

Now when she sleeps she may not be dreaming of him so much as of the day he leaves.

His sinecure as an instructor is lost. In 1944, he goes to sea on a ship that will take him to Australia. Norma Jean and he have been together for two years. She moves in with the Doughertys, who are out all day working, and takes care of the house. Before long she is working at a defense plant with her mother-in-law, packing parachutes and spraying dope on target planes. Like Gladys at the film studio, she is a hard worker. As if she senses that she is entering a period of great change for her, she is thriving with energy, gets an "E" for excellence from her employers, but is disliked by her fellow workers in return. She will be disliked even more when a photographer from the Army, David Conover, comes by one day looking for an attractive defense worker. Conover's assignment for *Yank* magazine is to show some young woman doing war work, and as Marilyn will comment later, "putting a girl in overalls is like having her work in tights—if a girl knows how to wear overalls."

Norma Jean has found the first focus of her life, and it is in a camera lens. She has much to learn about posing for a camera, but she does not have to learn how to pose. She has learned already what a hundred little moves of her figure will do for workers, servicemen, sailors, truck drivers, Marines. She knows how to offer the restrained gift of a smile. She is Lady Girl of the working class, and our own Rubens of the 4 × 5 Speed Graphic. Click! For if the photographer is usually seen as the artist, and his model as a species of still life, she becomes the artist when she takes a pose: she paints the picture into the camera, and few photographers will fail to pay her homage. At the moment, however, it must have been enough for Conover that he had found a promising model on that unpromising job, and he went beyond the limits he needed, posing her in sweaters, breaking out color film, taking her telephone number. Her career had begun: *Click, Pic, See, Salute, Laff,* and *Sir* were getting ready to greet her. A friend of Conover's named Potter Hueth saw the *Yank* contacts and was sufficiently enthusiastic to pose her several nights a week after work, then was so pleased with the results that in gratitude—she was working on spec—he made an appointment for her with Emmeline Snively of

the Blue Book Model Agency. Miss Snively (who was introduced, we may hope, once at least to William Faulkner) had a course she required of all her models, and it cost a hundred dollars. Norma Jean passed inspection—on reflection we are not surprised—and was told she could pay the fee out of her earnings. That did not take long. She was hired at once for ten dollars a day for ten days by a salesman for Holga Steel who needed a hostess for the company at an industrial show at Pan Pacific Auditorium. We can picture her as she sits at this exhibition. Her hair is a dark blonde, almost brown, and long and too heavy in its ringlets which are thick in a permanent's curls, her little nose is not yet little—in fact it is near to bulbous—and her upper lip is too short. She smiles, and there is a tendency for her nose to look too long (Emmeline will yet teach her to cash that smile with her upper lip pulled down—and the future Marilyn will quiver then subtly as a result), but these flaws are not merely so significant as her aura. She now realizes that men—not boys nor service personnel, but men—are flocking around her booth, executive businessmen full of financial *deeds* actually seem to like her. Deeds rather than dudes now like her! The clear sense of ambition is taking on its edge. In the ten days she works for Holga Steel, she also takes lessons at night in the Blue Book Model Agency School (fashion modeling, posing, makeup, and grooming) and calls in sick at Radio Plant where she has been working with Mrs. Dougherty. She has already come a distance from the girl who barely passed her classes and left high school in junior year. But soon she will even quit defense work: she can sometimes make as much in an hour of modeling as in a day of spraying dope. Since she is out all the time, Muggsie, the dog, begins to pine. When tension with her in-laws increases over her new work at night, she moves back to Ana Lower's house, *and does not bring the dog with her.* Muggsie will die before too long. It is "of a broken heart," Jim Dougherty will later say.

The war is over. Grace Goddard comes back with Doc from West Virginia and brings the news—since she is the only one to have been in touch—that Gladys, Norma Jean's lost mother, is feeling well enough to come out of the sanitarium. At the same time, Dougherty comes back on leave, his skin a dark yellow from atabrine taken in the tropics, and goes immediately to visit Norma Jean at Aunt Ana's. Guiles gives Dougherty's version of the scene.

> Norma Jean sat on his lap and they kissed unashamedly with Ana rocking in a nearby chair. . . . It was later, Jim remembers, that he saw the small pile of unpaid bills for dresses, shoes, sweaters and blouses from Bullocks. . . . "What happened to my allotment?" he wanted to know.
>
> "It always goes," she said airily. "All that is an investment in myself. I've got to have these things when I go out on a job. If you're dressed well, they pay higher fees. If you're in a hand-me-down, they'll try to take advantage of you."
>
> "Sure, Norma," he told her . . . "Sure, that makes sense." There was something over three hundred dollars in his wallet . . . winnings from gambling, savings from beer and women he'd declined to have. It was intended for one long blast with his wife, even a *new outfit* for her. He had imagined handing her a fifty-dollar bill.
>
> When she took the money she wept a little. . . . "I know it's a lot . . . I'll make it up to you some way."

Grace comes back from San Francisco with Gladys, who is dressed all in white, even white shoes, but the meeting is uncomfortable and distant between mother and daughter—Dougherty remembers Gladys as beautiful and close in appearance to Norma Jean except that she was not young at all. Soon Norma Jean is off with Jim on furlough, yet still modeling some of the time, and therefore not able "to make it up to you some way," for he looks on her modeling as a "cruel dedication." It is not too great a demand on our voyeurism to see a young husband in bed, while his wife, Mind all out in the electric field of her career, feels like a piece of insulation to his touch. He goes back to sea "certain he was losing Norma Jean and disgusted that he seemed to have tried to buy her back with his savings." In turn, Norma Jean takes the opportunity to rent an empty two-room apartment below Ana Lower's, moves Gladys in with her. The mother and daughter will live together for seven months into the summer of 1946 before Gladys decides (with what whole depression we can hardly conceive) that she wants to go back to her sanitarium home. According to Dougherty, Gladys was hardly cured. "She wasn't right, even then, way over the hill on religion. Always quoting the Scriptures." But then Scriptures are always totem and taboo to any Christian filled with dread. Of course, it is in the period she has been living with her daughter that Norma Jean would go away for a month with the photographer André de Dienes, and would also write to Jim and ask for a divorce. There has also been the first discussion of a movie career with Emmeline, who promises to find her an agent. So it has been a sea with more than a few new currents for Gladys, and patients just out of mental hospitals look upon new currents like sailors who do not swim. Gladys will alternate between enthusiasm and fright, pride in her daughter's career and fore-boding. Lonely nights. Norma Jean is out most evenings. Photographers take her to dinner, and illustrators. She is even meeting actors. Her career as a model has not been unsuccessful. Emmeline Snively gives the recommendation:

> "She was the hardest worker I ever handled. She never missed a class. She had confidence in herself. Quit her job at the factory without anything except confidence and my belief in her. She did something I've never seen any other model do. She would study every print a photographer did of her. I mean she'd take them home and study them for hours. Then she'd go back and ask the photographer, "What did I do wrong in this one?" or "Why didn't this come out better?" They would tell her. And she never repeated a mistake. . . . Models ask me how they can be like Marilyn Monroe and I say to them, honey, I say to them, if you can show half the gumption, just half, that little girl showed, you'll be a success too. But there'll never be another like her."

On a winter afternoon, Gladys goes over to visit Emmeline in her white dress and white shoes. Two small ladies sit in the palms of the lobby of the Ambassador Hotel and talk about Norma Jean's career. "You've given her a whole new life," Gladys assures her. We are frustratingly short, however, of other episodes or evidence on Marilyn's life with her mother—nothing further in Guiles nor anything in Zolotow, no interesting references by Marilyn to her mother. We cannot even begin to know whether Gladys feels terror of the future, lack of affection from Norma Jean (does the mother hear the whining of Muggsie's ghost?), or some stirring of hopeless old ambitions for a career herself. She is still only forty-five. We only know she goes back to the sanitarium that summer. It is Dougherty's impression that Norma Jean had to let her go back because the mother had a few hopeless habits. Gladys would go on wild shopping sprees the daughter could not afford, and was always ready to go off for a short walk and neglect to come back for days. But Dougherty was probably all but finally separated from Norma Jean by the time Gladys was re-committed, so he may not know the exact reason. In any case, Norma Jean says goodbye to her mother some time after she has gone off with André de Dienes in the spring. But since Dienes offers one of the few clear pictures of Norma Jean in this period, and his relationship to her has not been described by other writers, it may be fitting to open a new chapter for him.

He is a young Hungarian, who came to America in the move of émigrés who were fleeing Hitler, and he has made his living in New York as a fashion photographer. Like other young Europeans before him, he is vastly romantic in a strange land and wants to go West because he has read about cowboys and old mining towns ever since he was a child in Hungary. He also wishes to photograph beautiful young girls in the nude, and ideally photograph them in natural western scenes. Then he wants to make love to them. It is all part of his idea about America and the boundless promise of the West. His ambition is common enough today, but in the Forties, right after the war, not that many young men staked out so simple and precise a set of goals, and photography, still a relatively new profession, had a set of proprieties. If the secret itch of the artist was

once to paint his mistress naked, the core of writing may be to describe the sexual act and the core of acting to display fornication on a stage. As a corollary, the buried secret in a male photographer was once to photograph his woman nude, ideally her vagina, open and nude. It is a rule of thumb today: one cannot buy a Polaroid in a drugstore without announcing to the world, one chance in two, the camera will be used to record a copulation of family or friends. Everything technological now has the impulse to enter the act of creation, as much as art used to. Right after the war, however, a talented photographer did not rush to announce his desire to do nudes. Indeed, there was no market then. All magazines designed for fingering in small-town drugstore racks were filled with sweater girls—cheesecake! So Dienes, while able to content himself in romances with Ruth Roman and Linda Christian, had to delay his trip with a lovely woman through the West because he could not get one to go along. One day he called Emmeline Snively for a model. She did not know it, but according to Dienes, a few of her girls were hustling. He was in an open Hungarian mood. If a good model came, he would photograph her, and if a whore arrived he would give her ten or twenty dollars and take the afternoon off. Instead, the future Marilyn Monroe arrived. On the phone Emmeline had said, "André, you're in luck today, a brand-new girl, and she's lovely."

His first impression of the model who arrived was that she was beautifully made up. He thought there was something particularly clean and agreeable about her. "Not a whore, absolutely not, a nice young girl," he said. She had not been there five minutes before he was asking her if she would pose in the nude.

She didn't know. She wasn't sure. She was married, after all. Separated from her husband, but married. Now, Dienes was full of concern. She was precisely that Girl of the Golden West he had been looking for—he had actually been humming Puccini as he thought of his project—but the trip had to be innocent. They could take pictures and make love against splendid backgrounds where Indians had once lived. But nobody must be *hurt*. So he asked more questions, even got himself invited to dinner on some future date. When Norma Jean now excused herself from this interview long enough to go to the bathroom—his proposition must have made her nervous—he looked into her model's box to study the costumes she had brought to his studio. There was only a bathing suit. He took pictures of her that day in the bathing suit, and sent flowers to her home before he came to dinner, laid siege to Ana Lower or Gladys, he is not sure whom he met, "a fine lady and not young," and assured her of his regard for Norma Jean. She in turn said grace before the meal and assured him that Norma Jean's marriage was over, and he would hurt nothing.

So the photographer took off in a car with his model for a month in the West, and went up to Oregon and down to the Mojave, through Yosemite and above San Francisco in the redwood country, wandering to no plan, searching under desert sun for old mining towns and driving north into the snows. He did not sleep with her at first, he was not able to. She liked him, and she posed beautifully in all the clothes he had brought for the trip, but at night they took separate cabins. Since she traveled with a Christian Science prayer book, she prayed at lunch. In Yosemite there were only outdoor latrines, and

she confessed to him that she was afraid of the bears when she left her cabin in the middle of the night. Each morning they got up at five to be on the road early, but they did not make good time, for she was often carsick. Her hours passed in a state of dreaminess that left her oblivious of the environment, and this began to irritate him. Once he scolded her for never cleaning the dust off the dashboard. Still, he was very fond of her, and determined to get her to bed.

One evening, as they headed into the mountains, there was a snowstorm, and when he stopped at a lodge, there was only one bedroom open. They would have to share it. She asked him to drive on in the snow. He obeyed. They drove for several hours in a near blizzard before coming to another lodge. It too had only one room available. He was in an Hungarian fairy tale. "Norma Jean, I will sleep in the lobby, and you take the room. But we cannot go on." She laughed and said they could share the room. So he became her lover. "She was lovely and very nice, but finally it was something she allowed me to do to her." Since Hungarians are sometimes known for making love more elaborately than the Irish, it is possible Dienes had variations to offer that Dougherty might have looked upon as debased. While today one has to look into the highest ranks of the Republican Party before finding an American who is not polymorphous perverse, it was then 1946 and Norma Jean might have been surprised at such kinds of sexual variety. Certainly she did not give back any caress more tangible than gratitude. André de Dienes hardly cared. Her gratitude was what he was listening to. She had never, no, never, not before. . . . He was the first man, but for her husband, and with her husband, she had never, no, never. . . . It

55

snowed and they stayed in bed. Dienes was in love. For the rest of the trip, he would photograph her all day and sleep with her all night. He would study her as she became lost in a study of mushrooms growing beneath a tree—was she comparing them to differences she had now discovered in the penis of the husband and the lover? Did she wonder at God's design?

Or, did he ever photograph her in the nude? The answer is he tried. They fought about it. Once she even leaped out of the car while they were parked, and ran away a distance and screamed, "I won't! I won't! Don't you understand? I'm going to be a great movie star someday." After a while he gave up a little. He did not want to jar the edges of this idyll. Besides, they were going to get married. He had never been as happy in his life. Even when she forgot to lock the trunk of the car and half his photographic equipment, all of her new clothes that he had purchased, and most of his exposed film had been stolen, he settled for photographing her in dungarees. Some of those pictures are here present.

They would have a few conversations he still remembers. Once she even spoke of going back to New York with him to study law at Columbia. "Why?" She wished to do good for people.

And he in his turn, photographing her one day in the desert, said with passion, "You are going to go on and on and you will be very famous and have many pictures taken, and I will end as a hermit in a cave." And she laughed and said, "André, you are very sweet."

They came back to Los Angeles. They were engaged. Business took him to New York. In his studio there the walls were plastered with pictures of her. His friends thought him crazy. "She

is not that remarkable," they would tell him.

When he went back to Los Angeles, she was changed. He spied on her and discovered she was going out with other men. Their engagement was broken. For years he claims to have hated her, but from time to time would find himself accepting assignments to photograph her again, as at Jones Beach in 1950 when he took "the sexiest picture I ever made." Sometimes they would make love when they saw each other again, which was not often, and became more infrequent every year. Still, in this same year, 1949, unable to rid his mind of the idea that they might still be married, he went back to Los Angeles in order to be near her. But she would not see him often. He would hate her again.

The last time he saw her was in 1961. On impulse, he called her at the Beverly Hills Hotel and she asked him to come over. It was her birthday and she was alone, and drinking champagne when he arrived. Her mood was low. She was recovering from an operation for "internal troubles, female troubles," and the studio, she confessed, was trying to tell her she was insane. He thought, on the contrary, she had become "a fine, intelligent woman." They drank champagne for hours, and his mood entered into the sweet and awesome depths of what they might yet be able to do for one another again. After a long while, he tried to make love to her.

"André," he reported her to say, "do you wish to kill me? I have this operation! You must not be selfish." He left soon after, but he had a sudden rage at the thought of being betrayed, and tiptoed back, and waited on the porch of her bungalow at the Beverly Hills Hotel in the dark. No telephone calls came to her, just as there had been none that afternoon of her birthday, and none came now. At nine o'clock, she turned out the lights and went to sleep, and no lover came to replace him. After another hour, Dienes tiptoed away and never saw her again, not alive. And now he lives in a house which may be something like a cave, still a bachelor and more of a hermit and not as attached to the idea of sex every night as once he was, a vigorous man of middle height, still full of a workingman's energy and with eyes that blazed so clearly they were remembered as blue when in fact they were brown. A rugged hint of something like the features Harpo Marx might have had if he had been craggier and had not died too young is in the photographer's face. "That is the truth as it happened to me," said Dienes in his accent, "and I tell it to you all."

What he did not know is that in the last years of her life she never rented an hotel suite that did not have two exits. So she may not have gone to sleep early that birthday night in 1961, but on the contrary, have slipped out on him. The riddle of her personality is with us, in any case, as we hear this story, for the question of her sincerity is almost insurmountable. Of Dienes it is hard not to believe that he is telling the truth, and indeed it is as if the experience is still there in all of his senses and has never altered. But we can hardly know if she was serious about marrying him, or drifted through the month, and was more delighted than not when it was done. Again, as with Dougherty, the truth may be an actor's

truth, where she felt every emotion Dienes assumed she felt, but it was her role and not her identity he was given.

That is confusion enough, but it is confusion limited by supposing she told the truth to Dienes, and he was only the second man in her life. What if she were lying? She will yet become so superb an actress, and she is obviously so creative already that it must have been small effort for her to encourage him to fall in love with her. One must act toward a goal, and intensifying his love keeps the play alive. So we cannot ignore the possibility that when it comes to sex she is as consummate a liar as she will be with publicity—for that matter, it is hard for actors not to tell a lie: the premise of their improvisation becomes thereby purer. For it is not always easy to know if we are telling the truth. The lie, however, being definite, offers a foundation for a part, offers a *script*. Thus the lie gives substance to an actor's personality. So the biographer who cocks his ears like any bright dog at the remark to Dienes that she has never had an orgasm before (since this offers some clarity into her relations with Dougherty) is left later to contend with information that she says the same thing to one or two other men and so opens the question of whether something of the sort was offered to many. Indeed, she may have had many a lover before Dienes, or one or two, at any rate, we know nothing about.

Let us return then to the little of which we can be certain. She is young, she is lovely, she is clean, she is likable, she is dreamy and energetic by turns. She is capable of getting into love affairs and getting out of them. Yet she is still painfully shy, remote from herself. So she can be tender, yet cold-blooded—her love tends to

end when the role ends. So she is more and more single-minded about a career, as if not only sanity but life depends on this. Finally, she is a girl of nineteen possessed of a witch's skill in relation to the eye of a camera. Mushrooms are growing in the forest and she stares at them. The camera catches her. She is there to be caught. So her love affair with Dienes speaks also of her love for the still camera. She will yet use cheesecake as a lever to open the vaults of power in the movie studios, and they are doors guarded by ogres. Thus she is, with everything else, and all her lies, a princess with a wand to wave. Let us assume she is stroking her wand in that sweet month with Dienes and even loves him a little as the equerry whose service would refine her magic.

With this much clarity, we can still tell her story. The facts will not grow simpler. To her own lies will be added the ten thousand lies initiated by everyone's separate self-interest on a movie set. A mat of factoids awaits us. So the time is even approaching when the narrative must touch fewer events if we are to follow her at all. Still, our history now brought to the edge of her entrance into movie life, we may as well enjoy one more situation where we can have no certainty of who reverses the truth. It is just about our last glimpse of Dougherty and a good one. Back in Los Angeles after the divorce, he is obliged to pay for parking tickets she gets on her car because it is still registered in his name. He comes to see her.

Dougherty's version is by way of Guiles: "Are you happy?" he decides to ask by way of greeting.

The question seemed to have caught her by surprise. Jim recalls that she considered it for a minute or two, and then said, "I guess I should be. During the day, I'm fine. But sometimes in the evening, well, I wish there was someone to take me out who doesn't expect anything from me. You know what I mean?"

Jim knew what she meant and wondered if she would ask him now to take her out or wait a few days and call him up. The idea that she would drop him as a husband because he was in her way and then talk about her loneliness angered him. He brought up the matter of the parking tickets. . . .

"I'll pay the tickets," she said without hesitation. "In installments like everything else. . . ."

Finally, Jim got up to leave. As he stood in her doorway, she said, "We could go out sometime. I know I'd like that."

Jim said, "Okay. Sometime. Goodbye, Norma."

"Goodbye, Jim," she said. And Jim Dougherty walked down the stairs and out of her life.

Monroe's version, as told to Arthur Miller, is that when her final divorce papers had to be signed, Dougherty asked for a meeting at a bar, and there told her he wouldn't sign a thing unless she went to bed with him one more time. Another man can offer the charity of assuming Dougherty wanted a fighting chance—only a true lover dares to make a bet on the very last of his hopes. Of course, a woman might reject the charity by remarking that Dougherty still didn't feel paid for his three hundred bucks. According to Miller, Monroe never told the end of the story. We do not know how she got the signature. As for the versions—they offer their conflict. We can take the word of an actress or a narcotics cop. The life of a literary sleuth is no neater than a precinct detective's.

A group of Twentieth Century-Fox contract players, 1950

IV. SNIVELY, SCHENCK, KARGER, AND HYDE

It is fair to say she is a small sensation as a model. Cover pictures of Norma Jean appear on *Laff* and *Peek* and *See*. Dienes' photos are covers on *U.S. Camera*, *Pageant*, and *Parade*, which offers much prestige in the cheesecake trade, yet she is locked into the commercial avenues of the still camera and hardly ready for a movie career. She has not yet had her first acting lesson. Emmeline Snively, however, is like a character in a Hollywood fight film —a small-time fight promoter with the boy of his life, ready to turn the fighter over to a big manager, if only for the love of the game. So Emmeline comes up with a publicity item, and sends it to Hedda Hopper and Louella Parsons (who conceivably owe her a favor). The item is printed. Because Howard Hughes is on the front page of every newspaper after just surviving an airplane crash, and Norma Jean Dougherty does not sound like a model, the squib—a wholly functional factoid—reads as follows:

> Howard Hughes must be on the road to recovery. He turned over in his iron lung and wanted to know more about Jean Norman, this month's cover girl on *Laff* magazine.

It creates a little interest at movie studios. The most mysterious property of a factoid is that it is believed by the people who put together the factoid printed next to it. So in many a Hollywood mind, Howard Hughes *is* interested in her. Another Jane Russell? Even Norma Jean may not be convinced Howard Hughes didn't look at the cover. On this publicity zephyr she soars into higher altitudes of identity and decides to become a blonde, a blonde-blonde, which is to say honey-blonde, golden-blonde, ash-blonde, platinum-blonde, silver-blonde—the blonde will be on call.

This conversion has been a campaign of Emmeline's ever since our heroine first came into the Blue Book Agency. Norma Jean's own light brown hair, described scornfully by Emmeline as "dirty blonde," photographs much too brunette, whereas a blonde's hair can be controlled by exposure to print light or dark. But the psychological reason has to be deeper, equivalent perhaps in some recess of Snively's brain to the foot-binding of Chinese ladies—when you want the role, commit yourself to it. If you think to stand in the world for all to see, then give up your piece of identity. Norma Jean's resistance to the change has been intense. She has so little identity to give away that the act of becoming a blonde may blur the last of her few points of reference. Besides, it must be frightening for her to conceive of the further intensification of her sex appeal. As she will say in her Meryman interview more than fifteen years later, "I'm always running into people's unconscious." She is timid. We can do well to give her credit, then, for the bravery, desperate perhaps, to think to walk into the center of attention with all she knew of the violence loose in the unconscious of everyone around her.

Norma Jean went to Frank and Joseph, hair stylists, Hollywood: ". . . cut short, given a straight permanent"—farewell to dungarees and bubble gum—"and then bleached a golden blonde . . . styled in a sophisticated upsweep. She thought it looked artificial. . . . 'It wasn't the *real me*.' Then she saw that it worked."

She has her magazine covers, her divorce, her publicity item, her new hair, and now, by way of Emmeline, a Hollywood agent, Harry Lipton of National Concert Artists Corporation. When she is famous he will say "so unsure of herself—

that terrible background . . . it gave her a quality that set her apart." She gets in to see Ben Lyon, the former actor, who played with Jean Harlow in *Hell's Angels* and now is casting director at Fox. She is tongue-tied, helpless, bereft of film credits, not particularly well-spoken, "I've tried to pick up all the camera experience I can around the photographers who've used me," and a vision. Lyon, believing perhaps in Hughes' interest, orders a quick screen test, and in color—he wants her presence to stand forth rather than her lack of training as an actress. He gets Walter Lang (who is directing Betty Grable in *Mother Wore Tights*) to oversee the test after shooting for the day is done, and gambles on using a hundred feet of silent color film. Lang talks to her all the way, as if to steady her animal nerves. Under the lights, with three professional men concentrated entirely upon her, Lyon, Lang, and the cameraman, she must feel as if she has been bound into a surgical pit. The cameraman, Leon Shamroy, is quoted by Zolotow on his reaction to the test when looking at it in a Movieola next day. "I got a cold chill. This girl had something I hadn't seen since silent pictures. She had a kind of fantastic beauty like Gloria Swanson, when a movie star had to look beautiful, and she got sex on a piece of film like Jean Harlow."

"Flesh impact is rare," Billy Wilder would later say, "flesh which photographs like flesh. You feel you can reach out and touch it."

They are speaking in all the symphonic flatulence of hindsight. She will get a contract from this test—it will start at $75 a week, and if all her options are picked up, she will make $1,500 a week by her seventh year—she will actually be given the nod by Zanuck, who thinks she is a "gorgeous girl" and forgives Lyon for shooting the test without his authorization. Then she will be christened with her new name—we can join her as Marilyn at last!—but she will still languish for years to come: it is now late 1946 and more than three years until *The Asphalt Jungle*, six before *Gentlemen Prefer Blondes*, and nine years to wait for *The Seven-Year Itch*.

When Lyon called her in and gave the good news that she had been taken, she wept. All that prairie madness in the iron insane blood of her forebears must have relaxed. Perhaps she had an inkling of future events spinning into the void. She is reported by Guiles to have shaken her head in disbelief.

Then they talked about changing her name. Jean Norman in itself might have been suitable, but the shift away from herself was too small. It was to the advantage of the studio for an actor to make a substantial change in his name since it is more difficult to be unamenable if your roots are cut. Therefore she gave up sentimental ties to Jean Harlow and Norma Talmadge, and now could substitute Marlene Dietrich and President Monroe. Before she left the office, she borrowed fifteen bucks from Lyon to pay two weeks' back rent at the Studio Club. Much to his surprise, she would pay it back.

So Marilyn came to Twentieth Century-Fox (by way of *Laff*, *Peek*, and Howard Hughes' iron lung), and she would be there off and on until she was finally fired fifteen years later; that was several days after her thirty-sixth birthday, and she died in two months. If she would make money for that studio as few other stars ever had, she began as no more than an outside candidate for the third blonde (as impressive a position as trying out for third quarterback), there back be-

hind Betty Grable and June Haver, and took studio classes in voice and body movement and appeared under studio orders where she was supposed to appear—at conventions, openings of restaurants—one of a platoon of starlets and stock girls at a big premiere. She posed endlessly for stills, which went to such far corners and small towns of the newspaper world that nobody at the studio ever could measure their impact or soon react to it. "If the publicity department sent her out to the beach or the mountains to pose, she went and posed. She rode in parades in a costume. She stood on floats, one of a bevy of float-riding starlets." She was still for all practical purposes a model, but she earned less. Now, at the commencement of her true career, she comes near to disappearing. She is lost in the talent pool of a major studio, and if her agent nags at film executives to give her parts, no one seems enthusiastic about her talent. She is, if anything, more renowned for her lack of it, seen as a dumb and not so unvulgar broad. In her first year at Fox, in the period of two six-month options she is in two films. From *Scudda Hoo! Scudda Hay!*, a vehicle for June Haver, her own small part is just about entirely cut out; her second film, *Dangerous Years*, has a bit that gives her fourteenth billing among fifteen actors. Yet she is remembered at the Studio Club as being up at 6:30 in the morning and running around the block to keep the condition of her figure, and her roommate will recall the small dumbbells she used—souvenir of Catalina and Jim Dougherty. In her first summer at the studio, she studies at Actor's Lab with Morris Carnovsky and Phoebe Brand, an offshoot of the old Group Theatre in New York and so in the family line of Stanislavsky and progressive politics. (Carnovsky, Phoebe Brand, and Paula Strasberg will all be cited by the House Subcommittee on Un-American Activities during 1952.) They are part of a tradition going back to New York in the Depression when Communism was by actor's logic equal to bravery, integrity, and identity. No post-Leninist philosophers ever came out of the acting profession, and the postulates were left to simmer down to simple-shit—Marilyn would answer a question about Communists years later by saying, "They're for the people, aren't they?" —but there was a style to progressive actors and directors, a vocabulary, and if they possessed a foreign accent, all the patina of European culture was there for a Los Angeles blonde just turned twenty-one and never graduated from high school. Besides, much talk about the mechanics of acting possessed its own formal jargon. "Concentration," "sense memory," and "penetrating the subtext" had to impress a simple American mind with a prairie love of technology. She was indeed impressed, if she could hardly have understood much, for years later in New York she would seek out the Strasbergs when she already had her career, and she would finally know as much about concentration as any movie star alive—she would create parts in *Bus Stop*, *Some Like It Hot*, and *The Misfits* that were triumphs of the actor's capture of whole identity, but in the bewilderment of this first year at Twentieth Century, in what a daze she must have walked. At Actor's Lab she froze to the back bench and never spoke in class. (For that matter, she would never talk at Actor's Studio in New York a decade later.) Phoebe Brand, with whom she studied Elementary Acting, testifies, "I never knew what to make of her. I didn't know what she thought of the work. . . .

67

Frankly, I would never have predicted she'd be a success. . . . She was extremely retiring. What I failed to see in her acting was . . . her lovely comedic style. . . . I was blind to it."

Just as blind will be the studio executives. Guiles has her trying one desperate afternoon to get in to see Darryl Zanuck and is told by the secretary that he is "in Sun Valley." She goes back. "Still in Sun Valley." She is living at times on thirty cents a day—hot dogs and coffee—gets second lead in a play in a local Hollywood playhouse, but no talent scouts get in touch with her agent. Her only reward is that Huntington Hartford is introduced to her after the performance. Actually, she has another kind of notoriety in these years. Poor, and reduced to taking modeling jobs on the side, anonymous as an actress, she is also known as Joe Schenck's girl. The old producer has his chauffeur stop the limousine as she is passing on the studio street one day, for she has just given him a cover-picture smile. He could not feel more attractive if he were a camera lens. ("I'll focus on her," says Earl Theisen, "and then looking in the finder, I can actually see the sex blossoming out, like it was a flower. If I'm in a hurry and want to shoot too quickly, she'll say, 'Earl, you shot it too quick. It won't be right. Let's do it over.' You see, it takes time for her to create this sex thing.") We may as well assume she had seen Schenck's car approaching from all the way down the street, and gives her best performance in a lean season, for Schenck offers her his card, his phone number, and tells her to call him for dinner. Their friendship begins. To Zolotow she says, "The word around Hollywood was I was Joe Schenck's girl friend, but that's a lie." It is possible she was telling the truth, for Schenck

was almost seventy and by Guiles' description "beginning to resemble an aging Chinese warlord." Schenck's women were legend (he had treated them like prize leopards, mares, and poodles) but by now his sex life may have been over. Of course, sex dies hard in a sultan, and Hollywood was built on the contemptuous principle that if an actor was nothing but a mouth, what could an actress be? Hollywood had long sustained the obscene myth of the big producer installed in his private office, welcoming the little starlet in the middle of business hours, then locking the door, unzipping his fly—we can skip the moment when she goes to her knees. It is one of the few historical myths which lives in fact—rare was the Hollywood tycoon who did not like his eminence in such an act. So the gossip in Hollywood has to be graphic about legendary sensual mean old Joe Schenck, co-founder of Twentieth Century-Fox, and the unknown blonde he has lifted from a studio street, and indeed she visits him often, is regularly seen at small dinner parties in his hilltop mansion. But unless her sexuality has divided into twin compartments, Christian Science to one side and the other lobe of her mind capable of playing the totally ambitious girl who will never vomit over what she has to put in her mouth since she is in fact excited by the sexual pursuit of her ambition—all of which assumes some striking sexual metamorphoses to have accompanied her new blonde hair and new name—the likelihood is that Schenck and Monroe had, or at least also had, some kind of genuine friendship; if there was sex, it was not necessarily the first of the qualities he found in her. We are not going to know. There is, on the other hand, no reason why they would not find each other interesting.

He would have a pipeline into what was going on in the depths of the studio—he was inactive these years compared to Zanuck—and he probably also had an instinct that she could yet be a star. We can be also certain, however, that he did nothing to advance her career during all of this period. Having recently served four months of a prison sentence for perjury after bribing a labor racketeer, then turning state's evidence, to be pardoned by President Truman—what a gift to the Democratic Party must have been arranged!—he was more or less out of power at Twentieth, still respected, but kept to the side by Darryl Zanuck. He may not have been in a real position to help her, and may not have wished to advertise this inability in a showdown. Since it was one of his favorite remarks that he had to buy his friends, it was just as likely that he was testing her. She in turn may have been wise enough never to push him. Or, equally, she may have been keeping to a quiet faith in the coincidences of her destiny. Schenck, after all, had been married to Norma Talmadge.

Since she is our heroine, it would also be nice to believe that the secret they concealed from others was an intellectual companionship. It is possible. Despite her wit, she was not overbearingly bright, and if intellectual ability is comparable to weight lifting, she lifted no weight. She may have wanted to go to law school when she spoke to Dienes, but she did not have the sort of mind to connect a string of clauses and detect a flaw in her logic. Nonetheless, she had intelligence—an artist's intelligence—and her taste by the end of her career was close to superb. She must have had a profound sense of what was whole in people and false, for her own characterizations were sound—she knew how to enter a scene with the full aura of the character she played, and so able to suggest everything that had occurred on just the other side of the scene, the breeze she had smelled, the doorsill on which she stubbed her toe, the errant whimsy of a forbidden thought to be concealed, and five distractions appropriate to the character trailing like streamers. Even this early she must have seen life as some sort of divine soup of situations where every aroma spoke of the primacy of mood. Existence at Twentieth must have confused her profoundly, then, in this first year when she could hardly locate a logic to the mood of company streets, studio personnel, and movie sets. Schenck, with his profound knowledge of studio power and the habits of high movie executives, producers, and directors, the idiosyncrasies of technicians, the eccentricities of actors, and the private life of anyone who aroused her curiosity, had to be her guide into the shifting lights of the career she had chosen like a great love affair—the fearful love affair of her life. We can only imagine how much dedication Schenck saw in her, but that he saw something must be the assumption, for if he is not in love, why else see this child so often unless she is truly his protégée, and anointed by him to receive an old man's gold—those secrets he is at last obliged to communicate to another. Of course, we do not have to be too sentimental. She could have been full confidante, and still act as mistress to an old man (who could hardly be certified as not a dirty old man). A whole part of the horror which would be in her later could first have come from gifts of Schenck—we never know which curses, evils, frights and plagues are passed into another under the mistaken impulse we are offering some exchange of passion, greed, and sexual

charge. An old sultan with a thousand curses on his head is capable of smuggling anything into the mind and the body of a young woman—less is known about the true transactions of fucking than any science on earth. We can only measure where she might have been at the beginning of her acquaintance with Schenck and at the end. If possession took place, let us say she was possessed, even diabolically, by the need to become a star after just one year of knowing him, and if he was testing her ability to wait for a favor, she passed a grim test—her option was dropped after the first year at Twentieth. She was out of work for several months and had to go back to doing jobs as a model. Schenck finally interceded, not at Twentieth, but at Columbia with his "fellow pioneer" Harry Cohn. Since she was not only taken in, but assigned the second lead in a film, as well as given a dramatic coach, and singing lessons, and much special attention, Schenck must have called in a fair-sized favor from Cohn. (Perhaps Schenck knew where an old body was buried.) She made, at any rate, a film at Columbia, *Ladies of the Chorus*, a bad B-film about a young burlesque star (chaste!) daughter of an older burlesque star (classy) in love with a scion. It came out in 1948, and is the first movie where we can really see her; she sings, dances, acts, even has a cat-fight with hair-pullings, slaps, shrieks, awkward blows reminiscent of girls throwing baseballs—the film is terrible, but she is not. She is interestingly wooden in the wrong places (like a faint hint of the wave of Camp to come), and she sings and dances with a sweet vitality, even does her best to make one agree it is not absolutely impossible she is in love with Rand Brooks the scion (who must certainly be the plainest leading man any ambitious ingenue ever was assigned to love), but what is most interesting in the comfort of studying this actress who is to go so far is the odd air of confidence she emits, a narcissism about her own potentialities so great it becomes a perfumed species of sex appeal as if a magnificent girl has just walked into a crowded room and declared, "I'm far and away the most beautiful thing here." Of course, she is not. Not yet. Her front teeth protrude just a fraction (like Jane Russell's), her chin points a hint, and her nose is a millimeter too wide and so gives suggestion of a suckling pig's snout. Yet she is still close to gorgeous in her own way, with a sort of I-smell-good look, I-am-wonderful look. She is like a baby everyone loves—how wise are the tunneled views of one's own hindsight! But where does this assurance come from? Is it a product of the cover pictures, some spiritual sable donated to her by Schenck, or the sum of ignorance, and desperation converted by alchemy into a starlet's glow?

It is certainly a great deal to write about so indifferent a film. Her acting is valiant, and knows enough to be modest where the script is hopeless. Her taste is instinctive—she knows when to duck. But there is no reason to believe she will ever be an actress. Harry Cohn with his cruel wise nose for success drops her option after six months, and one cannot find fault. She emerges from *Ladies of the Chorus* only because we know she will emerge—the best thing to be said about her acting is that she blurs the edges of a wholly unreal story.

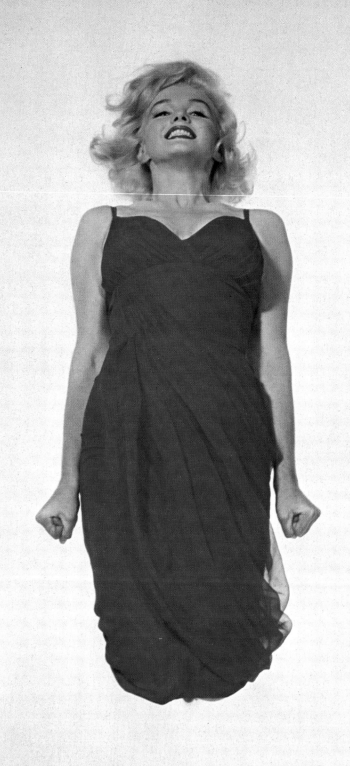

adies of the Chorus must have disappeared from memory two weeks after anyone saw it. Except for Marilyn. A part of her may have gained confidence after this film. Her roommate at the Studio Club is supposed to have asked her once, "If fifty per cent of the experts in Hollywood said you had no talent and should give up, what would you do?"

"If one hundred per cent told me that, all one hundred per cent would be wrong." It is a line to come out of the inner life of an artist, and so the dialogue is remotely conceivable.

However, we do not need more evidence than the film itself. She is just interesting enough to be fascinating to herself on the screen, for of course she will view it with every ambition of the blood. Her performance is bound to take her through an experience as large as watching Garbo or Pola Negri. The absorption must be equal to a fix of heroin; she can relax some of the tightest tensions of the long effort to locate identity. If there had been a question in her mind about a film career, we can assume it was less after *Ladies of the Chorus*. Besides, the plot was kind enough to underline her own myth: she was a working girl who would rise from the chorus and marry a son of high society. Of course, her life at this time was not without its parallel. She was now in love with Fred Karger (who had been her singing coach on the film), and his mother, Anne Karger, while not wealthy, must have seemed like the nearest Hollywood equivalent to landed gentry. In the years of silent pictures, as the widow of Max Karger who had helped to found Metro, she had kept open house, and could speak of the stars who had come often to her home, Nazimova among others. (One can hear Marilyn saying *Nazimova* in a voice that would anticipate

Jackie Kennedy.) Even that syndrome of destiny, Valentino, with his feet that fit Marilyn's feet, and his death that followed her birth, had been there to visit Anne Karger. How it must have appealed to Marilyn to meet the hostess, and how delighted was Anne Karger with Marilyn who, if being groomed by Fred Karger for second lead in *Ladies of the Chorus*, was yet without enough money to eat. How that appealed to a good cook like Anne Karger! The love affair between her son and Marilyn would end (despite Marilyn's and Anne Karger's little efforts to make it a marriage), but the sense is offered of a family whose good ties are so close that Karger chooses to move back in with his mother and six-year-old son after a divorce from his wife. He is by general description a man of some musical culture and the best of good manners. It is obvious he cared enough for Marilyn to cultivate her possibilities. He gave her evenings of dining in restaurants with candlelight by the sea and good wine for the table, they went to dance in some of the better clubs on Sunset Strip, and took trips to the desert—shades of André de Dienes!—but in all his care, and in all the skill with which he taught her the rudiments of music and voice, he also appears wary of any passion that offers too much heat, and more than a little distrustful of all women after the smash of his marriage. Besides, he is ashamed of Marilyn. Perhaps no other one of her lovers is ever so ashamed of her. We need only conceive of the magnitude of some of her innocent remarks. If her blunders had hooks, they would be big enough to gaff marlin. In his cultivated ear, he has to be living on the edge of boborygimous thunder. It is a love affair not unreminiscent of Henry Higgins and Eliza Doolittle, or Charles

Francis Eitel and Elena Esposito, except that the passion is on Marilyn's side. We even can suspect half of her love affair is with Anne Karger. If she needed both a mother and a father, it was a mother she needed first, and marrying into the Karger family would have suited her most intimidating psychological needs as perfectly as a superb vehicle will resuscitate an aging actress. Marilyn would have had a base for the career to come. This was, however, precisely what Karger did not need. He wanted a mother for his six-year-old son. So there is reason to believe he thought her not only too ambitious, but too sexual at this point. One can only offer a set of quotes from Marilyn ben Hecht fished right out of Factoidal Gulch, but there is always the hope it may be equal at least to a poor translation. Who knows? It is, at any rate, something like the portrait Marilyn wished to give of the Karger affair in later years.

> "A new life began for me. I moved from the Studio Club where I was living to a place nearer his house so he could stop on the way to work or home from work."

Sex on the way to work was the imprimatur of devotion in a Hollywood affair. More than one Hollywood star would yet brag of early morning blow jobs fresh as milk while having his studio lunch in the commissary, but those were slave affairs. Marilyn, looking for marriage, had to be more formidable. In this memoir she suggests (or is it Ben Hecht?—factoids, like amoebae, have no family line to trace) that Karger finally insulted her mortally by suggesting that if he dropped dead (keeping up with the need to make love to her?) it would be bad for his boy.

"Why do you say that?"

"Don't you see?"

"No, I don't see."

"Don't you see it wouldn't be right for him to be brought up by a woman like you . . ."

"You hate me," she said.

All we can see is Ben Hecht pic-plunking his ten fingers on the keys, but if we cut across the dialogue to the terminal fact—which is that Karger soon wed Jane Wyman after always making it clear he did not want to marry Marilyn—we can assume her narcissism, ineptitude, and huge ambition were a poor combination for a sensitive man. Meanwhile, her sexuality remains an enigma. It is the fashion by now (for the legend since her death was so fashioned) to see her as not really interested in sex nearly as much as the early publicity would promise. The testimony of a few of those who made love to her in later years suggests she was more likely to sleep with her brassiere on (for fear her breasts would sag) than to lie in abandon on an orgiastic bed, and there are all the stories of her curious innocence about sex—once after going to bed with Marlon Brando she said next morning to Milton Greene, "I don't know if I do it the right way," but then which of us does know? Every certainty in sex is followed by the recognition it is a plateau and there are peaks above. Sooner or later we all reveal our innocence about sex in a candid remark.

While it is true that numbers of her friends testify to just such innocence, to her sensitivity, her vulnerability (which of course is hardly a sexual constraint), and to the gentle nakedness of her nerves, her inability to protect herself, there is a common denominator to all such descriptions—they surround her only after she has come to New York and has had the modulating influences of life with the Greenes, the Strasbergs, and Arthur Miller. By then she was certainly enough of an actress to take on any new persona and keep it—a role of sexual modesty was at the least wise to reduce general resentment of her. Besides, whole parts of her psyche had been wounded, bruised, crushed, lacerated, amputated, thickened, and killed by then—the inside of her heart must have looked like a club-fighter's face—and she may have been just a little on the other side of sex. The question of biography before us now, however, is whether she was innocent in the early years of her career, as the last legend would claim, and that is hard to tell. While an actor's face and body can be the human equivalent of Potemkin's village, and glamour no more than a measure of the distance from the glow of the flesh to sentiments of sewer gas in the womb, not every woman who is transcendently sexual on the screen must therefore be transcendently frigid in bed. It is simpler to assume that sexual attraction is finally based on something in sex itself, or that for some years, at any rate, there is the power to find some sexual return in a phallus or vagina as well as in a mirror or a lens. The point is that Marilyn's private life in these first years is all but buried. Her secretiveness is commented upon frequently. Natasha Lytess, who became her dramatic coach at Columbia for *Ladies of the Chorus* and stayed in that relation for seven years (until precisely the end of *The Seven-Year Itch*), was also a species of housemother, since Marilyn, when down on her luck, would sometimes live with her. "I dared not ask her the simplest question about her life," Lytess would write. "Even an inquiry as to where she might be going on a certain evening would be re-

garded as unpardonable prying." A "veiled look" would come into her eyes. (Indeed, how frustrating a veiled look must be to a dramatic coach.) It is just about legitimate to wonder if it is the same expression Marilyn will show in *Niagara* when thinking of her adulterous lover. But then Natasha Lytess' first impression on meeting Marilyn is of a girl who was vulgar, artificial, and dressed like a "trollop." Lytess is writing out of the bitterness of being dropped after seven years in favor of Paula Strasberg, and has as well all the prejudices of a much cultivated European émigré reduced to giving dramatic lessons when once she has known and worked for Reinhardt—indeed her studio cottage at Columbia is formidable with books and a large photograph of the incomparable Max! No two women could seem less compatible—Lytess is, for example, calculating about money, where Marilyn will be generous, yet they form a team. Lytess will soon discover Marilyn's willingness to be serious about acting, and the power of her ambition, but it is worth something that she first sees Marilyn as the next thing to a whore because it is also the way others saw her, and the news photos and cheesecake we have of her over the next years show a young blonde who is unmistakably tougher, more sensual in her sexual display than the later Marilyn. It is worth reminding ourselves that if she presented herself this way, men, and Hollywood men to the fore, would so tend to react to her. If she is also a hint vacuous in many a photo of this period, well many a whore has had the same vacant look, indeed part of her vast attractiveness to the world, soon to be so evident, would come from precisely that expression which was ready to suggest sexual pleasure and love could be taken in separate doses, and with separate people. The need of the

high-density technological society will soon be for less family and more inter-connection in sex. Since sex is, after all, the most special form of human communication, and the technological society is built on expanding communication in much the way capitalism was built on the expansive properties of capital and money, the perspective is toward greater promiscuity. But we are talking of a sex queen, so let us force-feed sociology no more. It is simpler to make the novelistic assumption that she probably had a sex life of some promiscuity in this period. The argument has already been advanced more than once that a good actor can be the equal of a movie projector and a screen; if the projector is his will and the screen his skin, a total display of sexual energy can mean no more than that the energy within is void, we know that, but it is finally a British mode of acting, cold as its derivation from Coquelin. There is also the Method, which would have the actor become what he is playing, be possessed, be even the spirit of Priapus if an erection is called for in the subtext of the script, so it seems likely that if she were shy, withdrawn, nervous, and wholly insecure in many an interview, she may have been also on some secret catlike search through sex in these less recorded years and had many a one-night stand while searching for experience, communication, actor's enrichment, and identification—a pretty way to put it. The legends that derive from the harshest sexual gossip have her saying to her lawyer as she signs the papers for a big contract, "Well, that's the last cock *I* suck." The biographer can immediately ask, "Which contract, which lawyer?" and indeed the same story has been told about other actresses—one can better ask about which Hollywood star it has not been told—but the real measure of the broad and ugly stories about her is to be found in the huge resentment she aroused once she began, when successful, to give trouble at Twentieth Century-Fox. We anticipate a period still some years away, but part of the explanation for that vast rage may have been in the knowledge (of the most complacent cigar-smoking studio executives) that she was a girl who once could be had—at least by some. It is all supposition here. One can hardly stand up in literary court with a hundred signed affidavits of one-night stands. Let us leave it that Ana Lower died in this year, 1948, which could certainly have kicked Marilyn loose of Norma Jean's last restraints, and her roommate Clarice Evans of the Studio Club testifies that she had more dates than any other girl at the dormitory and never spoke about them. The best evidence, *force majeure*, is still in her photographs—she looks in these years like the most popular blonde in the most expensive brothel in Acapulco, and while the look is manufactured, it is easier to assume the raw material partakes of existence than that it does not exist, and her sex is altogether synthetic. The likelihood and the tragedy is that these are the years when she is giving more of herself than she will get back, and for too little, so that later when she is in love she will be able to offer less and must demand much more—at the least we know that she cultivates her sexual sweetmeats in the sexlands of swamp and plague.

78

t is a choppy period. Her agent, Lipton, describes her as moving around like "a flea on a griddle." In this period before her affair with Karger, she rents a little haunted house against the warnings of friends and leaves it soon after—it is interesting to suppose that promiscuity helps to summon a few ghosts, some spirits in her, and she has an experience or two in the house we will not soon hear about. Earlier, living in Burbank, an off-duty cop who had met her on the street and been attracted cut through a screen door to enter her apartment. Marilyn's screams bring neighbors and he flees, but in her mind it must be shades of the wrath of Jim Dougherty, who is now a cop as well. Then she is befriended by John Carroll the actor and his wife Lucille Ryman the talent scout. They take her in to live with them. Soon enough she attracts a teen-aged peeping Tom who brings a ladder to her third-story window. She must be living in the fear of violence, yet she almost breaks up the marriage—Carroll, who played supporting actors and occasional leads, has a strong resemblance to Clark Gable—and Marilyn walks around in a robe with nothing beneath. Finally, as Guiles reports,

> Marilyn took Miss Ryman aside one day and said, "Lucille, I want to have a little talk with you. You don't love John. If you did, you wouldn't be off working all the time. I think I'm in love with him." This announcement, Miss Ryman asserts, caught her completely by surprise. Whether or not Marilyn had been encouraged by Carroll to get the matter into the open is unclear, but she then asked, "Would you divorce him so we can marry?"
>
> When Miss Ryman recovered from her shock, she asked Marilyn what had prompted all of this, and Marilyn is said to have answered, "No one who is that good to me could *not* be in love with me." Miss Ryman then terminated the discussion, saying, "If John wants a divorce, he can have it."
>
> No divorce resulted from this confrontation and the crisis passed with no one outside the Ryman-Carroll household observing any special melancholy in Marilyn.

The haunted house comes after this, then the Bel Air Hotel, the Beverly Carlton, next a motel, and then the Studio Club again. Now begins her affair with Karger, and then she lives with Natasha, who tells her not to go out on so many dates because men "were interested in her as a human being and not as an actress." She also tells her to put on underwear, for Marilyn wears nothing beneath her dress, as if her skin is the true undergarment. Then she is dropped by Columbia and makes the rounds. Her agent gets her a bit in *Love Happy* with Groucho Marx. She has a classic moment—the famous undulating movement of her hips is now unveiled for the first time on film. It is an uproarious moment in the movie—the wild call of a strange girl's ass to Groucho Marx—he engorges his cigar in a leer.

"What seems to be the problem?" he inquires.

"Men keep following me all the time." She exits, Mae West in one swinging pocket, Jean Harlow in the other. It is uproarious, but she may have been desperate. Twice hired, twice fired, and she is approaching the age of twenty-three—Elizabeth Taylor, who is four years younger, is already famous. So she puts everything she knows of provocation, exaggeration, and the nascent art of Camp into the swing —"Take me from behind, I'm yours," say her undulating hips. A blonde with an anal bent is looking for the towers of power: no wonder Karger abjured her as high explosive.

But it is a Faustian contract she has made. The well-known agent Johnny Hyde will see her in *Love Happy* at a private screening and meet her soon after, then put in a call to Lipton to take over her management. Her future career will be designed by Hyde and he will bring her to the attention of every major studio executive in Hollywood before he dies, she will go to New York on a publicity tour for *Love Happy* and receive a very good reception from the press considering she is an unknown starlet with thirty seconds in a film, she will splash in the papers with three ice cream cones in each hand on a very hot June day beaming at New York, but back in Hollywood over years to come she will be branded as a freak, a sexual gargoyle, a joke, a hip slinger, a tail switcher, a tart who "throws sex in your face," yes, of course she would pay for keeping that walk in future years when executives would not believe she was a serious actress and cast her in roles which were slowly killing her, yes, a Faustian contract—it can hardly be the first she has made.

It is in this period that she is photographed by Tom Kelley for nude calendar shots, and according to Zolotow's interview with him Kelley thought she was "graceful as an otter, turning sinuously with utter naturalness. All her constraint vanished as soon as her clothes were removed. [Kelley] remembers the experience as extraordinary in its intensity." She signed the release Mona Monroe. The photographer said, "I can tell you this. Marilyn Monroe has more sexual vibrations than any woman I ever shot." Looking at the prints, we see her body is in superb condition. Ah, those dumbbells at Catalina. She is paid fifty dollars, which she needs for the installment on her car, and probably treats it as a buried episode.

What is more significant now is the interest Johnny Hyde has begun to take in her.

He is one of the biggest agents in town, one of the "best-loved" and "best-respected." Hyde was "wonderfully compact," as Elia Kazan would describe him, "short but nothing soft or small about him, nothing wasted in his body, and he had *good* manners. He was one of the few important men in Hollywood who had class."

She has a first meeting with Hyde at the Racquet Club in Palm Springs. "We had some drinks and we talked. . . . He listened to me when I talked. . . . He said I would be a very big star. I remember laughing and saying it didn't look like it because I couldn't make enough to pay my telephone bill. He said he had discovered Lana Turner and other stars and that I had more than Lana and it was a cinch I would go far." He had standards for comparison. Some of his other stars were Betty Hutton and Bob Hope, Esther Williams and Rita Hayworth. He had managed Al Jolson. Studio heads like Darryl Zanuck and Dore Schary, Don Hartman of Paramount and Jack Warner, were even cronies when they were not disputing with him over contracts, for he was close friends with his clients, and "golfed with them, counseled them on money problems and marital difficulties, wrangled with studio executives for them." He even drank with them.

Since he was the son of a Russian acrobat who had a vaudeville act with the modest title of Nicholas Haidabura Imperial Russian Troupe, and grew up on vaudeville stages as Johnny Haidabura until the name was changed to Hyde, he had no more education than Marilyn. Yet everyone agreed he had good taste—we need only conceive what a distillation of acrobatic exer-

cises went into retaining taste after years in Hollywood! So she was drawn to him—for his mind. He was one of the very few men who could teach her more about Hollywood than Joe Schenck. He was also fifty-three. She was thirty years younger and still not altogether out of love with Karger, whom she would use as a confidant during her affair with Hyde as if still attempting to impress the singing coach, but then Karger would hardly be attracted to her ability to rise in the world when that was the trait in Marilyn which had first made him uneasy. If he ever saw her as Sister Carrie, he was perfectly willing to let Hyde play Hurstwood. And the agent, small doubt about it, was disastrously in love with her. He had a family of four sons and a beautiful wife, Mozelle Cravens, "an ingenue he had liberated from Republic Pictures westerns." If he had also a history of affairs with many of his female clients, his wife, if not enchanted, none-theless seems to have managed to accept the prin-ciple that a creative agent like a psychoanalyst or a talent coach has to get into the guts of the talent in order to express his own talent. So for years he had been half a husband but a good one. Marilyn exploded this arrangement. Since he was forever taking her to Romanoff's or Chasen's to help publicize her, their affair was advertised before it may even have existed. Hyde was a sick man with a very bad heart. If he knew Mari-lyn for a year, his heart was so bad toward the end of the year that his chauffeur had to carry him up the stairs to his bedroom. In the earlier months of their relationship, however, when he was merely gambling with his heart rather than mortgaging its roots, there was no studio execu-tive who had not been alerted to the incandescent possibilities and unlimited future of Marilyn

Monroe. Since she was a girl with an unsuccessful B-movie to her credit, plus one burst of thirty seconds in *Love Happy*, plus snippets in *A Ticket to Tomahawk*, the gossip must have doubled. What a monumental experience the girl had to be in bed, reasoned top executives, if Johnny Hyde could lose his judgment. So word of the affair began to intensify. Mozelle Hyde heard. "I'm a tolerant person, but there is always a limit. I remember once Jimmy (my son) was down in the cellar looking over some old things of his father's and he found Marilyn's nude calendar . . . brought it upstairs." (Since Marilyn's posing for nudes was still unknown, the discovery of her photographed nakedness in Mozelle's husband's cellar papers must have seemed like obsession with a slut to the wife.) Mozelle finally confronted him. Hyde simply told her, "It's happened and I can't do anything about it." So the wife filed for divorce. Johnny Hyde asked Marilyn to marry him.

She wouldn't. It is one of the mysteries of motivation in her life. He would be, even after the settlement, a millionaire; Marilyn had no money. He respected her, and she must have needed respect in those years the way a terminal patient cries for opiates—to marry him would be to live in the atmosphere of his respect. He was also a great teacher, able to instruct her in the strategy of choosing roles. Already, his manner was refining her manner. (She will be curiously refined and special as Miss Caswell in *All About Eve*, a role he will obtain for her.) And he adores her. Love as well as respect is being offered to her. He will be a father. He will even die for her. His last arguments for marriage are close to a beggar's art. He cannot live long, he assures her, his death is a matter of months. She

will not be trapped with an invalid, no, he will be dead, and she will have his name and his resources, and she will make him happy for a little while. Still, she refuses. She loves him, but she is not in love with him. As if he knows that he is only a month or two away from his death, his professional time is devoted more and more to her future; he must anticipate all the difficulties ahead. He arranges a new contract at Twentieth for her. It is again for seven years, but now she will start at $750 a week. At least her finances will be secured and she will be active in film. He induces her to have plastic surgery. The bulb at the tip of her nose is subtly reduced—farewell to W. C. Fields—and a minor deficiency of her jawline is corrected with cartilage. Since the protrusion of her teeth has been taken care of by an orthodontist selected by Karger, her face is now in final altered form, and has reached the stage where she can launch an attack on a major career without any fundamental flaw of feature. And Hyde, with his heart wearing out, his thin body losing weight, and his fingertips pinching him warnings of the next and final heart attack, is still trying to induce her to marry him, yet having conversations with his business manager about how to leave Marilyn one-third of his estate if she won't. He dies abruptly, sooner than he expects, and she is specifically not invited to his funeral by the family, no, it is worse than that. She has been living with him in the house he bought after separating from his wife, and in the hours after his death, a lawyer representing Johnny Hyde's family calls and tells her to move out, personal belongings and all of her body pelf—out! But ministers dispute when kings die. Some of Hyde's friends and associates encourage her to go to the funeral.

As they file past the coffin, she throws herself across him and screams, "Wake up, please wake up, oh my God, Johnny, Johnny." She is led to the rear of the church. She is alone again with the wrath of Hollywood on her head, a blonde who killed a good man. In the immediate future she will pay for not marrying him.

By now it is no more than a game of intellectual speculation to wonder why she did not. If she had been calculating in many an act of her life, and well able to anticipate oncoming forces in her career, she had also, as Arthur Miller would remark, a kind of selflessness, even saintliness, from time to time, and it was possible, he thought, that one need look for no more motive than that she did not love Johnny Hyde and had too much respect for love. Money, said Miller, was never real to her, and so never a motive.

As one thinks of her, it seems true that money could solve nothing but petty embarrassments and aggravate her purest problem. It is always the dislocation of her identity to which we return, and the paradox of Johnny Hyde's devotion is that she adored him because he could shape her career and so be equal to furnishing the house of her identity. That was why she could hardly marry him. As his widow she would have to shift that identity for another, be then a merry widow, and a black widow, a woman known as Mrs. Hyde. What an obsession is identity! We search for it, because the private sensation when we are in our own identity is that we feel sincere as we speak, we feel *real*, and this little phenomenon of good feeling conceals an existential mystery as important to psychology as the *cogito ergo sum*—it is nothing less than that the emotional condition of feeling real is, for whatever reason, so far superior to the feeling of a void in oneself that it can become for protagonists like Marilyn a motivation more powerful than the instinct of sex, or the hunger for position or money. Some will give up love or security before they dare to lose the comfort of identity.

The next question must obviously inquire what fearful objects or monsters are to be encountered in such a void, but it is a question to postpone until the wings of death lay wet feathers across her face. Let us see her here in her honor. For, whatever motive, whether the "saintliness" of rejecting money (grave poet of the middle-class mind, Miller would indeed see the refusal of wealth as saintly), or to protect that identity so painfully coalescing, still she was bold enough to keep to a course that all of her practical friends must have considered madness, kept to it against all of her affection for Hyde, and all her fear of being alone when he was gone. Let us suppose she was pointed so clearly into the arrow of her own direction that, like Joan of Arc, she could hear a voice. Since she was considerably less of a saint—we must assume!—this voice merely told her not to marry. It could have been no modest command to obey.

Hyde? There are men who rush to their death as if they are in a race with something other. Gary Cooper, dying of cancer, said to Hemingway, "Bet I beat you to the barn." No, we do not know enough about Hyde to find a source for his desire to die with speed, no, we do not even know if the fingers of old Hollywood ogres are clutching at his wrists when his own heart finally opens an acrobat's fingers and flies out beyond the net.

V. MARILYN

Snively, Schenck, Karger, and Hyde! If she had been a bargirl looking to sue an ex-lover in a raunchy case, she would have picked her law firm out of the yellow pages with a name like that. She could now have used their advice. Hyde had helped her to get the part of Angela in *The Asphalt Jungle*, and helped again for the part of Miss Caswell in *All About Eve*. While both parts were small, she had been sensational in both, yet Dore Schary was not impressed enough to give her a deal at Metro, and Hyde barely succeeded in obtaining the seven-year contract (in half-year options) at Twentieth before he died. She had been known for years, first as a cover girl, then as a starlet with a flair for publicity, and for a long time as a kid with connections in the industry and therefore the poorest reputation. Now she was even going to be seen by a few as an actress with talent! Yet her career was in more confusion than her personality—Twentieth did not cast her for months and then only in a series of trivial films and small parts over the next two years. On loan to Metro, she did *Right Cross* and *Home Town Story*. For Twentieth there was *The Fireball*, *As Young As You Feel*, *Love Nest*, *Let's Make It Legal*, *We're Not Married*, *Don't Bother to Knock*, *Monkey Business*, *O. Henry's Full House*, and *Niagara*. They are all in varying degree unimportant films, and need little more description than their titles. *Love Nest* is worth a footnote in any history of cinema, for Jack Paar has a part in it, *We're Not Married* is comic, and *Don't Bother to Knock*, although a slow and disappointing piece of cinema, is worth study for a student of Monroe since she gives a serious performance in the part of a deranged girl with nuances of alternating numbness and hysteria, although she fails to project much menace. It is a role she does not go near again. She has a classic stuntman's ride in an automobile with Cary Grant in *Monkey Business*, a scene with Charles Laughton in *Full House*, and a starring role in *Niagara*, where she offers the only interest. Her best performance in this whole period is not even for Twentieth but RKO (across the fence from the orphanage), where she does *Clash by Night* with Barbara Stanwyck, Robert Ryan, and Paul Douglas, and steals all the publicity.

It is an abominable waste of the talents of the girl who was seen in *The Asphalt Jungle* and *All About Eve*. Her career echoes in the vacuum left by Hyde's death. Even his agency, in reaction, shuns her. She is without an important guide, and yet she is still the best and most interesting personality in all these film squiblets, bits, and tidbits, mangled nuggets, rushed productions, factory products, vehicles for other stars, items in omnibus movies, and supporting roles, all her hordes of supporting roles. Before this stretch is completed, they are billing her name on top no matter how small the part—she has emerged. Unaccountably and incredibly, she has emerged from this detritus of the insignificant, these films which are non-films, this burial ground of old movies. She emerges even as we look at the films today. She is more vivid on the screen than others. She has more energy, more humor, more commitment to the part and to the playing—she *plays* the roles, she gives off the happiness that she is acting, and that is indispensable for any cheap entertainment. Once actors become depressed in a work without value, then the audience is attending an obscene rite—which may be why bad art in theatre or film evokes such intimate rage. Instead, she is giving every sign of being an absolute bonanza in the gold country of the West, a sacred rite in the holy grove of film, and the studio is the last to discover what they have.

Nobody can ever estimate the damage this does to whatever reservoir of good will she has managed to carry up from childhood; it is not hard to comprehend her later detestation of directors and producers; her retaliations will be nihilistic. She will savage the best of directors with the worst, and push the cancer of wasted waiting time into actors she loves just as much as she will punish actors she detests; she probably is deprived by these early films of the last chance to become a great artist and still have a little happiness left for herself—no, she will become instead a sly leviathan of survival, and, Faust among the Faustians, will set out to become one of the world's most formidable monsters of publicity, all to advance that career she deserves and which the studio will begrudge her.

It is here that the sharpest and most cogent account of her actions is to be found in Zolotow and Hecht rather than Guiles, as if Zolotow who purveys old feature stories and Hecht who makes them up with all the joy other biographers look for in facts have thereby the better instinct for poking into Marilyn's tricks when the subject turns to publicity; so the portrait they give of her in these situations seems not only livelier but closer to the essential imbalance of her position in the year after Hyde is gone.

Marilyn testifies: "I used to have nightmares about Mr. Zanuck. I used to wake up in the morning thinking I have to make Mr. Zanuck appreciate me and . . . I couldn't get in to see him. I couldn't get in to see anybody that counted. . . . [Mr. Zanuck] told somebody in the front office . . . that I was just a freak and he didn't want to waste time on me." In her bitterness, she makes a nice comment (even if it is written by Hecht): "Studio bosses are jealous of their power. They are like political bosses. They want to pick out their own candidate for public office. They don't want the public rising up and dumping a girl . . . in their laps and saying, 'Make her a star.'"

No one ever seems to have disagreed with the estimate that Darryl Zanuck liked to put his own meat into a star's meat so that the product was truly stamped Twentieth Century-Fox. In his eyes she had to be Schenck's meat and Hyde's potatoes. No glory to his own sausage. Of course this is just a factor among twenty others—Zanuck has better reasons for not advancing her. His idea of a great movie is *Gentlemen's Agreement*. Marilyn simply does not fit his concept of what to offer the public—which is a three-word secret formula of Zanuck's which has brought in great sums of money for Twentieth Century-Fox in the past. The formula: "Make good shit." He does not hold the pulse of the American public, he inhabits its bowels. Marilyn Monroe is much too wicked for good shit. She ups the ante, a freak, and Zanuck likes a game where he controls the limits. He is hardly plotting against her, she is merely one of a hundred tendencies he is holding in firm restraint.

She now, however, has the indispensable rallying cry of the artist—a tangible villain to hate. And an art to espouse—herself. Since he, in her mind, is determined to obliterate her, she will in turn vanquish him. Like any great political leader, she will go to the people. He can cut off her acting roles, but he cannot control every last avenue of her publicity. So she returns to what she will always know—the still camera. And is the perfect pet of the shooting gallery at Twentieth Century where still photographers work with starlets. They welcome Marilyn back. She takes up where she began on her first contract three years before, and her publicity stills begin once again to cross thousands of newspaper desks, her face pops forth. Irrepressibly, she whispers in the ear of the man who looks at the photo, "You can fuck me if you're lucky, Mr. Sugar."

But she is a true general marshaling every aspect of her campaign, and not only shoots her guns out to the world, but into the charged centers of the studio. Zolotow portrays one salute to Darryl Zanuck on a day when she is called to pose for pictures in a negligee while supposedly relaxing in her apartment after a day of moviemaking at the studio. The pictures are of course to be taken at the shooting gallery. (In Factoid Manor, it does not matter; one starlet's apartment looks pretty much like another.)

> Marilyn decided to be dramatic. She changed into a negligee in wardrobe, and then she walked the six blocks to the gallery. Barefooted, her long hair streaming loosely behind her, her skin clearly visible under the diaphanous negligee, she slowly floated along the studio streets. The studio messengers, on bicycles, spread the news. By the time she started back to wardrobe, after posing, the streets were lined with cheering throngs of studio employees. The next day, items about her escapade appeared in the trade papers. She was the talk of the movie colony.

Was she mad, went a query through the studios, or a sexual bomb Zanuck did not know how to use?

> A few weeks later, the studio gave a party for a group of visiting exhibitors. Marilyn, together with other starlets, had been ordered to attend. Naturally, the main attraction was such stars as Anne Baxter, Dan Dailey, June Haver, Richard Widmark, and Tyrone Power. But when Marilyn arrived, an hour and a half late, it was she who was mobbed by the theatre operators and film salesmen. The exhibitors kept asking her, "And what pictures are you going to be in, Miss Monroe?" She fluttered her eyelashes, and said, "You'll have to ask Mr. Zanuck or Mr. Schreiber about that." Soon Spyros Skouras, the president of 20th Century-Fox, became aware that his leading stars were being trampled to death in the stampede for Marilyn.
>
> "Who is that girl?" Skouras inquired of one of his myrmidons. The myrmidon didn't know. He went to ask, and reported that her name was Marilyn Monroe and that she was a contract player. Skouras then asked the same question everybody else was asking. "What picture is she in?" Informed, rather nervously, that she was not in any forthcoming studio products, Skouras glowered. . . . Skouras growled, "The exhibitors like her. If the exhibitors like her, the public likes her, no?" . . .
>
> Zanuck gave orders that Marilyn must be worked into any film that was in production and could use a sexy blonde, and there are very few Hollywood films that can't use a sexy blonde. Supporting roles for her were found in *As Young As You Feel* and *Love Nest*.

Now she is making films, precisely those inconsequential mediocre films, and the publicity mills of prose are also working. Stories appear of her in *Collier's* and *Look*. "Miss Monroe's value during the past year has risen faster than the cost of living," go the words in "Hollywood's 1951 Model Blonde." Less than a year before, her friend Sidney Skolsky relates how in a depression she had said "that she'd keep working and that nothing—do you hear?—nothing would stop her from becoming a movie star. Then in the next breath she'd doubt that she could ever make it."

Of course, she was in a period when the inner life of a race car driver would be clear to her. She was living in publicity, and in all the perils of publicity. (The virtue of little identity was that she did not have to suffer too much embarrassment with publicity.) Since she was, however, the near-empty and close to wholly prevaricating center of every last piece of dialogue she was slugging into newspapers, she had to feel the gap between history and publicity. It was as the abyss between flesh and plastic. Just as one never knew when a piece of plastic would break because there were never proper signs of stress, so one could know no better when a factoid was ready to explode. That she worried about a few items in her past seems likely, for unless Johnny Hyde had been given the nude calendar of her by someone else (which would be a story in itself!), more likely it was in his papers because Marilyn wanted him to think about the problem of possible exposure.

Zolotow gives a version of how the calendar photo was finally revealed which is good enough to make a vintage film; the plot is as intricate as a three-cushion carom with English and draw, and yet believable since Jerry Wald—the happy model for *What Makes Sammy Run*—was the center of it. Wald, who had just finished producing *Clash by Night* at RKO, was blackmailed one day by a man who wanted $10,000 not to reveal what he had discovered. Into Wald's ear came the information over the phone that Marilyn Monroe could be seen nude in half the bars of America. Exposure might hurt the release of *Clash by Night*, especially if religious groups were to start a boycott. Wald, however —we *must* be watching a movie—listens to the arguments of Norman Krasna, the writer, who

thinks this will help the picture more than hurt it. Fell moment! We are at a turning point in publicity, and Eisenhower is not yet even President! The game plan is worked out as follows: Monroe is merely on loan to RKO, and the immediate notoriety will make people curious to see the film. If her later career is hurt, that can only do damage to Twentieth—and her seven-year contract. RKO may as well take the money and run (from the wind whistling in the orphanage windows). Wald has a new worry, however. What if the blackmailer loses his nerve and never exposes Marilyn? They decide to do it themselves. A tip is phoned to Aline Mosby of United Press. Mosby calls Twentieth. They pull Marilyn off the set of *Don't Bother to Knock*. Naturally she has been discovered just in the hour she is playing the madwoman under the director named Baker.

Now when Twentieth learns from her lips that she has, yes, posed in the nude, a novelist has a right to invent the following dialogue. "Did you spread your legs?" asks a studio executive.

"No."

"Is your asshole showing?"

"Certainly not."

"Any animals in it with you?"

"I'm alone. It's just a *nude*."

"You are going to deny you ever took those pictures. Some other blonde did the job. Somebody who has the misfortune to look like you."

She asks Sidney Skolsky for advice. A gossip columnist is a master plumber. He can gauge the likelihood of future news leaks. The story can no longer be contained, must be his judgment. So she tells the truth to Aline Mosby, which is to say she passes on the living factoidal truth: "In 1949 she was just another scared young blonde

struggling to find fame in the magic city and all alone. . . . She posed, stretched out on crumpled red velvet, for the artistic photo three years ago, because 'I was broke and needed the money!' "

Clash by Night does superb business and her name gets the most prominent billing on the marquee (although she has only the fourth lead). No storm breaks. In 1951 a movie star could hardly be discovered in the nude (for money) and survive, but she is an orphan in the land of Christ. Within a short time, studio executives who have been screaming at her are signing requisitions for Publicity to buy calendars and give them to the press.

She is clear. She is a phenomenon. There are mysterious properties to publicity. "Quantity changes quality," Engels once wrote, by way of indicating that one apple is a taste and one hundred crates of apples is the beginning of a business. (Of course, a million crates is one finger of a conglomerate with insurance, the Mafia, ski equipment, and the space industry—farewell to Engels!) We can leave it that a starlet in the lower depths of an option contract who receives more publicity than any star has performed some equivalent of breaking through the sound barrier. The influence of controls is reversed. When the news breaks two months later that she has only pretended to be an orphan (and in fact has a mother who is very much alive in a mental hospital and is even a charity ward of the state while Marilyn is making $750 a week), the tone of the new exposure, arranged by the studio as an exclusive to Erskine Johnson, the Hollywood correspondent, is hardly savage:

Marilyn Monroe—Hollywood's confessin' glamour doll who made recent headlines with the admission that she was a nude calendar cutie—confessed again today.

Highly publicized by Hollywood press agents as an orphan waif who never knew her parents, Marilyn admitted she is the daughter of a one-time RKO studio film cutter, Gladys Baker, and said, "I am helping her and want to continue to help her when she needs me."

Said Hollywood's new glamour queen: "Unbeknown to me as a child, my mother spent many years as an invalid in a state hospital. . . . I haven't known my mother intimately, but since I have become grown and able to help her, I have contacted her."

And the gap in her charitable instincts is covered. She has Gladys moved from a state institution to a private nursing home. Marilyn's business manager, Inez Melson, is made her guardian.

In the moral arithmetic of publicity, to be an orphan is a plus, while girls indifferent to their mothers' welfare obviously lose points. It is hard to think of a story which could damage her more. Yet she gets out free. She has already burst out of all standard frames of reference for publicity. Quantity changes quality! She is now the secret nude of America's dream life—secret precisely because it has been so public! Our heroine has been converted from some half-clear piece of cheesecake on the hazy screen of American newspapers (where focus always shifts) to another kind of embodiment altogether, an intimate, real as one's parents, one's family, one's enemies, sweethearts and friends. She is now part of that core of psychological substance out of which one concocts one's life judgments. (George Wallace is such a figure today.) Marilyn had become a protagonist in the great American soap opera. Life is happy for her one hour, tragic the next; she can now appear innocent or selfish, wronged or wrongdoer—it no longer matters. She has broken through the great barrier of publicity—overblown attention—and is now *interesting*; she is a character out there in the national life, alive, expected, even encouraged, to change each week. The spirit of soap opera, like the spirit of American optimism, is renewal; God give us a new role each week to watch, but a role that fits the old one. Because that, Gawd, is how we learn!

What deeper or more wonderful motivation can there be to her affair and marriage with DiMaggio? It will occupy her center of publicity for the next three years, and she will meet him after the story of the nude calendar has hit the wire services. Or is it just before? As with everything else about her, there is a double image to most of the facts.

She has a strange relationship with DiMaggio—strange because it cannot possibly be as mundane as she will later present it—and it is virtually undocumented, although choking in factoids. DiMaggio never gives much to an interview, and her version of him, when married to Miller, is spiteful, even reminiscent of the way she has already dismissed Dougherty. Yet DiMaggio will always be there when she needs him, and is probably her closest friend in the months before she dies. Certainly he is the first of the bereaved at her funeral. The enigma that remains is of their sex life. Was it a marriage whose good humor depended on the speed with which they could make love one more time, and lie around in the intervals suffering every boredom of two people who had no cheerful insight into the workings of the other's mind; or is it a failure of tenderness (and soon a war of egos monumentally spoiled)

between an Italian man and an Irish girl (by way of Hogan) who had been built to mate with one another, and would therefore have been able to thrive in any working-class world where marriage was designed for cohabitation rather than companionship.

These speculations belong to gossip unless we recognize that if it has not been sexual attraction, or some species of natural suitability, that brings them together, then her motivation is more than a little suspicious, and even suggests she has grown ruthless in the years since Ana Lower's death. While accounts of their first date excite a factoidal rhetoric with only the smallest resonance of reality—"There's a blue polka dot exactly in the middle of your tie knot. Did it take you long to fix it like that?" she is supposed to say after a silent dinner, while he is supposed to blush in silence and shake his head—still the tempo of their subsequent meetings takes on acceleration in proportion to her recognition of his fame. She knows nothing about ballplayers when she meets him—she might as well be the belle of Puerto Rico being introduced to Stein Eriksen—she is merely relieved, she confesses, that he did not have "slick black hair and wear flashy clothes." Instead he was "conservative, like a bank vice-president or something." (To someone as protean as herself, dignity would be indispensable in a man, a node of reference by which to measure her own spectrum of movie star manners, good and bad.) It is only over the next few weeks that she comes to learn he has been the greatest baseball player of his time, the largest legend in New York since Babe Ruth. With her capacity to measure status—she has passed already in her life from microcosmos of the social world into macrocosmos, there is not too much a headwaiter need do before she can detect by the light in his eye that he is feeling the unique and luminous spinelessness of a peasant before a king. She is on a date with an American king—her first. (The others have been merely Hollywood kings.)

On the movie sets, as items appear in the gossip columns about whom she is dating, the stage-hands and grips are more cordial than ever before. Proud and scornful hierarchy of the working class, tough, cynical, contemptuous and skilled, they have never as a collective group been re-motely as friendly before. That opens her do-main. She has already risen from freak to secret nude of the national dreamlife. Now she can rise again, be queen of the working class. For DiMaggio's wife is beyond reproach. When he comes to visit her on the set of *Monkey Business*, a picture is taken of Cary Grant and himself with Marilyn between. When the photo is printed in the papers, Cary has been cut out of the photo-graph. The publicity department at Twentieth is announcing the public romance of the decade. Down in Washington, ambitious young men like Jack Kennedy are gnashing their teeth. "Why is it," they will never be heard to cry aloud, "that hard-working young Senators get less national attention than movie starlets?"

Within the studio, there must be grudging rec-ognition at last that they have some sort of genius on their hands. She is not only going to survive her own millions of calendar nudes but will sell tickets to her films right off those barber shop and barroom walls. Every time a man buys gas at a filling station and goes in to wash his hands, her torso will be up next to the men's room door. Soon the story of her mother will come out and fail to hurt her—the public is too interested in the progress of romance with DiMaggio to wish to

lose her. And she plays the situation with all the aplomb of a New York Yankee. For the longest period she will refuse to admit they are more than "friends." No denial is more calculated to keep a rumor alive. There is even the possibility that her interest in DiMaggio begins right out of her need to play counterpoint in public relations. Mosby's wire-service story on the nude calendar has gone out on March 13, 1952, and Zolotow has her wit-nessing her first baseball game on March 17 when DiMaggio is playing in some special exhibition (since he is now retired), an event which would therefore have to take place almost immediately after their first meeting, although Guiles, whose chronology is more dependable, does not have them introduced until April. Either way, the sup-position reinforces itself that she certainly had a good practical motive for continuing to see DiMaggio.

His relation to her is obviously simpler to comprehend. If it is necessary to speak of her varieties of beauty, then a thousand photographs are not worth a word. Doubtless she is, when alone with him, nothing less than the metamorphosis of a woman in one night, tough in one hour and sensitive in another (at the least!), but she has also the qual-ity she will never lose, never altogether, a species of vulnerability that all who love her will try to describe, a stillness in the center of her mood, an animal's calm at the heart of shyness, as if her fate is trapped like a tethered deer. At her best, she has to be utterly unlike other women to him, eminently more in need of protection, for she is so simple as to live without a psychic skin.

If at this point her personality seems to have bubbled up into the effervescence of a style that will present her in one paragraph as wholly calculating only to offer next a lyric to her helplessness (of which the best glimpses have been caught in old newsreels), the answer is both, yes, both are true, and always both, she is the whole and double soul of every human alive. It is, if we would search for a model, as if an ambitious and sexual woman might not only be analogous in her particular ego and unconscious life to Madame Bovary, let us say, but rather is a woman with two personalities, each as complex and inconsistent as an individual. This woman, then, is better seen as Madame Bovary and Nana all in one, both in one, each with her own separate unconscious. Of course, that is a personality which is not seriously divided. One unconscious could almost serve for Nana and Bovary both. It is when Nana and Joan of Arc exist in the same flesh, or Boris Karloff and Bing Crosby, that the abysses of insanity are under the fog at every turn. And there is Monroe with pictures of Eleonora Duse and Abraham Lincoln on her wall, double Monroe, one hard and calculating computer of a cold and ambitious cunt (no other English word is near) and that other tender animal, an angel, a doe at large in blonde and lovely human form. Anyone else, man or woman, who contained such opposite personalities within his body would be ferociously mad. It is her transcendence of these opposites into a movie star that is her triumph (even as the work she does will eventually be our pleasure), but how transcendent must be her need for a man ready to offer devotion and services to *both* the angel and

the computer. How large a requirement for DiMaggio to fill. The retired hero of early high purpose too early fulfilled, he is now a legend without purpose. Yet he is not forty and adulation is open to him from everyone. How natural to look for a love where he can serve.

Of course, he is a hint too vain for the prescription. Somewhat further along in their affair, when Marilyn is making *Niagara* and is high on the elation that she has been given the lead in *Gentlemen Prefer Blondes*, they spend a few days together in New York. Zolotow gives a good description of their social differences:

> At Shor's, Joe's friends sat with them and talked about the 1952 pennant races. She was bored. She wanted to see the new plays. She wanted to go to the Metropolitan Museum and to visit the hot jazz spots, like Eddie Condon's. Joe didn't care for theatre, music, art. His world was the world of sports, his cronies were sports-loving men like George Solotaire, men who lived in a closed masculine world of gin rummy, sports, betting, money talk, inside jokes.

That is a world which can take on dimensions of risk in Hemingway, or pathos in Paddy Chayefsky's Marty. It is also a world where women can be mothers, sisters, angels, broads, good sports, sweethearts, bitches, trouble, or *dynamite*, but are always seen at a remove, as a class apart. It is a world of men whose fundamental habit is to live with one another and compete with one another. Their habit is not homosexual but fundamental. Its root is often so simple as having grown up in a family of brothers, or known more happiness with their father than their mother—the days of their lives have been spent with other men. Women are an emotional luxury. Of course, like all luxuries they can be alternately ignored and coveted, but it is false to

97

Joe DiMaggio and Marilyn, 1953

the whole notion of that world, and impossible to understand DiMaggio, if it is not seen that the highest prize in a world of men is the most beautiful woman available on your arm and living there in her heart loyal to you. Sexual prowess is more revered than any athletic ability but a good straight right. It is precisely because women are strange and difficult, and not at all easy, that they are respected enormously as trophies. It is part of the implicit comedy of DiMaggio's relations with Monroe that he would expect her to understand this. There is a story of a very tough man, told in New York bars, who revered his wife and lived with her for twenty years, and at the end of that time she said, "Why don't you ever tell me you love me?" He grunted and said, "I'm *with* you, ain't I?" Women who can live with such men obviously have to comprehend their code. It is as if DiMaggio expects her to understand, with of course never a word being said, that he has not arrived at his eminence in Toots Shor's along with Hemingway and one or two select sports writers and gamblers because he is dumb or gifted or lucky but because he had an art that demanded huge concentration, and the consistent courage over the years to face into thousands of fast balls any of which could kill or cripple him if he were struck in the head, and closer than such danger, engage his ego in the perilous business of each working day being booed or cheered depending on how he passed the daily test of pressure. If he had been a New York Yankee, and therefore in the highest part of that sporting establishment honored by the corporation, the diocese, and the country club; if DiMaggio with his conservative clothes and distinguished gray hair was a considerable distance from the athlete who gets up in the morning with his head axed by a hangover and blows his nose to get the sexual gunk of the night before out of his nostril hairs (which act excites him to give no farewell kiss to the garlic and bourbon breath of the sleeping sweaty broad of the night before), then stumbles out in white shirt and tie into early morning sunlight to take his place at a communion breakfast, and get up on his feet in his turn with other ballplayers and prizefighters to tell the parochial kids how to live, cleanly, that is, as Americans; if DiMaggio has too much class to be part of this hogpen of whole hypocrisy (he is a Yankee and the best), still he has all the patriotism and punctilious social behavior that is still required of great athletes in the early Fifties: his propriety has to reinforce the romantic image he must hold of himself and his love for her. His communion to her, his gift to her, is that he loves her. He's there, isn't he? He will certainly be her champion in any emergency. He will die for her if it comes to that. He will found a dynasty with her if she desires it, but he does not see their love as a tender wading pool of shared interests and tasting each other's concoctions in the kitchen. He is, in fact, even more used to the center of attention than she is, and probably has as much absorption in his own body, for it has been his instrument just so much as her anatomy has become her instrument, and besides, the body of a professional athlete is part of the capital of a team, and numbers of trainers have spent years catering to it. Indeed, the one of her associates he likes the most is Whitey Snyder, her makeup man, who looks like a cross between Mickey Spillane and a third-base coach. DiMaggio can understand and get along with the man who helps her to keep her professionalism in shape. The easiest thing he can understand in her world is Snyder talking about how he does her

face: "Marilyn has makeup tricks that nobody else has and nobody knows. Some of them she won't tell me. She has discovered them herself. She has certain ways of lining and shadowing her eyes that no other actress can do. She puts on a special kind of lipstick; it's a secret blend of three different shades. I get that moist look on her lips for when she's going to do a sexy scene by first putting on the lipstick and then putting a gloss over the lipstick. The gloss is a secret formula of Vaseline and wax . . ." It is like listening to a trainer hint at the undisclosed blends of a superliniment, or an athlete describe how he bandages himself, but, finally, DiMaggio cannot have the same respect for movie people that he has had for athletes who pass tests. He has discovered the wheel. They are people with false identity. Phony.

And she has to be suffering all the anguish of living with a man who will save her in a shipwreck or learn to drive a dog team to the North Pole (if her plane should crash there) but sits around the apartment watching television all night, hardly talks to her, is not splendidly appreciative of her cooking yet resentful when they eat in restaurants, acts like a maiden aunt when she gets ready to go out in the world with a swatch of bare bosom, and, incredible pressure upon her brain, wishes to end her movie career! She needs, ah, she needs a lot. No heroic man of hard-forged and iron identity (with both his souls wed into narrow-minded strictures and athletic grace), no, she needs a double soul a little more like her own, a computer with circuits larger than her own, and a devil with charm in the guise of an angel, something of that sort she certainly needs, but *wholly* devoted to her. Because the keel of her identity has at last been laid

—she is her career, and her career is herself. No lover can shift this truth—as quickly let a wife ask Thomas Alva Edison to abjure his laboratory! She will never get what she needs in the full proportion of her needs—never enough creative service to satisfy taste and tender wit—a man who can anticipate that if she claims to love anemones they must still not be too violet, a slave of exquisite sweetness who will foresee appetites and develop them by art and surprise, someone who—full lament of a woman—someone who will bring her *out!* Instead she has DiMag, worth the front page of the New York *Daily News* every time he smiles. DIMAG SMILES!

So their affair goes on, they fight, have reconciliations, fight again. They separate, and they love each other more on the phone. He will be in New York and she will make a film. He will come to San Francisco and she will go to New York. They reunite in Los Angeles, or she goes to visit his restaurant at Fisherman's Wharf. They surreptitiously move clothes into each other's apartments—then tell the newspaper world they are still only friends. For near to two years it goes on. He wishes to marry, but she is uncertain, then he will go away for a few weeks in disgust, or refuse to accompany her to a function where she most certainly wants him along. On one night in 1953 when she is given a *Photoplay* magazine award, DiMaggio is so outraged by the cut of her dress that Sidney Skolsky has to take her to the dinner. Joan Crawford will be equally censorious: "Sex plays a tremendously important part in every person's life," are her words to columnist Bob Thomas. "People are interested in it, intrigued with it. But they don't like to see it flaunted in their faces. She [Miss Monroe] should be told that the public likes provocative feminine personalities; but it also likes to know that underneath it all, the actresses are ladies."

Is this the voice of DiMaggio in Miss Crawford's mouth? "I think the thing that hit me the hardest," said Marilyn, now offering an exclusive reply to Louella Parsons, "is that it came from her. I've always admired her for being such a wonderful mother—for taking four children and giving them a fine home. Who, better than I, know what it means to homeless little ones?"

She is also shaming DiMaggio. He, too, is being cruel to the homeless little one. Yet is it possible he is the one responsible for the fact that she has never been more attractive than in these years? She looks fed on sexual candy. Never again in her career will she look so sexually perfect as in 1953 making *Gentlemen Prefer Blondes*, no, never—if we are to examine a verb through its adverb—will she appear so fucky again. It is either a reflection of her success at the studio, or the secret of her sex with DiMaggio, and that is one secret she is not about to admit. She will look more subtle in future years, more adorable, certainly lovelier, more sensitive, more luminous, more tender, more of a heroine, less of a slut—but never again will she seem so close to a detumescent body ready to roll right over the edge of the world and drop your body down a chute of pillows and honey. If all this kundalini is being sent out to an anonymous human sea, her sex flowing forever on a one-way canal to the lens and never to one man, it is the most vivid abuse of kundalini in the history of the West, and makes her indeed a freak of too monumental proportions. It is easier to comprehend her as a woman often void of sex in the chills and concentration of her career, but finally a woman who has something of real sexual experience with her

men, for she tends to take on the inner character of the lover she is with, something of his expression. In the best years with DiMaggio, her physical coordination is never more vigorous and athletically quick; she dances with all the grace she is ever going to need when doing *Gentlemen Prefer Blondes*, all the grace and all the bazazz—she is a musical comedy star with panache! Diamonds Are a Girl's Best Friend! What a surprise! And sings so well Zanuck will first believe her voice was dubbed, and then will finally go through the reappraisal, ulcerous to the eye of his stomach, of deciding she may be the biggest star they have at Twentieth, and the biggest they are going to have. Yes, she is physically resplendent, and yet her face in these years shows more of vacuity and low cunning than it is likely to show again—she is in part the face DiMaggio has been leaving in her womb. "Take the money," he says to her on one occasion when she is talking about her publicity, and something as hard and blank as a New York Yankee out for a share of the spoils is now in her expression.

Still, she is a wonder in *Gentlemen Prefer Blondes*. The play has run for two years on Broadway, and the part of Lorelei Lee has been minted by Carol Channing. It is analogous to the difficulty Gertrude Lawrence is to face in making *The Glass Menagerie* after Laurette Taylor. Yet *Gentlemen* becomes the best picture Monroe has made so far. She comes into the film looking like a winner, and leaves as one—not inconceivable that DiMaggio has put a sense of victory into her.

If she has had her first acting lesson not six years before, and never been near to working on a New York stage, it has no significance before her grasp of cinema. She inhabits the frame even when she is not on. Just as she had once preempted the art of the still photographer and painted herself into the lens, now she preempts the director. In this film, and in *Some Like It Hot*, to a lesser degree in *The Seven-Year Itch* or *Bus Stop* or *The Misfits*, it is as if she has been the secret director. The picture has been set by the tone of her personality, set just so fully, let us say, as Ingmar Bergman leaves his mood on every scene. But Bergman at least has a mood that is suitable to such impressment on material; he lives in the vapors of evening and the hour of the wolf: all the hoarded haunted sorrows of Scandinavia drift in to imbibe the vampires of his psyche—he is like a spirit vapor risen out of the sinister character of film itself. She, however, is merely a sexpot on a romp, there with Jane Russell in the Battle of the *Bulge* (as a columnist with ineluctable newspaperese is bound to put it), a young actress enjoying herself immensely in a film, or so it seems, and yet a species of musical comedy history is being made, for her personality infuses every corner of the film as if she has even picked the scenery to work for her. Of course, she has not, she has merely accommodated herself to the background and the costumes, but how she steeps herself in the existence of that film, how she lives in harmony with Jane Russell. Never have two women gotten along together so well in a musical. So the movie rises above its pretext, its story, its existence as a musical, even its music, and becomes at its best a magic work, yet it is a comic bubble without weight or solemnity, another piece of spun sugar come up out of everything

banal in entertainment. She must be the first embodiment of Camp, for *Gentlemen Prefer Blondes* is a perfect film in the way early Sean Connery–James Bond films were perfect. In such classics of Camp, which would arrive ten years later and more, no actor was ever serious for an instant, nor any situation ever remotely believable—the art was to sustain non-existence, counter-existence, as if to suggest that life cannot be comprehended by a direct look—we are not only in life but to the absurd side of it, attached to something else as well—something mysterious and of the essence of detachment. So in *Gentlemen Prefer Blondes*, she is a sexual delight, but she is also the opposite of that, a particularly cool voice which seems to say, "Gentlemen: ask yourself what really I am, for I pretend to be sexual and that may be more interesting than sex itself. Do you think I have come to you from another place?" She could even be a visitor who has studied the habits of humans—the unhappy suspicion crosses our head that if she were a saint or a demon we would never know.

In any case, it is the first film which enables us to speak of her as a great comedian, which is to say she bears an exquisitely light relation to the dramatic thunders of triumph, woe, greed, and calculation: she is also a first artist of the put-on —she dramatizes one cardinal peculiarity of existence in this century—the lie, when well embodied, seems to offer more purchase upon existence than the truth. The factoid sinks deeper roots than the fact. The oncoming desire to inhabit the interior of the put-on and thereby know one's own relation to a role (in such a way that others cannot) will affect a whole generation in the Sixties. They will rush into the shifting mirrors of the put-on—it is the natural accompaniment to sexual promis-

cuity. "I had a great piece of ass last night," says the husband to his wife. "You did?" "No, in fact, I didn't get laid at all." In a world where everyone must lie, the put-on becomes a convention, an oasis, a watering hole where two liars can rest for a moment in mutual recognition of the impossibility of reaching any reality across the burned-out desert. (In the Seventies, America would even be ruled by a President who could put in a claim to have rediscovered the political put-on as he folded his hands in prayer when the truce was signed in Vietnam.)

But she is so early in her put-on, and so different in her style. Maybe that is the reason Zanuck valued her lightly—he could just not find her sexual meat and potatoes, not palpable to him, and he was right!—they may not have been palpable. She is so special, so suggestive of someone possessed. She is even reminiscent of a medium who has to go through more and more arduous emotional labors to locate the spirits of the sexual seance she would invoke. So to begin to speak of her first triumph also requires one to speak of the first signs of her future breakdown. It is in *Gentlemen Prefer Blondes* that she begins to be late to the set and to fight with her directors. As time goes on, one can even suspect she fights with directors in the way a medium will seek to eliminate those guests who are too hearty or hostile at a seance, as though she can express her own art only after she has neutralized more active life forces around her. In an interview with Zolotow she said, "I do not believe I could ever take the road of religion, and yet I believe in many things that can't be explained by science. I know that I feel stronger if the people around me on the set love me, care for me, and hold good thoughts for me. It creates an aura of love, and I believe I can give a better performance." With each film she will make from now on, she will report later for work each day. On *Some Like It Hot*, her greatest film, there will be days when she answers the nine o'clock call at four in the afternoon, and Billy Wilder will suffer with a spasm of his back muscles through the film, while Tony Curtis and Jack Lemmon stand around in high heels for hours and curse her impotently for the delay. Of course, nothing will waste an enemy's curse faster than letting him wait. Yet we may as well go further and assume the real motive to her lateness came from the instinct of a medium who needed a way to draw on all those psychic forces not easily available, but forces she is nonetheless obliged to pick up for her art. The price was a medium's toll: insomnia, pills, groundless fears, and the need for a palace guard. Even before she is a star, she has assistants—her dramatic coach, her hairdresser, and her makeup man—later there will be others, and it will become the style of her life. Even before she and DiMaggio are done with one another, she is close to being mistress of a coven.

Certainly in their years together DiMaggio is carrying on a species of exorcism which is doomed to fail. It is his project to wean her from films and encourage her to retire and make a family. It is not so impossible as it seems, for she is still in good enough health to recognize how films strip her of existence while she is working. She can be aware of what she pays. All that exuberance on the screen is beginning to leave her empty, livid, and insomniac. So there are hours when she will listen to him, and hours when he will almost succeed in his first battle, which is to get rid of Natasha Lytess, who has disliked DiMaggio on sight. It is a perfect mutual repulsion. To Na-

tasha, DiMaggio is interested in Marilyn only as a human being, not an Actress, and therefore is a vandal. To DiMaggio, Natasha must seem still one more pretentious European, nervous and bigoted, who will speak only of art while lifting your uncultured money. Not difficult to imagine Natasha's expression when Marilyn mimics the face of DiMaggio playing cards with George Solotaire, nor any more elusive to conceive of DiMaggio's contempt when Marilyn tells him how Natasha has obtained funds from her for medical operations she did not have.

How adroitly is Marilyn divided. In this period it is as if she is looking to live in the two houses of every opposed desire. She is not only sharing apartments in San Francisco and Los Angeles with DiMaggio but has also been taking dramatic lessons in two opposed schools. Natasha has become indispensable to her on a set, and the first of the means by which to exasperate a director, because Marilyn looks immediately for Natasha's approval whenever a director is satisfied with the take: if Natasha does not nod, Marilyn will insist on another take. Powerful Natasha! Still, Marilyn has also been going to school with Michael Chekhov and manages to keep him apart from Lytess. They never meet. She maintains Stanislavsky and Coquelin at odds in her. If she bends over to straighten a stocking in *Monkey Business* and reveals a leg which could belong to a Petty girl, it is not because she has been born with just such beautiful legs, but rather because they are slim enough to put to work, and she has studied Vesalius on anatomy (and herself in the mirror) long enough to know how to arch an arch and turn an instep. So she is comfortable before the still camera in that school of Coquelin which calls for an energetic heart and a cold mind. (As one weeps on stage, one is also ready to modulate the sobs and thereby conduct the audience through *their* emotion.) Natasha, who has been dramatic coach at a studio, is of course attached to such technique. On a movie set, an actor must produce quick results—it is too expensive if he doesn't. Certainly, young actors, at the puppet's end of a production string, have to be able to twitch on order, a way of saying that they have to be in service to their own will, which suggests they are obliged to be phony in every relation but the liaison between their personality and their will. Since an actor usually recognizes he wishes to become an actor about the time he becomes dimly aware he has only a small sense of identity, that in fact if he were a philosopher he could not posit such a condition as identity, the school of Coquelin offers quick rewards for such a psychological strait, but deepens the actor's uneasiness. Subtly, the technique is encouraging him to become more skillfully phony. By way of psychoanalytical jargon, it could be said that actors schooled in Coquelin will find *support* for their personalities in such techniques: will learn to build an armor to contain the shapelessness of their psyche (and presumably even win battles with that armor and so gain identity). Actors in the Method will *act out*; their technique is designed, like psychoanalysis itself, to release emotional lava, and thereby enable the actor to become acquainted with his depths, then possess them enough to become possessed by his role. A magical transaction. We can think of Marlon Brando in *A Streetcar Named Desire*. To be possessed by a role is *satori* for an actor because one's identity can feel whole so long as one is living in the role. Ergo, actors, particularly uneducated actors, tend to prefer the Method. It is more exciting, more satisfying

when it works, and dispenses to some degree with the need for schooling in manners, accents, movement, voice and diction, even as Abstract Expressionism can try to ignore oil painting technique.

Of course, the greatest virtue of the Method also becomes its professional shortcoming. Method actors find it more difficult to do meretricious parts since one cannot be possessed by a role which has no inner life. There is then no spirit to emerge from a mood and enter you. The worse the role, the more one needs an external style to project. No wonder actors hate bad roles and worship good playwrights. An actor can only squander energy in a bad role—he cannot be reimbursed by discovering new sides of himself as he plays the role. Instead he must consume his little hoard of identity and tarnish his hard-acquired style by offering charm to lines which never begin to probe into his personality. Living with the wrong part is like living with the wrong mate and having to make love every night. Not hard to imagine what a tormenting question then has her training become to Marilyn. She has every need of Natasha, who is sensitive to what Marilyn must do on the set for results, but Natasha is also too loyal to the demands of a bad script. Marilyn's growing instinct is to work by the Method. In an interview in *Redbook* years later, she tells of playing Cordelia to Chekhov's Lear:

"I was out of the room for seven seconds. When I came back in, *I saw a king before me*. Mr. Chekhov did it without changing a costume or putting on make-up or even getting out of his chair. I never saw anything happen so fast in my life. . . . So little was done in so short a period of time that I really became Cordelia."

Once the scene is over, she has Chekhov pounding the table. "They don't know what they're

doing to you!" he cries out against that Hollywood which refuses to see her potential.

No reason for the story not to be a factoid—except that she possesses the talent to play Cordelia. Like a doctor who is no better than his patient, she is no better than her surroundings. Of course, she is also no less—already she must sense her present ability to rise to great roles in a cast of great actors. And is also perfectly ready, good democratic talent, to bother Chekhov with her lateness as much as she will bother others. Once, told by him to drop her lessons because she keeps throwing his schedule into confusion, she sends a note:

Dear Mr. Chekhov,
    Please don't give me up yet—I know (painfully so) that I try your patience.
    I need the work and your friendship desperately. I shall call you soon.

                                Love,
                                Marilyn Monroe

So all the while Joe DiMaggio is trying to get her free of Natasha Lytess as a way to pry her loose from acting, she is searching more deeply into her profession. She even, at Mrs. Chekhov's suggestion, takes lessons in mime for a while. Since everything, however, must be at odds in her life, she is also particularly flamboyant in publicity these years. Rare is the week she does not receive her factoidal award: "The girl most likely to thaw out Alaska," or the 7th Division Medical Corps will choose her as "the girl we would most like to examine." After *Niagara*, she goes to the Miss America contest in Atlantic City and is photographed with every one of the forty-eight girls. Then pictures are sent to newspapers in each of the forty-eight states. A custom fit: *Miss North Dakota with Marilyn Monroe. Marilyn will soon be seen in* Monkey Business *with Cary Grant*. She poses with four women in uniform, a WAC, a WAVE, a WAF, and a SPAR, and dumps a bushel of cleavage into the middle of four plain (and electrified) ladies in uniform. "Don't anybody stick a pin in these balloons," could be the swallowed thought in her full-mouthed smile. An army officer tries to kill the picture. (Is he being paid by the studio?) Naturally, every newspaper rushes to print it. DiMaggio hates all of this. The suggestion is doubtless arising among his friends that he does not know how to keep a leash on his broad. It is as if she steps into a situation where there is publicity, and cannot restrain herself. A pure fragment of her personality leaps into power, and overthrows every one of her demands to be taken seriously. At Camp Pendleton, where she has gone to entertain Marines (and help convince the studio she can sing and dance well enough to do Lorelei Lee), she stands out in all her scantily clad meat before ten thousand gathered men and says, "I don't know why you boys are always getting so excited about sweater girls. Take away their sweaters and what have they got?" The demon of publicity in her mind is laughing at ten thousand Marines and ten million men all picturing a bevy of sweater girls with the sweaters lifted, bare breasts high, oops, whoops! She is one golden hellion in her rush to get the golden monkey at the end of the jungle trail, she will even propose, when Jane Russell and she are invited to press their hands and feet into the wet cement at Grauman's Chinese—shades of Valentino—that they ought to register their breasts in that cement and their buttocks as well. It is an irony to anticipate Women's Liberation, but there is no liberation in the air—she is probably disappointed when the suggestion is refused.

Yet for all that power which enables her already to pass through a crowd in a comet of charisma, she is small and broken and helpless when she meets other actors she will work with, and only knows how to appeal to them with her vulnerability, or disarm them with her lack of presence, her uncertainty, her need to be taken care of. So she will charm Robert Ryan and Barbara Stanwyck and Paul Douglas in *Clash by Night* until the late occasion when Douglas bellows, "That blonde bitch is getting all the publicity." So she will put herself at the mercy of Jane Russell, who ends by adoring her (and handing her the film). So she will put herself in trust to Betty Grable and Lauren Bacall in *How to Marry a Millionaire*, and Grable—who will be deposed in this film as the premier blonde at Twentieth Century—is moved nonetheless to mother her. She is the doe come to the clearing in the forest, and the hunters lower their rifles. She is not even necessarily false. She is like a champion who has won the title with only a few fights. His manners are sweet and deferential. He does not know how he won, or who can as quickly take him out with a punch. He has no experience of heights. Even the kid who brings the sandwiches looks menacing.

But such an analogy has too many limitations. It is rather as if all her anger and ambition can brazen out in publicity, and all her charm attach itself to curious powers when she plays a script, but she has developed next to no ability for talking to other actors, or playing the theatrical game of discovering which actor will dominate the other.

Indeed, she hands over her game cards before the game can begin. She knows so much about the strategy of a career, yet next to nothing of the tactics of small talk, she is a witch not a warrior and wins more when she loses (even as the buttocks of a witch once possessed will possess the bugger). But then she is too distracted to obey even the formal logic of small talk. "How old are you, Stevie?" she asks Lauren Bacall's son, who is playing on the set.

"Four."

"Why, you're so big for your age. I would have thought you were two or three."

We can go back to that moment when Della may have been close to strangling her. It is as if the child has been left half in life and half in the special powers of death. We count backward as we go toward oblivion.

Zolotow gives a description of her at this time which captures the near to monarchical phenomenology of her life. Since Twentieth has made *How to Marry a Millionaire* with financial trepidation—can a light comedy sit comfortably on their new and enormous CinemaScope screen?—the finished picture which gives every promise of being a success, excites plans for a huge world premiere on Wilshire Boulevard. DiMaggio won't go. She wants to be a serious actress, he points out to her. Yet she rushes to hustle over to a circus premiere. Skolsky can't go. So she goes by herself. Zolotow describes a day that begins with Marilyn retching as she tries to drink orange juice and gelatin powder. Then she drives over to her dressing room at the studio where they will work to make her "all platinum and white tonight."

Gladys gave Marilyn a straight permanent. Then she bleached and tinted her hair and set it. . . . Gladys painted her fingernails and toenails with platinum polish. Her slippers, her evening dress, her long white gloves arrived from wardrobe, together with two wardrobe women. A messenger boy delivered a box with diamond earrings. Her furs had come that morning. . . . Except for the white fox fur stole and muff, and her panties, everything she wore belonged to the studio. . . .

Roy Craft dashed in to kiss her on the cheek, and wish her luck and say that the town of Monroe, New York, had changed its name for one day to Marilyn Monroe, New York. Telegrams arrived. Phone calls from friends, demi-friends, pseudo-friends. Joe finally called from New York. He said he missed her. He said he loved her. He hoped she understood. He was praying for her. His heart was with her. He was sorry they weren't together. She said bitterly, "Give my regards to Georgie Solotaire."

"Whitey" Snyder began changing her face, powdering her shoulders, pencilling lines around her eyes, putting the high gloss on her lips. The wardrobe women helped her into the strapless evening gown.

Unchastened by Joan Crawford's pronouncements, Marilyn had chosen a dress made of white lace lined with flesh-colored crepe de Chine and embroidered with thousands of sequins. It had a high waist, and it curved under her breasts revealingly. A long white velvet train trailed from a gold belt. The long gloves were drawn up the length of her arms. The stole was placed around her shoulders. She put her right hand into the muff and with her left she carried the train as she walked outside to a waiting studio limousine.

The time was seven-fifteen. It had taken six hours and 20 minutes.

Outside the Fox-Wilshire, for five blocks in either direction, traffic is being rerouted. Thousands of people are sitting in bleachers or pressing up to lines of police in front of wooden sawhorses. She sits on the edge of her seat in the car so as not to wrinkle the dress—she would be happier standing erect in a chariot. When they see her, the screams of the crowd rise up into the night with the searchlights, then reverberate over the boulevard. "Marilyn . . . Marilyn." Flashbulbs in the lobby, microphones, television cameras.

She had been invited to several supper parties after the premiere, but she was tired. The studio limousine returned her to the studio—now almost deserted. A wardrobe woman waited in dressing room M. It was almost midnight and time to end the masquerade. Off went the gloves, the earrings, the shoes, the gown. Off went the false face, erased by cold cream and paper tissues. . . . She got into the slacks and the sport shirt and the loafers. She placed the muff and the stole in their boxes, carried the boxes to her car, and dumped them in the back seat. She felt fatigued but not sleepy. A restlessness pervaded her. She drove out by the sea, cruising along the highway for a long time. When she got home, she drank a glass of orange juice mixed with gelatin and took three Seconals.

"That night," concludes Zolotow, "she was the most famous woman in Hollywood." And could not sleep. She could not sleep when she won. In later years she would also be unable to sleep when she lost.

VI. MS MONROE

All the while she is fighting the studio and they are fighting her back. She wants more money and the right to choose her script and director. They refuse. By the end of 1953, *Niagara*, *Gentlemen Prefer Blondes* and *How to Marry a Millionaire* will gross $25,000,000 for Twentieth, more than any other movie star will earn for a studio in those twelve months. Yet she is not yet being paid $1,000 a week (while working with Jane Russell who gets $100,000 for the same film), and even has to fight for a decent dressing room. Executives tell Marilyn she is spoiled. "Remember, you're not a star," they tell her.

She has one of her better moments. "Well, gentlemen, whatever I am, the name of this picture is *Gentlemen Prefer Blondes*, and whatever I am, I *am* the blonde."

It would seem in retrospect as if they could re-negotiate her contract or sweeten the choice of films. Her resentment already exhibits itself in the form of slowdowns and will yet cost them hundreds of thousands of dollars, even millions, but they cannot be conciliatory, for she is attacking the foundation of the studio system, and that base is built on decades of entrenched waste. Studios in the early Fifties are still factories with whole companies of actors on contract, and over-staffed departments forever seeking to enlarge themselves. Like government spending, the system seems to function in a time of expansion, but television has already done its first damage by reducing the volume of people who go to movies. The solution is going to be worked out with fewer theatres, better movies, and a higher priced ticket; but at this point, the studios are still geared to turning out fifty films a year for chains of exhibitors—even if the exhibitor chains are about

to be separated from the production companies, thereby intensifying the crisis. When that finally arrives, half the studio executives will be obliged to retire. But that is later. She is premature. She is tipping the system just when anxiety is at its greatest.

At such times, executives look to advertise those aspects of their system that are most spectacular, which is to say, profitable. She is the most spectacular. At a cost in salary of $50,000 a year, she has brought back $25,000,000, a return of 500 to 1. That is a statistic to show a board of directors. It is about the only one they can show. The cost of every film is multiplied half again by overhead, and hundreds of seven-year option contract players have gone through the studio mill and never helped to gross a dollar. It is an economic procedure that penalizes actors for success while enforcing their obedience to mediocre films. The contract player is part of a slave corps, aesthetic filler to be stuffed into the sausage of the product, a lost morsel in Zanuck's exploration of the American appetite for shit. Obviously wasteful, it is still a system that has managed to survive for decades because of the psychological rewards it offers executives. Its demise has to be accelerated if they open her contract. Every other contract player of value will soon demand a raise. So they hold the line against her, then double their resistance when it comes to her choice of films. Somewhere in the root of his unconscious, every studio executive must have a glimmer of the concentration camp in which he is incarcerating actors (whose souls will slowly expire from lack of nourishment in meaningless scripts). So the executive also knows that once actors begin to choose scripts, the studio system is dead, the studio executives are next to dead. For they, after all, have devoted their lives to making money out of meaningless productions. What will be their moral crime before eternity —asks the unconscious—if one can also make money with *good* films.

They resort therefore to the social reflex of a slave system: punishment. They send her up the river to northwest Canada. She is in a "Z cowboy film"—it is Monroe's concise description of *River of No Return*. She will be the only woman and, surrounded by strong male actors (who will presumably break her balls), is also drenched in scenes with a boy actor (who will steal them) and with a director (Otto Preminger) who is famous for grinding actors' bones (balls and all) in the maw of his legendary rage. Frightened perhaps, she calls on DiMaggio to accompany her —they can have a vacation in Banff—but predictably they fight before she leaves, and she is alone except for Natasha Lytess, until DiMaggio must come up in response to Marilyn's cry for help— she has torn a ligament in an accident on a raft and doesn't trust the local doctor. DiMaggio arrives with a good doctor. It is the surest route to a woman's heart, and stands out by contrast to everything else in this deteriorating situation. Lytess, at war with Whitey Snyder (who is sympathetic to DiMaggio's desire for Marilyn to get out of movies) declares to Marilyn that she must make a choice between Whitey and herself. In turn, Preminger discovers that his boy actor has been demoralized by a conversation with Lytess (who has told him that child actors lose their talent "unless they take lessons and learn to use their instrument"). She is barred from the set by Preminger, who tells Natasha in his German accent "to *just* disappear." Marilyn says nothing, but obviously gets in touch with Zanuck, who

intercedes for fear Marilyn will quit the production. Lytess is reinstated. The film is somehow finished. That is Preminger's forte—to finish. Of course, it is the most demoralizing movie in which Marilyn has ever played a lead, and must be the worst of Preminger's films. In its aftermath— shuddering no doubt at the fadeout on her red dance hall shoes lying in the dust—she feels close to DiMaggio, and then is brought even closer by the sudden death of his brother who drowns in a fishing accident. She promises at this time to marry him, and sets a date, which she begins soon to delay again. For she has met a man who has opened her mind to the possibility of starting her own production company.

DiMaggio is like the hero of a farce. Whenever he is closest to achieving his aim, the forces of the plot converge and wipe him out. While there is something near to ludicrous in his hopes to take her away from acting, the desire is less comic if we assume the theme of suicide is always present. He has to see moviemaking as a danger, and feel close to success after *River of No Return*. For the first time since becoming a star, she has been trapped in a script, has gone through a species of creative death, and been obliged to recognize that the studio is powerful enough to do it again to her, and will. She has to consider the possibility of retiring while still champion. Yet a few weeks later she meets Milton Greene, out from *Look* magazine to do a cover story on her. He is the most talked about fashion photographer in New York, his good taste is legend, his humor is sweet as an ocean breeze on a day of summer inversion. "You're just a boy," she says in surprise when she meets him.

He smiles back. "You're just a girl." She adores him like an old friend after an hour.

In the next hour they are talking about making films together. If DiMaggio is finally close to separating Marilyn from her professional ogres, a soothsayer has flown in, a man of fashion to give Marilyn the sweet conviction that she, too, is chic. DiMaggio will now be able to settle for a marriage, but not the renunciation of a career. Indeed, she will marry him as the last high card she can play in a studio publicity game for high stakes; she chooses to marry only after Twentieth has put her on suspension for refusing to do *Pink Tights*, a film she considers as bad as *River of No Return*. In fact, she is doing her best to drive a spike into every studio executive's raging heart—to the press she confesses that she "blushed to the toes" at the thought of playing a "rear-wiggling schoolteacher doing a cheap dance." Yet the studio is obliged to lift the suspension. For a wedding present! The bride of Joe DiMaggio can hardly be kept rear-wiggling. Delighted with her success at studio card games, she disappears with DiMag for a couple of weeks in a snow-covered lodge above Palm Springs. Let us hope he has a honeymoon, for soon enough he will begin to live once more in farce and be obliged to put up with a robber bridegroom: there is reason to believe she is still in love with the ghost of an old passion for Arthur Miller.

We can even wonder if she has told Joe about it. Years ago, before she even met DiMaggio, she was introduced to Miller on the set of *As Young As You Feel* just after Johnny Hyde's death in December 1950, and saw him again at a party at Charles Feldman's house not a week later. At that time she rushed home to give her reactions to Natasha Lytess, with whom she was living. "It was like running into a tree!" she said of Miller. "You know—like a cool drink when you've got a fever. You see my toe—this toe? Well, he sat and held my toe and we just looked into each other's eyes almost all evening."

Later that week, back in New York, Miller wrote her a letter. "Bewitch them with this image they ask for, but I hope and almost pray" —he is a Marxist, after all—"you won't be hurt in this game, nor ever change."

There was more correspondence and phone calls. She spoke to Natasha of being in love. Perhaps they had an affair in 1951—we can presume to know her well enough to think it is hardly to the point. She would not need an affair to conceive of love for Miller, and the fact that his wife had helped to support him through all the years he was unsuccessful put one more grave responsibility upon an ordered man. Miller, already in his twenties during the Depression, had a personality that spoke of the ability to bear years of penury, and so probably felt comfortable in taking no more than a first taste of Marilyn in 1951 before withdrawing to dream of her.

Of course, it could never be said he gave her no encouragement. During that communion while he held her toe (which must have been an experience more thoroughgoing to her than fifty fornications), she confessed to Miller that she wanted someone to admire, and he recommended Abraham Lincoln, altogether unaware, of course, of any resemblance to himself. "Carl Sandburg," he suggests in his letter, "has written a magnificent biography." No, Miller may have led a restrained life compared with other playwrights, but had to feel pleasure that this exceptional young starlet was attracted to him. It must have been like a scent of perfume in a prison cell. And she in her turn had to make a complete equation of literary greatness to Arthur Miller. How could any play have moved her more than *Death of a Salesman?* She was herself a salesman—there was probably not a nerve of her intelligence that would not give a whole response to the lines, "Way out there in the blue riding on a smile and a shoeshine. And when they start not smiling back, that's an earthquake. And then you get yourself a couple of spots on your hat, and you're finished." He had written the psychological history of her life in the part of Willy Loman, for it could say no less to her than that every moment of existence went into sustaining one's identity, and the moment one weakened, it was over. Since a good actor always marries a good role as the first way to get out of the narcissist's circle, it is natural to revere a good playwright. Like God, the playwright can fashion a superb mate—a character in whom can rest one's search for identity. She must have given Miller up in all the sweet sorrow of losing an ideal love and an ideal man, and now could use the memory as a scent to ward off the direct impingement of DiMaggio. Joe D. could fill everything in her, she must have suggested, but the lonely summit of her mind. Other men were there to think of then. Guiles gives an account of DiMaggio meeting Fred Karger at a small gathering after his marriage with Marilyn has ended in divorce, and when the two men find talk to be difficult, Karger sits at the piano. DiMaggio listens, broods, thinks perhaps of Marilyn's description of unrequited love for Karger and holds up two powerful arms. With "operatic melancholy" DiMaggio announces, "These hands! They're only good for hitting a ball with a bat." Of course, it is hardly a characteristic moment (and, since the sister, Mary Karger, Marilyn's close friend, is also there, we can

wonder if DiMaggio does not intend the story to get back to Marilyn, and touch her). He is, after all, not without his own flamboyance. If Joe is a man to dress conservatively for dinner, he has also a closet full of sport clothes, and red predominates. His hands are now also good for hitting a golf ball. It has become his major activity in life other than serving as front man for his restaurant. Indeed, in the middle of the nine months Marilyn will be married to him, while they are living in San Francisco, she will spend many a night sitting in a rear booth of his restaurant. It is tempting to see her with a bandanna, and alone, doing her nails while waiting for her husband, but in fact she draws crowds. Still, the specter of a future as the bored wife of a saloonkeeper may come to visit her.

That is later, however. Her marriage begins with a display of publicity works. After the honeymoon, they go back to San Francisco and live in a prosperous house belonging to the DiMaggio family. Joe's sister, Marie, comes in to cook and run the household. Almost immediately, they are off for Japan. DiMaggio is mixing business with a wedding trip, for he is also going on a baseball tour with his old coach, "Lefty" O'Doul. In his mind, the scenario of marriage calls for the husband to become the center of attention. He has no chance. From the day of their marriage, she has become the leading female character in that great American movie which runs in serial each day in the newspapers of the world. Not until the funeral of Jack Kennedy and the emergence of Jackie Kennedy will a woman occupy so central a place in American life again. They start to get off the airplane in Honolulu, and are mobbed. "Thousands of Hawaiians ran out onto the field. . . . Strands of her hair were

actually torn away." Taken in a convoy to the airport lounge, she is promised Japan will be more civilized. It is worse. A stampede of the crowd toward their plane, and an eight-mile drive in an open convertible to downtown Tokyo with Japanese lining the street to scream "mon-chan." She is more "monchan" than anyone in the Orient since Shirley Temple.

Crowds surround their hotel. She must sneak out for sightseeing, or to visit the Kabuki The-atre. In the morning she can go to watch DiMag-gio coach baseball with O'Doul, or study the two men playing snooker in the game room at night. "No matter where I've gone or why I've gone there, it always ends up that I never see any-thing," she will soon write by way of Ben Hecht.

At a cocktail party in Tokyo where high-ranking Army officers meet the DiMaggios, she is invited to take a quick trip to Korea and enter-tain American fighting troops. DiMaggio has the unhappy choice of accompanying her as a flunky —he can smile at the troops—or stay in Tokyo to do his job and suffer in her absence. He chooses the second course, and she takes off for Seoul, and is then shuttled by helicopter up to rear areas of the front lines where the First Marine Division is waiting on a winter hill. She asks the pilot to fly low over the assembled soldiers, and then with a separate airman holding each of her feet, she leans out of the helicopter, no, *hangs* outside to wave and blow kisses, all the while asking the pilot to make more passes over the troops. It is her strongest public appearance since she walked the six studio blocks in a negligee, and naturally excites the Marines to break ranks and crowd up on the landing pad. As she lands, she sees road signs: DRIVE CAREFULLY—THE LIFE YOU SAVE MAY BE MARILYN MONROE'S. It is a newsman's

love affair: G. I. Joe meets America's most gor-geous doll. Officers and enlisted men dispute over her attendance at company messes, and when she entertains it is in regalia.

> Marilyn changed from an olive-drab shirt and skin-tight pants to an equally clinging gown of plum-colored sequins, cut so low it exposed much of her breast to the frigid winds. She was decked out with rhinestones to go with her first song, "Diamonds Are a Girl's Best Friend." Her singing voice was slight and was always amplified . . . now she had an ordinary mike. In mid-performance, she stopped singing and walked over to a soldier in the wings who was about to snap her picture . . . She gently plucked a lens cover from his camera saying, "Honey, you forgot to take it off."

The ovation roars up from the thousands. There is a newsreel of her shivering in the dark winter afternoon air, her chest exposed and her blonde hair flying out like her arms. She coquettes and wiggles her shoulders in a quick showgirl's cooch, thus setting up an automatic wail in the troops, she sings and shivers, her voice *is* small, and yet she is like no other entertainer. "I swear," she says in recollection, "I didn't feel a thing, except good." She is the acolyte of Hemingway's dictum that whatever makes you feel good is good. For this hour of her life, she needs no one to admire. "I guess I never felt I had an effect on people until I was in Korea," she will say years later. She looks beautiful. She is happy. She may never look so immensely happy at any other time. And sings "Do It Again" so well down into the last innuendo that the Army requests her not to sing it at other bases. She is too happy to refuse.

At the airport farewell party she tells the assembled officers and enlisted men, "This was the best thing that ever happened to me. I only wish I could have seen more of the boys, all of them. Come to see us in San Francisco." A great laugh, and she is on the plane and in a fever of 104 degrees from all the sexual promises sent to her across the winter winds by men she would never meet. She is sick for four days in Japan. Once again, DiMaggio is the nurse. What a sweet convalescence. Actors love extreme change around themselves.

Warrior back from the wars, she is obliged to be bored in San Francisco. There is a limit to how long she can visit the restaurant, smile at his family, go out in his cabin cruiser—it is named *The Yankee Clipper* after himself—or seek to be a good stepmother to his twelve-year-old son, who, for that matter, is away at school. They begin to have fights. Later, when she is divorced from him, she will tell ugly stories which quickly become exaggerated, so that Lee Strasberg will, for example, be under the impression DiMaggio is a brute who in a fit of rage once broke her wrist. The story when reduced by Arthur Miller comes down to an episode where the ballplayer in a fury at something she said slammed a suitcase shut, and her hand was accidentally caught and bruised. Whatever was going on, murder or boredom, she must have been afraid she would lose something interesting. So she goes back to films, accepts a part in *No Business Like Show Business*. The script is patently inferior to *Pink Tights*, and instead of playing with Frank Sinatra she will have Donald O'Connor for a leading man. When she wears high heels, O'Connor looks six inches shorter. Worse, Ethel Merman is in the film. She can hardly sing in competition with Merman. Dan Dailey, an old pro from the days of *Ticket to Tomahawk*, is used to dancing at his best and hamming at his utmost in atrocious scripts. There is also Johnny Ray, at the top of his vogue. She feels like an amateur among veterans and is shamed by the speed with which they pick up routines. She is out of practice and has not made a film in eight months, indeed, is only making this one as part of an arrangement to get *The Seven-Year Itch*. And in the house she has rented with DiMaggio in Beverly Hills, there is neither peace nor family life. She comes home exhausted from the studio and they eat out every night. Sullenly. She has lost some respect for him. DiMaggio has been invited to join a holding company by a businessman who suggests "that it might be helpful if Marilyn would appear at certain affairs planned by the new company—sales meetings, conventions, and possibly stockholders' meetings." DiMaggio, apparently, has not said no. He has been weeding out her attachment to leeches and phonies! But he has not said no on the instant! Leon Shamroy, the cameraman who gave Marilyn her first screen test eight years before, sees the DiMaggios one night in a fancy Chinese restaurant. They do not say a word through the meal.

She has also become a wretched housekeeper. There are open toothpaste tubes, clothes on the floor, water running in the sink, electric lights burning—it is nothing to the slovenliness that will come. Billy Wilder gives a description of the back seat of her black Cadillac convertible: "There's blouses lying there and slacks, dresses, girdles, old shoes, old plane tickets, old lovers for all I know, you never saw such a filthy mess in your life. On top of the mess is a whole bunch of traffic tickets. . . . Is she worried about this? Am I worried about the sun rising tomorrow?"

It is as if the energy one employs in holding one's identity together cannot be wasted to put objects in order. Small wonder the back seat of her car looks like a crash pad. She is an animal who needs the funky familiar of her lair.

The war with her husband carries over to the set. He comes to visit one day. He is no longer the shy suitor who was mugged at *Monkey Business*. Now he consents only to have his picture taken with Irving Berlin, and announces that he has really come to listen to Ethel Merman sing. The "Merm" is also a favorite at Toots Shor's. We can guess Marilyn's reaction.

She is working four hours a day with her singing coach, trying to work her way back into shape, but collapses three times on the set during shooting. For her big dance sequence in "A Tropical Heat Wave" she brings in Jack Cole, her choreographer in *Gentlemen Prefer Blondes*, but the number will prove a critical disaster. She is pushing for effect, and looks pasty in a Carmen Miranda costume. Her skin seems to have lost tone. She is drinking. Her eyes look flat when they do not look dead. She has never looked less attractive in a film. So she wears black panties and a flamenco skirt open up the front, and thereby looks as if she is giving flashes of pubic hair every time she kicks a leg. The guardians of the republic kick her back. Hedda Hopper does a furious column. Ed Sullivan will write, "Miss Monroe has just about worn the welcome off this observer's mat. . . . 'Heat Wave' is easily one of the most flagrant violations of good taste this observer has ever witnessed." The fan mail has lines like, "Marilyn Monroe sickens me and even my children." The abuse will come later, but as if she senses how bad a film she has made, she finishes the last week of shooting with a low-grade infection, and goes without a day's rest to the set of *The Seven-Year Itch*.

Now she rallies. As if she has been drilled in the metaphysical differences between two strikes and three, she will be at her best. Marilyn is plump, close to fat, her flesh is bursting out of every strap, her thighs look heavy, her upper arms give a hint that she will yet be massively fat if she ever grows old, she has a belly which protrudes like no big movie star's belly in many a year, and yet she is the living bouncing embodiment of pulchritude. It is her swan song to being a sexual object—the last fucky film she will make —and how she makes it! She proves once again that she is as good as the actors she works with, and she and Tom Ewell do a comic march through the movie. As The Girl upstairs, a TV model in New York for the summer from Colorado, she creates one last American innocent, a pristine artifact of the mid-Eisenhower years, an American girl who *believes* in the products she sells in TV commercials—she is as simple and healthy as the whole middle of the country, and there to be plucked. It is an unbelievable performance for an actress who is on the edge of separating from her husband, has two atrocious films behind her, is in psychoanalysis, drinking too much, and all the while thinking of breaking her contract and beginning a new life in New York to make movies with a photographer who has never produced a film.

It is an impossible load for an ordinary woman.

It is a next to unendurable strain for a strong woman of firm identity, but it is natural for Marilyn. There is one grace to possessing small identity—it is the ability to move from one kind of life to another with more pleasure than pain. If this lack of identity becomes a progressive burden in a static situation (for everyone else tends to build and prosper more than oneself), a lack of psychic density also offers quick intelligence in a new role. This is not to say that she is heaven on the set of *The Seven-Year Itch*. Usually she is several hours late and often keeps the company in irons while forgetting her lines, but she is resilient, how she is resilient in this film.

As if she has been picking the opportunity, she has a critical fight with DiMaggio while on location in New York. He has accompanied her after much debate, and is on the street with several thousand New Yorkers on the night she is filmed standing over a subway grating with Tom Ewell. As the trains go by underneath, her skirts billow up. It is so hot in the city she presumably loves the rush of air on her thighs. She plays it in innocent delight, a strapping blonde with a white skirt blown out like a spinnaker above her waist—a fifty-foot silhouette of her in just this scene will later appear over Times Square. In Eisenhower years, comedy resides in how close one can come to the concept of hot pussy while still living in the cool of the innocent. "Oh," she says in a Betty Boop voice, "I always keep my undies in the icebox."

Witness DiMaggio with these thousands of spectators crammed on hot New York night streets to get a glimpse of Marilyn in white panties and powerhouse thighs over a wind blower on a subway grating. The scene is more indecent to DiMaggio than he ever conceived. The sound of New York snickers takes his ear. It is a jargon, based on sewers, whoors, and delicatessen—"Look at that pastrami!" Unable to endure any more, he tries to get away. A group of newspapermen cut him off on the way to Toots Shor's. Toots is around the corner from where they are shooting! The aristocracy at Shor's will have their unsaid reaction. One of the reporters says it instead. "What do you think of Marilyn having to show more of herself than she's shown before, Joe?"

A newspaperman on the street is the existential equivalent of a surgeon who goes into cutting because he likes to discover the route by which meat falls away before the knife. DiMaggio gives no answer. He will have his war with Marilyn as soon as she gets home. A monster of jealousy all these years, he will not even trust her to smile at a bellhop. Hotel guests in nearby rooms hear shouting, scuffling, and weeping before the dawn. In the morning, DiMaggio is on his way to California.

Two weeks later, back in Los Angeles, she announces to the press they are getting a divorce. She is sick and can see no one. DiMaggio shoulders through newspapermen and leaves to drive to San Francisco with the friend who had been best man at his wedding, Reno Barsocchini. He takes with him "two leather suitcases and a bag of gold-handled golf clubs." The Associated Press reports, "the news hit Hollywood like an A-bomb."

A few days later, Marilyn is back at work on *The Seven-Year Itch*. Her work is faster and more concentrated than before. Sometimes Wilder, to his surprise, can cut and print on a first

or second take. New identity. Good film. "Rachmaninoff," says The Girl upstairs in the honeyed happy-doll voice.

She continues to see DiMaggio from time to time. He will even months later be her escort to the premiere of *The Seven-Year Itch*, although they are reported to fight before the evening is out. It is like a calculus of partial derivatives. The lack of complete commitment to the marriage creates a lack of finality in the separation. It is as if they cannot excise what was never finished, and the conclusion returns that they were locked like sweethearts, egoistic, narcissistic, petulant, pained, unwillingly attracted, and finally together for sex. If Marilyn almost never gives a hint of this, and will indicate to many a friend that she was bored with him, poor Joe, it is hard to explain why when they saw each other again in 1961 she was quick to explain he was a companion. Nothing was happening with DiMaggio, she assured her friends, because she was "cured." It is not the way a woman speaks of a man to whom she was sexually indifferent, and indeed her affair with Yves Montand, which will effectively break up her marriage to Miller, and can hardly be concealed as not directly sexual, offered curious similarities. Montand like DiMaggio was Italian, of peasant stock, and they even shared a general physical resemblance.

But then it is characteristic of her to play leapfrog in love and work. She will start with Miller, then go to DiMaggio, come back to Miller, and pick up again with DiMaggio, just as she will alternate from Lytess to Chekhov back to Lytess and then on to the Strasbergs and the Method again, just as she leaves Hollywood to live in New York to return to Hollywood to leave again and return to die. She is entering a period of her life when the weight of the past will make her as sluggish as a dinosaur's tail. She might as well be feeding a family within herself—those separate personalities of her past—and if her general lack of identity has enabled her to be an angel of nuance in one hour, and a public relations monster in the next (with the moronic glee of the emptiest ambition in her eye), if she has been mercurially quick and will be as quick again when need arises, still she is approaching the years of crisis that come to all men and women who have managed to survive with little sense of inner identity, a time when the psychic energies of early success begin to exhaust themselves, and the ability to change over radically for each new situation diminishes at the same time one's reputation for unreliability begins to grow—it is then that the backwater of foul and exaggerated bad legends begins to enter the reactions of strangers at the sound of the name.

So she is at a moment in her life when events do not force her decision—she is in the rare situation of being able to wait and choose, the worst of times for someone like herself, for the tendency (since she cannot concentrate long enough to clarify her thoughts) is to find all projects becoming polluted with ambivalence. If she is at a crossroads, she can be certain that the longer she waits, the muddier it will get. Yet what a choice to make! Her need for security is probably greater than ever, doubled by her divorce from DiMaggio. As she will read in a few weeks, she has worn out her welcome mat with Ed Sul-

livan, which is equal to having exhausted the tolerance of the New York Archdiocese. DiMaggio was her precise welcome mat, and so pressure will soon be building on the studios if she remains. And now she will also be open to attacks as a sex star twice divorced which will be different from being the zany lady married to DiMag. No, the New York *Daily News* won't be on her side no more. Needless to say, the best blow of the gossip columnist is a quick kick to the ear once your head is on the ground, and this is still the age of Kilgallen and Winchell. Alone, she has to be more vulnerable, for gossip columnists have a continuing political relation with the studios that restrains them from attacking movie stars on contract, yet a good column still depends on a minimal quota of murderous remarks. (We read a gossip column to keep up after all on which celebrities are being killed this day—it lifts our depression.) Unattached to DiMaggio, or the studio, she would be on every columnist's free list. Nobody would have to explain this to her.

She can then hardly fail to be relieved when the studio, delighted with her latest work, starts to woo her with attentions she has never received before. There is talk (at last!) of tearing up her contract and giving her a better one—if it is, one may be certain, vastly inferior to what other stars are getting, still it is an improvement. To celebrate the finish of *The Seven-Year Itch*, her agent, Charles Feldman (who has also been her co-producer) throws a party for her at Romanoff's. Samuel Goldwyn, Leland Hayward, Jack Warner, and Darryl Zanuck come as well as Claudette Colbert, Doris Day, Susan Hayward, William Holden, Jimmy Stewart, Gary Cooper, Humphrey Bogart, even Clark Gable, who com-

pliments her on *Gentlemen Prefer Blondes*. Joan Crawford is not invited. It is Hollywood's way of welcoming her to the Establishment. Two days later, DiMaggio accompanies her to Cedars of Lebanon Hospital where she will have a minor "gynecological operation," which may make it possible to have children. Louella Parsons writes that Marilyn's "glad the divorce won't be final for a year because it leaves the door wide open . . . about a reconciliation." It is a good move in a complex publicity game, and probably contributes to bringing Milton Greene out to Hollywood to talk to her about the plan they have already discussed to start her own film company. Again the risk appeals to her, but it is such a risk! Greene has no real money, although he is confident of raising money when the time comes, a fair assumption. In the meantime, he will support her in New York from what his photography brings in. He has even worked out a way for her to break her contract with Twentieth. There has been a threatening letter written to Marilyn by a studio executive when she would not do *Pink Tights*, and this can be used as a legal pretext that her option was not taken up. Greene's lawyer has also charted a high road for the case, which will be to claim Twentieth was enforcing degrading roles upon her and "every person has a basic right to stay decent." It is just enough law to worry Twentieth. With a senile judge and an out-of-phase moon, Twentieth could even lose the case, for contractual law staggers under a library of precedents that are closer to mutations than clarifications. At bottom, the law is being used in the way it is usually employed, as a wrestler's grip for advantage in the future against mutual torture in the present. The gamble was that Twentieth would suffer more than Greene. "As soon as the bills started coming in," Greene told Zolotow, "I knew it would cost me about fifty thousand dollars a year for the three years that remained on the Twentieth contract. . . . At the very minimum they would lose a million dollars a year without Marilyn. . . . I figured the odds were favorable, and the stockholders would start screaming." They did. In the year Marilyn was in New York before a new contract was negotiated with Twentieth, Greene was to be presented many offers, each superior to the one before (and in private was offered bribes). The final contract was a victory. She would be paid $100,000 a picture for four pictures over seven years, and could make other films with her own company, yes, a perfect move when completed, but she could not know that in advance when Greene came out to Hollywood after her operation. So the move to slip back to New York with him was bold, for she took the less secure of two possibilities and took it in the face of what might be stubborn and vindictive opposition from the studio and a debacle in the papers—she could not know. As the less predictable and more elegant move, it must have come out of the same voice in herself which would not agree to marry Johnny Hyde. She had a talent rather than an identity, and if there was a logic in her life it was to rip up the roots—Do It Again! —and follow her talent to New York. In an artist that is the exercise of saintliness, for it is saintly to follow the best thing one has discovered in one's life no matter the cost, and there is no way to comprehend Monroe unless we assume that her deepest experience in life was the act of playing in a superb role.

That she has also a dream of love with Arthur Miller which will be as large in her mind as the love of Eleanor Roosevelt for Abraham Lincoln is also part of her vision, but at least it is a vision. Not every girl from an orphanage becomes a star and then dares to desert Hollywood. Since she is also one of the toughest blondes ever to come down the pike (there in the concentrated center of her misty blonde helplessness) we can also assume that the bad reviews on *No Business Like Show Business* give her a push. She is a traveling omnibus of motives and moves most quickly when a variety of reasons coincide best with the multiplicity of herself. Holding Milton H. Greene by the hand, and endowing herself with the name of Zelda Zonk, she takes flight with him for New York in December 1954, and disappears from view.

To a newspaper circuit which had her fighting with her studio again—she would not do *How to Be Very Very Popular*—and in new romances with Milton Greene, Jacques Sernas ("the libidinous Lithuanian"), Mel Torme, Marlon Brando, and Sammy Davis, Jr., the disappearance was dramatic, an interruption of the national soap opera. There was natural consternation when she reappeared in three weeks as the head of Marilyn Monroe Productions before a press conference of a hundred reporters.

"What makes you think you can play serious roles?"

"Some people have more scope than other people think they have."

She had been living in seclusion in Weston, Connecticut, with Milton and Amy Greene, and the picture of those few weeks, when it is told by the Greenes, is not far from idyllic, for Marilyn's friendship with Milton speaks of some wistful longing of the past, as if he is the friend she never had in the orphanage, and she and Amy

act like finishing-school girls on a romp. It is not an automatic picture to make of a fashion photographer, a movie star, and a wife who is Cuban, patrician, and a New York model; we are hardly ready to picture all three in some wicked pie of absolute glee at the thought of celebrities, business types, lawyers, agents, press, and half the thunderheads of Hollywood all busily trying to locate Marilyn while the three of them get ready to sail across the financial seas in a washtub. Yet the recollected tone is of just such happiness, and images are offered of the two women rolling in maniac mirth on the carpet—"we wet our pants"—while Milton assures Bob Hope on the phone that he doesn't have any idea where Marilyn can be found, and so she won't be able to go along on Mr. Hope's trip to visit the troops in Alaska, no sir.

Amy Greene and Marilyn steal out from the house in Weston with Marilyn dressed in a brown Prince Valiant wig with a pillow stuffed under an old dress. She is pregnant! They go shopping for antiques. Another time and still another Amy takes her out in costume. By the fourth occasion, Marilyn demurs. "She was tired of looking pregnant. She *wanted* to be recognized," laughs Amy.

So they go out dressed in casual wear. An adolescent in a drugstore spots Marilyn and goes to get his friends. When Amy returns to the car, she hears a thump behind the rear seat. Marilyn has hidden in the trunk. A picture of pillow fights, hoots, screams, and hours of playing with the Greenes' boy, Josh, is offered. Marilyn buys him a pajama bag called Ethel and a huge stuffed bear named Socko.

Guiles, however, presents Amy as a hint disturbed by Marilyn's sudden entrance into the Greenes' life. In turn, Marilyn is not comfortable with Amy, who

> was the most organized human being she had ever encountered. Even the simple act of emptying a brimming ash tray was transmuted to a graceful act. . . . Marilyn was to come to a conclusion which she later confided to Miller that Amy's subterranean strengths had a tinge of the devious.

Of course, this is the picture Marilyn gave to Miller, who was implacably opposed to the Greenes and so would be likely to recall every negative remark. In turn, Amy Greene would speak with malicious delight of Marilyn's remarks about Arthur. After they were married, Marilyn showed Amy a book of love poems in Moroccan binding with gold edges and said, "Arthur paid for this with his *own* money." It is obvious, if indeed we did not have other evidence, that Marilyn was inclined to throw herself positively into each relation, and save negative reactions for another friend, hostile to the first, who would be happy to hear them. It is characteristic of those with little identity.

Zolotow gives, however, another portrait. " 'I got the feeling,' " he has a woman witness say,

> "that Amy looked down on Marilyn Monroe as a stupid little bitch. Amy was better dressed, more chic, more sophisticated, and much cleverer than Marilyn. She even looked better. In fact, you couldn't believe that this queer little duck you saw sitting around the Greenes' was really Marilyn Monroe. I remember we played charades, the girls against the men. We went into a bedroom to select the sentences. We had some quotations from poetry and things like that, and then somebody said how about the title of a book, and Amy looked over at Marilyn and said, 'Come on, Marilyn, give us a book title, will you? You're always reading all those books.' I got the feeling that Amy was implying that Marilyn

was a phony about being intellectual and didn't read any of the books she pretended to read and that Marilyn knew Amy had this low opinion of her mind. Or maybe it was that Amy resented all the gossip going around that Milton was having an affair with Marilyn and she wanted to show us that she was in command of the situation.

"What happened later convinced me of this. About half past twelve we all got hungry—oh, there were about ten of us—and Amy turned to Marilyn and ordered her—she didn't ask her, she ordered her, the way you would a servant—'Marilyn,' she said, 'Marilyn, go in the kitchen and make sandwiches.' And Marilyn obeyed her. She went into the kitchen and made sandwiches and coffee and served them to us."

Of course, in the next paragraph, Zolotow has Milton Greene subleasing a three-room apartment for Marilyn in the Waldorf Astoria Towers, mortgaging his home, cashing his securities, and borrowing to the end of his credit to support Marilyn's expenses, which come to $1,000 a week, of which $500 goes for "beautification"—a personal hairdresser on salary, podiatrists, manicurists, masseuses, and fifty dollars a week for perfume. Three thousand dollars are spent for clothes in two months during the spring of 1955. Since Greene is obviously taking the largest gamble of his life, and looking to jump from years of sinecure as a high-paid fashion photographer to a producer who will be able to make films that appeal to his good taste, Zolotow's account of Amy Greene could only suggest that she was trying to spike his gamble. But Amy Greene would argue the opposite. "My God, she was so beautiful, and I was just a couple of years out of a convent." Amy tells a story about one night in New York when she happened to mention that she would love to see Sinatra, who was appearing then at the Copacabana. Marilyn said,

"Get dressed. We're putting on our best." An account ensues of the two women readying themselves over the next couple of hours. Then Marilyn, made up with all her skill, in white dress and white furs, goes with the Greenes to the door of the Copacabana. "We had no reservations, of course, not even a phone call for warning, and Marilyn smiled at the dragon who was standing at the door and he fell back, and we just moved forward through Mafia bouncer after Mafia bouncer until we got to the room where Sinatra was singing, and of course there wasn't a seat available or even an *aisle* for that matter, and Marilyn just stood at the rear of the room not moving and one by one the customers turned to look at her and the show slowly stopped and Sinatra finally saw her, and said, 'Waiter, bring a table here,' and we were conducted, we were virtually *carried* through these nightclub *gargoyles* at their tables with their wives and their mistresses after they'd schemed and begged for reservations and of course we were put directly under Sinatra and his microphone, there could not have been a space closer to him, God *knows* what they did to the people they pushed back, and then Milton, Marilyn, and I were sung to by Sinatra, he sang the entire set to us alone, and in the middle, Marilyn kicked me in the foot and said, 'You like the table?' 'Bitch!' I whispered back."

Later, after Sinatra has joined their group, they start for his dressing room. Four bouncers form a diamond around them, one to the front, one to the rear, and two on the flanks, and they try to proceed, but the crowd is reaching in on all sides. "I panicked," said Amy. "Marilyn was very calm and kept saying to me, 'Just keep moving and don't be afraid,' but I was hysterical. You see,

they couldn't get past the bouncers, but they could reach in with their arms, and they would, until they got to Marilyn, and then they'd stop and pull short as if she were some sort of divinity and they were afraid to touch her. Of course, I was getting buffeted in the process. Those faces reaching in were the worst I ever saw. But Marilyn wasn't fazed." Amy Greene looks up from the memory. "No," she says, "I didn't look down on Marilyn at all."

Marilyn will be in New York more than a year before she goes back to Hollywood. From the end of 1954 until the beginning of 1956, her career if at all analogous to a river is most certainly going around its major bend. Perhaps 1955 in New York is the happiest year of her life. *The Seven-Year Itch* will come out to rave reviews and movie crowds waiting in line, thereby demonstrating to Twentieth how desperate they had better be to get her back. As the year goes on, she and Milton Greene will develop a clear sense that they are going to win. She will not only have her production company actually producing a film, but will work out a new and much improved contract with the studio. She is in the position of tasting victory over a powerful enemy—how many ever reach such vengeance? But then she is like a Shakespearean hero in those middle acts when good fortunes accumulate. Her love affair with Arthur Miller is begun—in the most confident part of her personality can she fail to see it as destined? How can the greatest playwright in America (or at least the greatest by her devout measure) not

naturally be wed to the most exciting actress in the land? With her infallible instinct in publicity —as superb in its readiness for bold lines of play as the most unorthodox grand master of chess— she springs out of the divorce from DiMaggio into the added velocity of a romance with Miller. Yet as if the success of her career and the promise of fulfillment to her dream of love are but two enrichments, and she is meant for more, she begins to study with Strasberg who is impressed, indeed enchanted, with her talent—he will later tell Joshua Logan "that he had encountered two film personalities of really great potential in his work at the Studio, Marlon Brando, and quite as good as Brando is Marilyn."

Some hint of the confidence she feels in the middle of this period is suggested by a story of Gardner Cowles, who was then publisher of *Look* magazine. He was approached by the distinguished George Schlee, known as the lover of Greta Garbo, but also functioning as a species of superior troubleshooter for Aristotle Onassis. Since this was in just the period before it became known that Prince Rainier of Monaco wanted to marry Grace Kelly, it had apparently been decided quite separately by Onassis (who owned half of Monaco), that Rainier ought to marry some movie star of vast renown in order to improve the glamour of Monte Carlo, which was in this year near to moribund. If very little in the world of finance could be shown to work in functional relation to publicity, the volume of gambling most certainly did, or so Onassis must have reasoned. Who would dispute the socio-mathematical maxims of our own Aristotle? His first choice evidently was Monroe, for Schlee came to Cowles, who had become friends with Marilyn, and asked the publisher to relay the message. Cowles discussed it with her in Connecticut, where Marilyn was visiting the Greenes. Would she be interested, he wondered, in marrying Prince Rainier?

What did he think she should do?

Cowles allowed that she might consider the proposition. But, he inquired, "Do you think the Prince will want to marry you?"

Her eyes were full of light. "Give me two days alone with him, and of course he'll want to marry me."

The offer can prove no more than a two-day sensation in her life, since not long after this weekend the news will break that Rainier is going to be engaged to Grace—either the Prince has worked out a line of action independent of Onassis, or George Schlee is being cut off from information. But how interesting to suppose Marilyn did dream of herself on the throne of Monaco for a weekend, since it offers a hint of her buried snobbery—an emotion to consider when she makes *The Prince and the Showgirl* with Olivier. Besides, she was in the middle of her affair with Miller. Perhaps they had had a fight that weekend. How bizarre her life had become. She had so much power, and in such a vacuum. No wonder three men, each possessed of his own artistic integrity, would nonetheless compete over the next year to fill that vacuum. A comedy sharp enough for the eye of Shaw must be buried in the details of how Arthur Miller, Milton Greene, and Lee Strasberg jockeyed with one another for control of her mind and possession of her life, but the comedy is not that they were meretricious small-minded studio producers, or like DiMaggio without a talent to develop her talent, no rather it is how each worked in his own way to *elucidate* her skills—

they would bring her *out* with a vengeance—and yet, so Shavian are the properties of a power vacuum, were finally obliged, all three, to go to war with one another. What compromise must each have made of the subtlest reflexes of his private and artistic integrity! Yet who is to judge them? We must conceive of her in 1955, the most magical and marvelous heroine of New York—she is a movie star in serious search of an education by which to develop herself. No matter how the envy of New York was ready to deride her, confusion had to collect. For who could comprehend her? No sex star had ever left Hollywood before at the peak of a career. It was remotely possible she was serious. Besides, few were ready for that shy waif with a strangled little voice, that face close to plain in the absence of makeup, her wholly insignificant presence when she was not in a professional situation. Hedda Rosten, later to be her close friend, describes their first meeting at her home in Brooklyn. Sam Shaw, the photographer, dropped by to visit the Rostens with a girl he had been photographing in the rain. She looked like a high school kid. Her hair was down and soaked through. She wore a black skirt and a cotton blouse. She had the look of a very sweet seventeen-year-old, Hedda Rosten recalls, and since she didn't catch the name, they had the following conversation.

"Oh, no, I'm not a New Yorker," the girl said. "Just got here a few weeks ago."

"What sort of work do you do?"

"Well, I'm studying at Actor's Studio."

"That's nice." Mrs. Rosten was impressed. "Have you been in any plays recently?"

"No, I've never done anything for the stage."

So it continued. Later, after the women had

become more intimate, Hedda's husband, Norman, a friend of Miller's, would sometimes be her escort.

One evening in late summer of 1955, she attended a party in Brooklyn Heights given by some of Rosten's neighbors. When they reached the house and he introduced her as his "friend, Marilyn Monroe," nobody believed him and they went ahead with their drinking and conversation. Rosten, perhaps frustrated by the people's disinterest reintroduced her several times only to get an unconvinced "Yeah, sure," from his host and others.

Who in New York could recover from the shock that Marilyn had made her voyage with a personality as modest, as uncertain, as vulnerable, and as bereft of social skin as this girl without guile who told unendurably sad stories of rapes and rebuffs in childhood. It was natural to see the tenderness embodied in that talent. How soon must each of her guides in New York have become convinced that her talent must absolutely not be tampered with by anybody else, for others would not know how to bring out the best in her. Yet if she begins three major relations this year in New York and each of these artists, Greene, Miller, and Strasberg, is finally devoted to serving her (until the finances of one, the personal life of the second, and the throttled ambition of the third have all been invested to the hilt), still each man must begin to think of how she could in turn serve him. It was impossible not to. Was there a writer alive in New York that year who would not have named some one of his literary properties for which she might be superbly suited as a tenant? Or an actor who could not begin to put a show together? Or an impresario . . . ? (Even Mike

Todd wanted her to ride on a pink elephant in a gala at Madison Square Garden, and of course she did.) High-mindedness, self-interest, and the need to protect a talented lady is enough to turn any artist into a partisan. Of course they go to war with one another. And she will use each of the three against the other two. Why should she not? They will all use her. The comedy is that no one of them is as noble as the dream they share of her potentiality delivered. It is a cruel comedy, and will yet contribute to costing her a life.

So we may as well attempt to comprehend them. There is Greene, the least known in reputation, and probably the most injured by her. It is certain he takes the largest overt gamble and comes near to bankruptcy by supporting her through all of this year in which she makes no films. After she is married Greene will eventually be inched out, inch by expelled inch, and Marilyn, under Miller's guidance, will end the partnership just as the company is ready to make real money. She will announce to the press that she sees no reason to give half the proceeds from her work to Mr. Greene. Still Greene will settle for considerably less than he could have asked. It is possible that of the three men, he had the simplest kind of love for her. In any case, he was married, she was married—it was not a position for infighting. He could serve as a buffer in her relations with directors, and always provide her with a poetic glimpse of the future. If he had the kind of mind that could comprehend her childish glee at the thought of being seen on a pink elephant in Madison Square Garden—Mike Todd had made his proposition through Greene—he was also capable of saying to her toward the end of their partnership, "Some day, when you've had enough of a white picket fence and babies, and want to make a film again, I'll tell you who to make it with, and this has nothing to do with me."

"Who?"

"Make it with Chaplin."

Of course, Greene was right. It was with Chaplin she should have made a film. We can see Greene's vision of the sort of film it might have been in those photographs he took of her in black net stockings. No ordinary relation reveals itself there between photographer and model, rather a mist of glamour, tenderness, amusement, sex, and subtle sorrow. They would tease each other for years. "Milton H. Greene," she would say after listening to an explanation, "you talk in circles."

"It's the way I walk."

They would laugh, but the relation was dependent on Marilyn's belief that he was absolutely selfless in his devotion. Once Miller was able to underline any evidence of self-interest, Greene had a position which could only deteriorate, and did. That, however, was more than a year off. She would yet make two of her best movies with Greene.

Still, the photographer (whether tender friend, romantic dalliance, or some part of giggles in bed with Amy and Marilyn) had to be outmatched by the playwright. Marilyn was not indifferent to status, and Miller was her equal and more. For Broadway was dominated by the presence of two playwrights, Tennessee Williams and Arthur Miller. Of course, that is a species of critical mystery if one compared their work, but Marilyn was not about to. Williams had already done *The Glass Menagerie, A Streetcar Named Desire, Summer and Smoke, Camino Real, Cat on a Hot Tin Roof*, and had a literary style as comprehensive in its influence on the theatre of the Fifties as had been Hemingway's influence on the novel, while Miller had only a workmanlike style, limited lyrical gifts, no capacity for intellectual shock, and only one major play to his credit. If there were some who applauded *All My Sons, The Crucible*, or *A View from the Bridge*, there were many who had not. He was a major playwright on the basis of *Death of a Salesman*. Of course, that play had given a deeper emotional experience to New York theatregoers than any other work since the war, and he was the only American playwright of stature who was not homosexual in his themes or his life. He was also much respected in Europe, where the inferiority of his style to Williams' would be less evident in translation. For that matter, he was revered by the whole hardworking half of the American theatre that was left wing and had voyaged from Odets and the Group Theatre to Actor's Studio while looking for a hero. Miller was the only candidate remotely available. He had dignity, looked the part, spoke in leftist simples that might conceivably be profound, was reminiscent of such tall spare American models of virtue and valor as Lincoln and Gary Cooper, and so could certainly serve as a major figure for the Jewish middle class of New York (who were the economic bedrock of Broadway). From that point of view, Williams was merely a distiller of exotic perfumes, a theatrical occult, whereas Miller knew how to compose drama out of middle-class values. No one else in that period did. So his audiences recovered long sought for echoes of Ibsen and O'Neill. They could encounter their own middle-class sense of themselves, study their devotion to values imposed from without (which is the aching core of middle-class life—allegiance to an identity one did not request). When Miller began to strip his characters of their values, the audience, particularly at *Death of a Salesman*, experienced a sensation of unique emotional power; their minds —in a year when no one was yet familiar with the phenomenon—were blown. The phrase is used up today but the sensation then was not. It gave life.

So he had done it once, and in a way no one ever forgot. Even people who did not like *Salesman* found to their horror that the play made them weep. But he had not done it with equal power before, nor been able to do it again in *The Crucible* and in *A View from the Bridge*. His creative life had become first cramped, then wholly constipated, and the early years of the Fifties turned out a discouraging period in which every description of him as a theatrical giant must have left Miller feeling like a giant in chains. The good and great work would simply not come. He remained locked in Brooklyn in a marriage of fifteen years' duration whose best life had long cooled, and was maintained as the first prominence in the American theatre more from the drama critics' patriotic need to insist upon a heterosexual than from any natural right to hold the post against the ever oncoming new productions of Tennessee. If Miller was ever disturbed by the thought that he might be an overrated or expired talent, he had then much to lose, for his idea of himself after *Salesman* had become immense. (Had he been an actor, such loftiness of presence would have always had him cast as the Admiral or the President.) He was sufficiently pontifical to become the first Jewish Pope, he puffed upon his pipe as if it were the bowl of the Beyond, and regaled sophisticated New York dinner parties with tedious accounts of his gardening and his well-digging, he was a Hamsun and Rolvaag of the soil, a great man! —one had to listen. Of course, by such measure he was an enigma, for his verbal ideas were banal, his processes of reasoning while not disagreeable were nonetheless not remarkable. His best intellectual presence was in his boyish grin, which for a great man was disarming. But he had no new work. The stinginess for which he was famous—find the witness to testify that Miller had ever picked up a check—now seemed to have become a species of creative thrift. He was tight, he was tied up, he was abstemious— an artist in a time of such orderliness and depression can feel he has nothing to write about. Experience repeats itself with the breath of a turnip.

We must picture this tall and timid hero of middle-class life, as guarded in his synapses as a banker, when he is visited by the return of a dream, a blonde and indescribable movie star as wild in reputation as the buried dynamos of American life (of which he has seen so little), and she is as delightful in her presence, as funny, as changeable, as interesting, and as remarkable as any adolescent dream of a heavenly blonde. Yet this blonde heaven wants him. There is a touching passage in *After the Fall* which may give the flavor of this period:

QUENTIN: I'm glad you called; I've often thought about you the last couple of years. All the great things happening to you gave me a secret satisfaction for some reason.

MAGGIE: Maybe 'cause you did it.

QUENTIN: Why do you say that?

MAGGIE: I don't know, just the way you looked at

me. . . . Like . . . out of your *self*. Most people, they . . . just look *at* you.

A little later she tells him he is "like a god." Other men would have laughed at her, she says, or "tried for a quick one."

> QUENTIN [*to Listener*]: Yes! It's all so clear—the honor was that I hadn't tried to go to bed with her! She took it for a tribute to her "value," and I was only afraid! God, the hypocrisy!

He would be inhuman if he did not have sufficient ambition to recognize that a marriage to Monroe would be theatrically equal to five new works by Williams. Besides, there was all of the experience of her life to enrich his own literary experience, a diamond mine for any playwright looking for another big play.

Still, how she must have terrified him. Where his work was not conspicuously innocent of sex, he tended to be a hint puritanical; he came out of that long line of Jewish middle-class lore which sees any heavy commitment to passion as a dire transaction. If he was thrilled by her, he must also have been shivered with her reputation. How many times had he not heard tales? "She was chewed," he would also write in *After the Fall*, "and spat out by a long line of grinning men! Her name floating in the stench of locker rooms and parlor-car cigar smoke!" Yes, if he is a repository of dignity, he is also no fool. He knows she offers him not a gift but a gamble. If they marry, he will be a target of envy and evil talk; if they fail, an object of ridicule. A man who has lost confidence in his creative power sees ridicule as the broom that can sweep him to extinction. It is not easy for an artist with the psychology of poverty to move into what may be a cornucopia of possibilities or equally a maelstrom.

Probably she, in turn, could not be excited more by his caution. She is not unlike a handsome actor who runs away from eager women all day only to go out and buy his sex that night. It has to be a novelty to desire a man who is not certain he wants her. Shades of Fred Karger, a pure male thrust of desire must rise in her at the thought she is the seducer. Plus all the joy of being able to educate another. For how well she can do this we have a clue in the seduction of Tony Curtis in *Some Like It Hot*—never does she look so happy in a sex scene. So, for all of a year, does she chase Miller until he is caught, and it is a sweet history of walks and long talks in modest Brooklyn. But then such modesty of means in Miller has to appeal to her enormously. In her reaction against Hollywood, the streets of Brooklyn Heights speak of the gentility of an easier nineteenth century. With her awareness of mood, how keenly must history come into her pores on the lavender hue of Victorian brownstones at twilight and the muffled cry of the foghorn up from the harbor—it is a year in which Miller will begin to believe that he can dare to end his marriage, separate from his children, and find a hope of love with her, yet it must also be evident that gaiety and depression shift in her psyche like the cloud wisps on each and every chop of wind, and he has not only a mistress but a new child who is utterly dependent upon him. In all misers must live the outsize fear of squandering their substance for too little—how happy must Miller feel at the discovery he can give his best to a woman of large possibilities greater perhaps than his own—it is the supposition one seems able to extract from the happiness of his face on the day they are married.

She has also been introduced to Strasberg. Cheryl Crawford has brought her to his home, and we can see Marilyn's entrance: Jacqueline Susann might as well be presented to the shade of T. S. Eliot. Before Strasberg's eyes have passed Brando and Jimmy Dean, Rod Steiger, Eli Wallach, David Wayne, Geraldine Page and Kim Stanley, Viveca Lindfors and Shelley Winters, Maureen Stapleton, Julie Harris, Monty Clift, Tom Ewell, Tony Franciosa, Paul Newman and Eva Marie Saint. In Strasberg's eight-room apartment, with high bookshelves rising up to high ceilings on every wall, editions in German and French and Italian on sofas, on tables, on the floor, in a house more laden with theatrical memorabilia than the office of Natasha Lytess, Marilyn has to be quickly reduced to her familiar idea of the nugatory—an empty box-office blonde ignorant of acting, theatre, culture, or technique. Now she is before the man who knows more about the Method than anyone in New York. He scowls at her.

Zolotow gives a clear description of Strasberg's appearance:

> He was on the small side and he looked undistinguished. His cheeks had the dark stubble of men who always look unshaven. He was wearing a dark-blue shirt and no tie and a badly fitting rumpled suit. He looked like a harassed small businessman, a drugstore owner maybe, or a delicatessen store owner who was on the verge of bankruptcy.

It is a good description as far as it goes, but it could go further, for it does not communicate Strasberg's peculiar force. If he looked exactly like that storekeeper on the edge of bankruptcy, he had also all the detestation of humanity you would find in such a man, a dank hostility that seeped out of Strasberg into every crevice of the ego of the unhappy player before him. Holding the cross of high theatrical culture overhead, as if exorcising an incubus, Strasberg could have played the chaplain in a dungeon mortuary where the services would provide no music other than his icy voice. Veteran performers went weak at the thought of performing before Strasberg. For good cause. He invariably looked as if he had just caught a whiff of some hitherto buried stink. He would watch a performance at the Studio without a quiver of emotion, and then in the silence that followed the discussion of the actors and the class, he would begin (with an air of annoyance at the simplicity of other opinions) to speak. He could talk for fifteen minutes on a scene that had taken five, he could go on for half an hour if the subject was worthy of analysis. He had one illimitable subject to which he always returned—it was the elusive question of how an actor might find a route from his own personality to the part he should play, and it was probably inconceivable to Strasberg that this process could be faultless. He would see the flaws in the most superb performance. Chief engineer of spiritual mechanics, he was able to trace a performer's inability to deliver an absolute maximum of emotion at climax to that faintest slip of concentration which had occurred picking up a pack of cigarettes some minutes earlier. It is possible there was no critic of acting in New York so incisive as Strasberg. Watching a performance at the Studio one could, if left to oneself, retain no more than some general impressions of excellence, together with the vague sense there had been some disappointing lack of excitement one could not quite explain. By the time Strasberg finished discussion, the separate pieces of the actor's performance had been taken apart, and one was no longer confused by the performance. One knew its faults. It was possible to acquire some real part of an actor's culture in those years merely by listening to Strasberg at the Studio. One would, however, pay for it. Strasberg was not so much articulate as verbose. He had an unpleasant gift for presenting his sharpest perceptions in a welter of banalities. One learned with fatigue. Even as he successfully demonstrated to actors how to bring life to their performances, he exuded his own distaste for life; he was like a surgeon of unremitting gloom who made his incision, collected his fee, and accepted no praise. It was the humiliation of his life that he could not direct a successful play.

He had had more influence upon actors than any other personality of the theatre, and had directed his share of plays, but they never succeeded. The answer might have been simple. Perhaps no play had ever been written that was sufficiently gloomy to contain the depressed ego of an actor after he had worked under Strasberg's direction for several weeks.

It is part of the excitement of her year in New York that Strasberg should have been therefore taken with Marilyn so quickly. He had seen her in films and not been impressed (which may have been the measure of his inability to look at films, or his general hostility to movie stars who had not begun in the theatre), but when she came to him, came modestly forward as acolyte to savant, his formidable powers of observation opened. He was, yes, willing to give her private lessons. "It was almost," he said later, "as if she had been waiting for a button to be pushed, and when it was pushed a door opened and you saw a treasure of gold and jewels. It is unusual to find the underlying personality so close to the surface and so anxious to break out and therefore so quick to respond." This quickness, he remarked, was "typical of great actors."

So began her introduction to the technology of the Method, her immersion into "justification," "objectification," "adjustment," "concentration," "contact," and "mood," a two-hour lesson twice a week until she was ready for the ordeal of showing herself in his school where, good modest high school girl, she would sit in a class of thirty and never say a word. Assigned to do a scene with an actor named Phil Roth, Guiles gives the dialogue of a phone call:

> "Hi!" the soft voice came through. . . . "This is Marilyn."
>
> As a joke, Roth recalled later to Strasberg, he pretended to draw a blank. "Marilyn who?"
>
> In case she dialed a wrong number, she explained, "You know, *Marilyn*. The actress from the class."
>
> "Oh! *That* Marilyn," Roth said. And Marilyn showed up a little later, breathing heavily from the five-flights climb to his walk-up apartment. She glanced about the littered room, looking troubled. "You need some woman to look after this place," she said, and . . . before beginning their assignment together, she swept the floor, put all the papers in neat stacks, and emptied the ash trays.

She is not only learning still another way to exercise her profession, she is also immersed in a role—she is the nice kid in New York who helps fellow actors with their apartments. What a wistfulness she must feel in this period at all those lives she has missed. She contains so many ages within herself. Fearful glimpses must already exist of middle age and a condition near to madness—she is approaching thirty—but since to look like a high school girl is her fundamental costume these days how much more she must retain of all those fragments of life held over from the unfinished relations of her childhood.

Meanwhile, she continues to work with Strasberg in private, does exercises, improvisations, scenes from plays. With his encouragement a pattern begins to emerge. He is slowly seducing her over to the idea of deserting films (except as a way of making money) and working in the theatre. The keel of the comedy is laid—if she works in the theatre, quite possibly he can direct her. It is certain she needs him. As the year goes on, he encourages her further. Deeper and deeper she goes—into psychoanalysis at his bidding. And Strasberg grooms her for a performance of Anna Christie at the Studio. May we assume he is more gentle with Marilyn than with most? She begins to work with Maureen Stapleton for her debut at the Studio, and confesses to Stapleton that with her tiny voice she is afraid she will not be able to project. Then there is a phone call from Milton Greene, and Marilyn goes into the next room to take it. Soon Maureen Stapleton is able to hear every word through the walls. Marilyn is shouting. She hangs up, she comes back. "Honey," says Maureen, "you don't have to worry about projection. You could project through steel walls."

Still, it is a huge test to play at the Studio, and a fair exhibit of her courage, for she will expose the unshielded surface of her extrasensory and full perceiving skin to the critical spite of highly skilled actors who have worked for years with none of her recognition. By Strasberg's report of the occasion, she played Anna with high sensitivity. He later said, perhaps a little generously, that despite the considerable talents of Maureen Stapleton, Marilyn walked away with the scene. He "foresaw a long and rewarding career for her on the stage." Arthur Miller, who had discussed the role with her in her apartment at the Waldorf Towers, was now also impressed with her talent. It has indeed been a big year for her in New York—she has gathered the admiration of fathers and peers. There has been only one flaw in her work. She can exhibit every emotion but anger. Nothing of the near-violent anguish of Garbo has shown in Monroe's Christie. Just the pain. It is as if she calls on a part of herself that has nothing to do with acting when she is feeling rage. Even if her hostility will soon be visible everywhere in her professional relations, it is not amenable to art. Nor does Strasberg appear to have discussed that with her. Perhaps he thinks it premature, since already he has been obliged to suffer from comic returns. The day after her success at the Studio in Anna Christie, Monroe wakes up with laryngitis. The unspoken thoughts of the audience seem to have strangled her after all. Whether Strasberg knows it or not, the timetable for a debut on stage must be revised.

Still, the first sixty days of 1956 are splendid. The year begins with Twentieth signing its contract with Milton Greene; she can now do William Inge's Bus Stop for Joshua Logan. Miller leaves his house in Brooklyn and moves to Manhattan. He is preparing to go to Reno for a divorce. Soon after, she does Anna Christie at the Studio, and presents herself in full décolleté at a press conference with Sir Laurence Olivier. Greene has bought the rights to The Sleeping Prince by Terence Rattigan, al-

ready played in London by Olivier and Vivien Leigh and now to be called *The Prince and the Showgirl*.

Monroe is going to co-star with Olivier! She has worked her portage from *River of No Return*. Asked to speak about her at the press conference, Olivier offers: "An extremely extraordinary gift of being able to suggest one moment that she is the naughtiest little thing and the next that she's perfectly innocent—the audience leaves the theatre gently titillated into a state of excitement," a most English and elegant taking of the sensual pulse, and Marilyn in her black velvet sheath cut low enough for either breast to be ready to pop loose, breaks a shoulder strap—nobody takes a press conference away from her! She succeeds in getting such a great majority of the questions that she looks to divert attention back to Olivier for fear he will be miffed. He probably is, and the questions of the press are hostile. She is grilled on the breaking of her shoulder strap—has that been a stunt? She is also asked to spell Grushenka. Yet she is certainly beautiful again. Gone for this hour is any high school girl.

She is also in full regalia when she returns to Hollywood in March 1956, Milton and Amy Greene in tow, to meet a huge turnout of press at the airport. Since her lessons with Strasberg must cease while she is away, Logan has been talked into accepting Paula Strasberg as her dramatic coach. That is the end of a job for Natasha Lytess. Natasha has been kept on salary as head drama coach at Twentieth while Marilyn was gone, but she has not heard a word. Now, according to Zolotow, Marilyn is "deathly afraid of Natasha Lytess, afraid Miss Lytess would do something to her." But let us take the quotation in full. It is long and once again under suspicion as a factoid,

but true or false, it does open an insight into the nature of Monroe's acting.

> Miss Lytess had made no threats but Monroe was terrified—terrified, perhaps, of the projection of her own guilt. . . . Until *Bus Stop* went into production, Natasha believed she would continue at Monroe's side, then she received a lawyer's letter notifying her that her services would not be required any longer. The studio took her off the payroll. It must be a mistake! Natasha tried to get Monroe on the phone, but Monroe was never there when she called. Natasha made no secret of her bitterness. "I did more for her than a daughter," she said, "with just a motion of her fingers, she could have told them she wanted me to stay at the studio even if she didn't want me herself on this picture. So this is my reward for sitting with her until midnight and two a.m. night after night, trying to teach her to become an actress."

Much has been made of this cruelty by detractors of Monroe (of whom there were enough at the Studio) and for years she had obviously been capable of cutting people off. She had dropped Dougherty and Grace Goddard as well as her first agent Harry Lipton; she would speak poorly of DiMaggio in the Miller years, and would soon cut off Greene, and then eventually Miller; she was not a woman to be loyal to a relationship that was done. Still, there seems something excessive in the end of Lytess, as if Marilyn is sufficiently terrified not to want her within physical range at the studio. Perhaps a hint can be found in Natasha's memoirs, where she makes her own extraordinary remark that Monroe had need of her the way "a dead man needs a coffin." It is a statement to throw light into the darkest corners of acting, for beyond the Method, and its sense memory and justification, is magic, incantation, spell, and necrophilia. In the depths of the most merry and roistering

1962

moments an actor can have on stage there is still the far-off wail of the ghoul. For a good actor is a species of necrophile—he makes *contact* with the character he is playing, inhabits a role the way a ghoul invests a body. Indeed, if the role is great enough, the actor must proceed through a series of preparatory acts not unrelated to magical acts of concentration, ritual, and invocation. The very exercise of "sense memory"—perhaps the deepest procedure of the Method—required the evocation within oneself of all the details, impressions, and finally the senses of an experience that was past; one was literally attempting to reincarnate experience as a way of preparing to reincarnate the spirit of a role; so the dialogue between a drama coach and an actor, if serious enough, bore little relation to teacher and pupil, or coach and athlete, and more was like the psychic life between witch and wanton. It was as if Monroe's fear of Lytess was the legitimate fright one could feel at daring to replace one's first witch with another, and it is certain that in the movies she will now make Paula Strasberg will be detested fully as much as Lytess ever was by most of the actors and crew, a small dowdy dumpling of a woman, described with cruelty by more than one associate as a black mushroom (for she was often dressed in a big black hat and black squat shapeless gown), and there is no doubt that in her fierce, even greedy, attachment to Monroe's welfare (and Monroe's money) she gives fierce services for fierce pay, and keeps others off Monroe or at least jolted away from dealing with her directly, a black-clothed body of a sorceress to intercept all cess, good and bad. She is always the most detested figure on a set and the butt of the most picayune and mean-spirited gossip. Even when she is praised, one can feel ovens of lividity

behind the remark. Josh Logan speaks: "A warm Yiddisher Mama with words of advice and caution pouring from her in torrents, all out of love and interest," and we flee such love and interest. It is hard sell on a witch.

This is not to suggest that Monroe had become any innocent victim. It is more to the thesis that she herself puts into her artistry the transmutations of a sorceress; how characteristic that on the set she is often a spiritless "sloth" until she can reach those inspirations she will need for a scene. It is even a sociological phenomenon that out of progressive acting groups with left-wing insights upon social problems should come precisely this species of witchcraft, even if it is never perceived remotely as such by Strasberg or anyone about him. Nonetheless, Actor's Studio is not without comparison to a cavern where mysteries of acting are invoked in soul-shifting states of ceremony.

Excellent. We are fortified with a tool to comprehend a few of her actions in the films she will make through the last years of her life. They are to be her best films, the fulfillment of an art—they will also be made with a clanking of chains, and a molasses-like set of impedimenta to the movement of schedule, the near-breakdown of director after director, the hatred of her fellow actors, and an occasional collapse of her methods of work as those methods become more undisciplined and inchoate to the eyes of her colleagues with every film. Yet her art deepens. She gets better. Her subtlety takes on more resonance. By *The Misfits* she is not so much a woman as a presence, not an actor, but an essence—the language is hyperbole, yet her effects are not. She will appear in these final films as a visual existence different from other actors and so will leave her

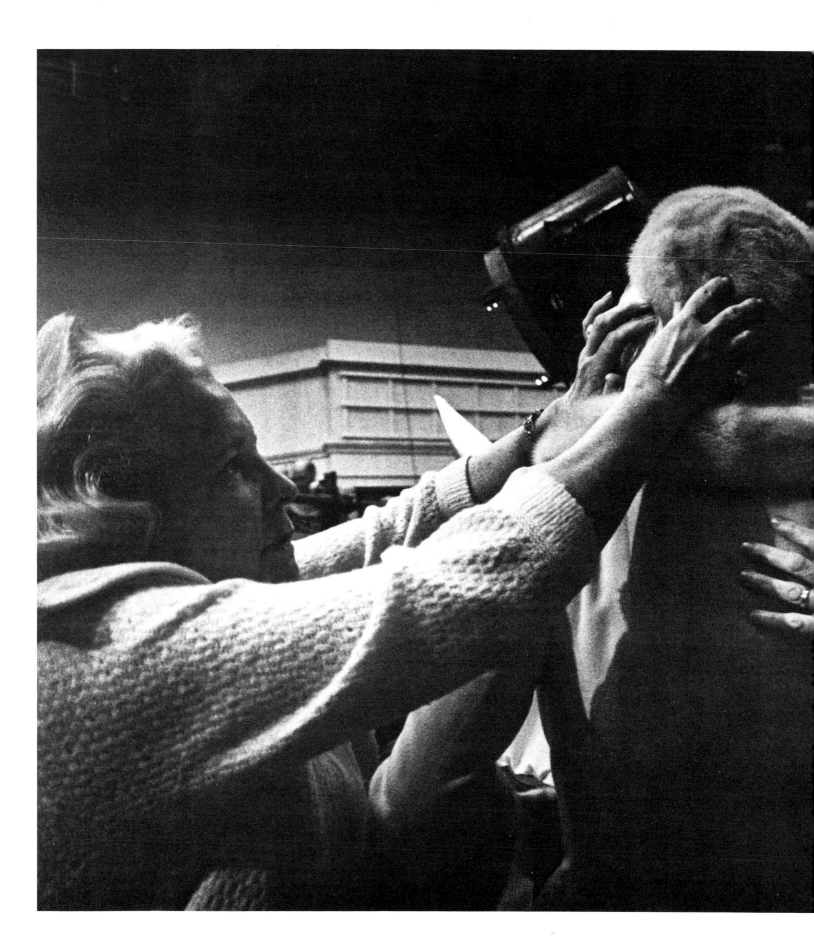

legend where it belongs, which is on the screen.

But since *Bus Stop* is the last good film she makes that does not guarantee a crisis each shooting day on the set, it is worth a word. In Logan she had a director who respected her and had the instinct to recognize (with much warning from Strasberg and Greene) that she must be allowed all of a long time-consuming meandering way to achieve her effects. Yes, Logan knew enough to work with Paula Strasberg, and with Milton Greene, who designed a dangerous chalk-white makeup, "almost a clown make-up," for Marilyn's role as Cherie, a tawdry southern cabaret singer, chalk-white precisely because she played the role of a girl who sang until the bars closed and lived on coffee and aspirin. It became a makeup to give pathos to the character—a talentless singer who dreamed of a great career.

She was up for the role. She had learned from Strasberg. Discarding preliminary sketches for her costume, she chose ratty clothes and looked for ripped stockings out of wardrobe with crude stitches, she purchased a sad small-town southern glamour by these funky clothes (a perfect piece of objectification), and brought to life some physical trappings of the biography she was to play, Cherie! and thereby began to create a comic role so sad, so raunchy, so dazzling in its obliviousness to its own poverty of talent, that some would consider it her greatest film. For certain, it is the only film she ever made where she was ready to present a character independent of herself, even down to accent—it is not Monroe's voice we hear but the blank tones of a dumb southern drawl, she communicates continents of basic ignorance in each gap of the vowels (southern nasalities are once again off in orbit), and her eyes roll and dart to the corners, as restless yet as lifeless as agitated marbles each time she talks about the promiscuities of her past. She has the blank schizoid fever of poor southern white trash, she is blank before moral dilemmas, blank before provocation, blank before dread—she suggests all the death that has already been visited upon the character in the mechanical hard-remembered way she clicks the switch for her red spotlight during a song and dance. So *Bus Stop* becomes a vehicle for Monroe, but the rest of the film suffers, the crowd scenes might as well have been done by a unit director from MGM, and much of the atmosphere established by supporting actors has the hyped-up hokey sound of bit parts in a stock company too long on the road. It is as if Logan has been able to direct her, but cannot give credibility to much else except for one triumphant scene of betrothal between the leading man, Don Murray, and Monroe at the end, all the better apparently for a history of feuds and squabbles between them. She becomes savage in her relations with Don Murray, and in a scene where she is supposed to slap him, whips the tail of her gown across his face so hard he suffers several cuts, an unprofessional roughness for which she prepares to apologize, but cannot. Instead she bursts into tears and yells at Murray, "Damn it, damn it, damn it—I won't apologize to you, no, no." It is as if the spirits forbid her. Once when Murray asks her why she continues to talk in a southern drawl after their work for the day is done, she replies, "Cain't you-all see ah'm making contact with my character?" Whatever love may be lost between them is actor's love.

The film comes out to reviews that take her seriously for the first time as an actress, but to her pain she is not even nominated for an Academy Award. (The prize goes that year to Ingrid Bergman for *Anastasia*—the heart of Hollywood has decided to forgive Bergman for Rossellini.) However, Miller comes out of Reno soon after the shooting to join her in New York. They are getting ready to marry.

VII. THE JEWISH PRINCESS

t is, of course, an orgy of publicity. Who could prevent it? The newspapers shift their new predictions for the date of the nuptials from edition to edition, and even Miller's "No comment" becomes a headline on his return from Reno. Now there are fifty variants on one fertile idea: the Great American Brain is marrying the Great American Body. Because Marilyn is taking up the faith (Reformed Synagogue), the New York *Post*, whose base of readership is suburban liberal, trade union, middle class and —in the absence of other sheets—progressive, goes in for tooth-sucking analyses of the wedding to come, plus an interview with Arthur Miller's mother. "She opened her whole heart to me," said Mrs. Miller, who then told how Marilyn was learning to make gefilte fish, borscht, chicken soup with matzoh balls, chopped liver, tsimis, potato pirogen—Marilyn is obviously going to have to come her way from Dougherty's carrots and peas.

Now the House Un-American Affairs Subcommittee provides an interruption to their plans for marriage. Looking for publicity, they summon Miller as a witness to explain why he was not granted a passport in 1954. That is an old case, which has been brought up again only because Miller is re-applying for a passport; he desires to go to England for the making of *The Prince and the Showgirl* and has been quietly negotiating with the State Department, who act as if they are prepared to refuse him again (under the terms of a regulation ready to deny passports to people "supporting Communist movements"— although by 1956 that has become an embarrassing power). It is four years since the peak of the McCarthy days and, next to testing a new hydrogen bomb, Miller and Marilyn are the most newsworthy item in America. Everybody in Washington understands that the Un-American Affairs Subcommittee, which has been altogether out of the news, now hopes to regain some of its lost attention by being able to cite Arthur Miller for contempt should he refuse to testify. Since publicity is a subcommittee angel, they are naturally slavish in their secret respect for Marilyn. So they also offer a secret deal: if Miss Monroe will pose for a picture with Chairman Walter of the Subcommittee, Miller's difficulties may begin to disappear. Miller refuses. He is even warned by his lawyers not to tell anyone. Who will believe such farce?

In the meantime, the hearings are given headlines. Marilyn endears herself to everyone from liberal Democrats to the *Daily Worker!* She tells the press her fiancé will win. There is a newsreel clip that shows her in the midst of an interview at this time on a lawn outside a Washington home, and she is never more beautiful. She looks in love. It could be said, if we are to invest in the logic of sentiment, that she looks deeply in love as she slowly replies out of a profound and pretty confusion to the questions which are asked of her. She seems bemused, as if thinking of pleasant hours with Miller rather than of the questions besieging her now. Of course, she is probably on sedation. We must live in two lives whenever we think of her one life.

It is still a year in which a movie star can be persecuted in the press for open left-wing associations, and so the suggestion that her fortune is committed to Miller's fortune gives her status as a heroine. She is beginning to capture the imagination of America's intellectuals; grudgingly, they are obliged to contemplate the remote

possibility that she is not so much a movie star as a major figure in American life—of a new sort! Of course, they will not move too far in this direction until her death. But since European intellectuals are agog at this new portrait—America persecuting its outstanding author and most attractive movie star in a neo-McCarthian wholly sophomoric hysteria, et cetera—the State Department quietly intervenes, Chairman Walter quietly breaks his wind, and Miller and Monroe have held their first fort. He gets the passport. They can be married and go to England to make the movie with Olivier.

So Marilyn is indoctrinated by Rabbi Robert Goldberg from the environs of New Haven on some general tenets and theory of Judaism (for two hours!), embraces the faith, enters the fold, and is told there is no afterlife. (What is the pride of Reformed Judaism if it is not the absence of an afterlife?) A double-ring ceremony takes place in Katonah at the home of Kay Brown, Miller's literary agent, and follows by two days the unscheduled civil ceremony in White Plains, which had been quickly arranged on Friday evening after an horrific press conference on early Friday afternoon at Miller's farm in Connecticut. That was when Myra Sherbatoff of *Paris-Match* was killed chasing their newsworthy automobile, and four hundred people by Zolotow's estimate (he was there) gathered around Milton Greene to hear how they would be given twenty minutes for newsreels, twenty for still photographers, thirty for reporters, a technological ceremony for the stifling midday landlocked heat of a Connecticut farm in the end of June.

"Give him a kiss, Marilyn," sing the photographers.

"One shot of the lovebirds, please."

One nightmare. Yet we have pictures of the day, and she looks happy. Death, press hysteria, Congress, and religious vows soon to come—it is all part of the *tohu-bohu* (if we are to use a good Hebrew word) of what has always been her public life.

Still, how beautiful they look in their wedding pictures. Staid Arthur Miller has been a scandal to his friends ever since he came back from Reno, for he and Marilyn sit in entwinement for hours. Like Hindu sculpture, their hands go over one another's torsos, limbs, and outright privates in next to full view of company, a questionable activity to perform in front of cynics, but it is as if the hero and heroine will each declare to the world that no matter the extent of *her* sexual scholarship and *his* meager schooling, they meet as equals in the godly art. They are lovers, and that is the only law of balance in sexual thermodynamics. They will immolate the past with the heat of the present. He buys her a gold wedding ring and inscribes it, "*A to M, June 1956. Now is Forever.*" It is a fervent response to whatever sentiments of confidence he hears pounding in his heart.

There is in retrospect a dialogue on the wedding day of Quentin and Maggie in *After the Fall*.

MAGGIE: . . . you said we have to love what happened, didn't you. Even the bad things.
QUENTIN: Sweetheart—an event itself is not important; it's what you took from it. Whatever happened to you, this is what you made of it, and I love this!

A few lines later Maggie says, "There's people who're going to laugh at you."

QUENTIN: Not any more, dear, they're going to see what I see. . . .

MAGGIE: What do you see? Tell me! [*Bursting out of her*] 'Cause I think . . . you were ashamed once, weren't you?

QUENTIN: I see your suffering, Maggie; and once I saw it, all shame fell away.

MAGGIE: You . . . were ashamed?

QUENTIN [*with difficulty*]: Yes. But you're a victory, Maggie, you're like a flag to me, a kind of proof, somehow, that people can win.

It is his rallying cry. One can hardly remain a left-wing writer if one does not believe that the people who are coming up from the bottom have enough goodness to win, have enough moral wherewithal to deserve to win, yes, she is his living testament, for she—his blessed heroine—is up from the people. So she becomes the affirmation to replace all lost left-wing certainties.

Of course, Miller, like many a playwright before him, is too complex a man to remain in one consistent piece. He is also a *practical* poet and much immersed in studies of money coming in and money going out. There is more to life than affirmations of passion and sexual vaults over the past. Miller is always asking Greene about Marilyn Monroe Productions, its details, its plans, its financing, its projects, its difficulties, until Greene says to him, "Be a husband! Leave the corporation to Marilyn and me." No, there is no quick love between Miller and Milton, nor much more between Miller and the Strasbergs. Lee Strasberg will give Marilyn away at the double-ring wedding, but Arthur, still keeping his opinion to himself, does not approve of Actor's Studio, nor Strasberg's mode of teaching that makes actors "secret people," and "makes acting secret [when] it's the most communicative art known to man." (Never has the inborn antipathy of the progressive mind for the dialectical hitch been more in evidence!) We can be witness to a small part of their first meeting. It is at Strasberg's home before the marriage, and one can anticipate Marilyn's excitement. But it all goes wrong. Marilyn begins to talk of a special record— Woody Herman playing Stravinsky—which Lee Strasberg has let her hear. Arthur wishes to share this pleasure, and Strasberg puts it on. A marvelous record, says Arthur, where can one purchase it? Can't be done, Strasberg assures him. The record is one of a kind. Arthur looks at it. It has a commercial label. May be hard to find, Arthur suggests, but not one of a kind. Most certainly is, says Strasberg, ending the discussion. It is evident to Miller that Strasberg is trapped in a boast he must have made on another occasion to Marilyn that the Woody Herman–Stravinsky record was unique. No, no quick love between Miller and Strasberg.

Still, for a honeymoon they will all go over to England to work on *The Prince and the Showgirl*, Millers, Greenes, and Strasbergs. A troika! Strasberg is no happier with Greene. A half year earlier, consulted by Milton as to the advisability of taking on Olivier to be director of the film as well as its leading man, Strasberg committed himself to no more than a mild opinion that the possibility "was a good idea." Greene immediately took this speech as his opportunity to cable Olivier a firm offer as director. A misunderstanding, they might agree, but who could be certain, including Greene himself, that the secret motive may not have been to cut off flirtation with any possibility that Strasberg might direct his first film—or did Greene wish to ingratiate himself with Olivier for future films? Who could know? In business, ambiguity poisons several more relations than betrayal.

Marilyn travels as her own kind of queen. Shades of Zelda! The Millers fly to England with twenty-seven pieces of luggage (of which three are Arthur's—like Barry Goldwater, he is ready to hold on to his socks!). There is $1,500 in overweight luggage, of which $1,333.33 is her share, and they are deluged by hundreds of press at the airports in New York and London. Guiles reports Miller in a near state of shock as they are conducted from terminal to plane, "strange arms under their elbows . . . no air to breathe . . . voices become a muffled roar . . . a little like drowning." Miller shows just such torture in his expression for photographers. The corners of his mouth have become the creases in the smile of a stone dragon. Given the dragon's stern principles, this wrack of publicity will never end. Perhaps he will suffer most when he finds himself trying to enjoy it. There seems a will to torture himself reminiscent of Richard Nixon being jovial on command.

At London Airport they are met by Sir Laurence Olivier and wife Vivien Leigh. A photographer is trampled in the crush. Off they go with a thirty-car caravan to a "large rented estate" at Egham in the royal grounds of Windsor Park. They have been expecting a "cottage" but find an English country mansion. All one-family homes in England, they are assured, are cottages.

Ga-ga is the prose of the English press. One London weekly prints a special Marilyn Monroe edition. That is an honor given to no human since Queen Elizabeth's coronation. "She is here," says the London *Evening News*. "She walks. She talks. She really is as luscious as strawberries and cream." *The Seven-Year Itch* has had exactly the kind of success one would expect in England, where many an Englishman can identify with Tom Ewell. Miller is naturally expected to be clever, superb, well-spoken, and romantic—a tall knight who has been ready to go to war with bloody McCarthy. England offers its oyster.

She was invited to be the patroness of a cricket match for charity at Tichborne Park and to taste the rockbound solitude of the island of Aran; the Scottish knit goods industry was preparing for her a lifetime collection of hand-knit cashmere twin-set sweaters; a group of teddy boys invited her to join them for a bit of fish and chips in Penge, a London suburb.

But it is comedy. For the Millers are tied in class knots. English accents, Olivier's in particular, have to certainly remind them that she is a girl from a semi-slum street and he is a boy from Brooklyn. She says the wrong things at her first press conference. The British do not care if she is witty, or refreshingly dumb, but she must choose to be one, or be the other—instead, she is pretentious.

"Do you still sleep in Chanel No. 5?"

"Considering I'm in England now, let's say I am now sleeping in Yardley's Lavender." That will waft no balm to English noses. It is like coming out four-square for Catholicism at Notre Dame—they have heard that already.

"Can you give us your tastes in music?"

"I like, well, jazz, like Louis Armstrong, you know, and Beethoven."

"Oh, *Bee*thoven?" We hear the nasal flush of Anglican tides in the Bay of Beethoven. "What *Bee*thoven numbers in *particular, Miss* Monroe?"

She gives a hopelessly American reply. "I have a terrible time with numbers." Now the recovery. "But I know it when I hear it." No worse mis-

161

take! You do not offer something to the English unless you deliver it altogether. They are not tolerant of conversations that belly-flop from one unfinished line to another.

In turn, Miller is hopelessly stiff. No more do the English need his chill. They have their own castles for chill. Miller is described to Zolotow by a London friend as "cold as a refrigerated fish." They turn down invitations to fashionable parties, and invite no one in return. Off to a very bad start.

Soon they begin to recognize new trouble. Olivier *hates* the Method. Where is Milton Greene, who had the genius to make him the director? It is possible Olivier is the foremost representative in all the world of the school of Coquelin. An actor does well to do his home-work, and come to the set with characterization superbly in hand. One does not wallow in depths. One delivers the point. Eli Wallach can speak of taking Olivier to Actor's Studio to watch the Method in operation. The reactions of Sir Laurence then are to show that he is not to be party to this revolution.

It can be said with no great strain that most of the male and female population of England are good amateur actors, well schooled in Coquelin. One lives in the creation of one's manner; one delivers the manner on call. None of your crude American fumbling toward the point while gorging on the charity of all. Can we conceive of a worse situation for Marilyn? She is an extermination camp to millions of cells in each of the brains of her co-workers as she gasses their patience—yes, Tony Curtis will speak of kissing Hitler, and Olivier will tell Milton Greene he is ready to "squeak!" What makes it even worse is that her troika is pulling next to no

chariot for her. Milton Greene is smooth as rum and butter with Olivier, and Miller has been lumbered by English upmanship and secretly respects Sir Laurence much too much. Strasberg delivers Big Bertha pronunciamentos from safe London, miles away from the studio. "Why does Olivier say he had difficulty with her," he remarks in later years. "I would say she had difficulty with him," but he is an outmoded gun for wars like this.

While Olivier has been warned in many a note from Logan to be patient with Marilyn, and not to raise his voice, nor expect "disciplined stage deportment," and Olivier has promised to iron himself out "nice and smooth," it is likely Olivier is contemptuous of the situation even before the film begins. He has already done *The Sleeping Prince* as a play with Vivien Leigh and so is conceivably in this for the profit rather than the glory of Marilyn Monroe's profession. Monroe, on the other hand, carrying all the secret snobbery that has led her to consider becoming Princess of Monaco, has to quicken to the thought she is playing with the monarchical actor of them all—her own secret coronation! We can measure the great and royal hollow of the orphanage by the size of her noble ambition now —yet there is Olivier brimming with hostility he cannot even begin to swallow at Logan-like injunctions to take care of darling little spoiled *lèse-majesté* wild animal actresses and Method madness and American money, upstart Millers and ogre Strasbergs, goes out, does Sir Laurence, and roils Miss Monroe's ego royally on the first week of work by saying, "All right, Marilyn, be sexy!" One might as well ask a nun to have carnal relations for Christ. Olivier has exposed that little gulf, wider than the Atlantic, between Method and Coquelin. In common-sensical Coquelin it don't take long to get sexy. If God was good enough to give it, throw it, babe! Indeed, the more unheralded English actors on the set have been looking at her with giggles. They have been waiting for the sex machine to start.

But in the Method, one does not get sexy. She calls Strasberg in London. Her voice burns wire. "Lee, how do you become sexy? What do you do to be sexy?" She cannot be soothed. Olivier has jammed into the tender roots of ontology and revealed his secret contempt for her. "The naughtiest little thing. . . ." Balzac, describing a bourgeois who purchased a false title, could do justice to her wrath. Now Olivier will get *her* treatment. He will learn, naughty little English boy, that sexiness is not a shiver in the pickle but the whole evocation of the whole woman in relation to the whole role: Marilyn proceeds to get ill. Quickly the cast is instructed by Greene not to giggle when she appears, and indeed, in reaction, are now funereal at the sight of her.

Soon they are in the familiar clutch of not knowing whether she will show up two hours late, four hours late, or not at all. Morning after morning, Miller phones that she is sick. In fact, she is back on quantities of sleeping pills. Arthur is beginning to discover the maelstrom. ("I have a terrible time with numbers.") Nights go by when she cannot sleep at all. The unnumbered count of pills goes up. Then the gamble. Does she splurge for a few more and get a couple of hours sleep, thereby to stagger forth in drastic stupor for a working day, or should she pass into morning without sleep and try the job on stimulants? And red-rimmed eyes? Or does she skip the job and miss another day?

He is on vigil. Already there are intimations that the bucket by which she lowers herself into the well is tied to a frayed rope. It is fair to wonder if Miller is still full of love, or whether rage at her habits is now begun with him as well. He is a most ambitious man. In his own way, he is as ambitious as she is, and if she had only been an actor in the school of Coquelin—small detail!—and could get the work out on time, they could go far together. During those days in Washington when he fought for his passport he must have thought once or twice that no national office was necessarily too small for him. The public loved them so! Instead, after years of cramped work, he is now doing less writing than ever. He is her god, her guard, her attendant, and her flunky. Old friends, much impressed with his importance in the past, are now horrified to see Miller pasting up news clippings of Marilyn in a scrapbook, or standing around to approve her stills. Greene, who reads the situation better, senses that Miller is immersing himself in all the corners of movie business by way of preparing to replace him.

Still, how she must irritate Miller with her endless journeys to the simplest point. He is becoming all too aware of her capacity to inflict damage in secret wars. He cannot help it—he has sympathy for Olivier. Honest Jewish lover, he must write "a letter from hell" and leave it for her to see. (Perhaps he thinks it will give the proper reorientation to her heart.) When she reads these few lines (left on his desk open) she phones Strasberg again. Guiles gives the recollection:

She was so overwrought in telling the story it was not easy to determine precisely what the notebook entry had said, but Strasberg remembers there was indignation in her voice. "It was something about how disappointed he was in me. I was some kind of angel but now he guessed he was wrong. That his first wife had let him down, but I had done something worse. Olivier was beginning to think I was a troublesome bitch and that he [Arthur] no longer had a decent answer to that one."

The Strasbergs naturally would believe in later years that the episode was "the seed of her later destruction." Miller as naturally would see it as one episode among many. Marilyn, always ready to shift the burial ground of each corpse in her past, would say after she broke with Miller that he had called her a "whore." In *After the Fall*, Miller will recreate the episode and give this language to the note: "The only one I will ever love is my daughter. If I could only find an honorable way to die." What a nightmare is beginning for him. It is the cauldron in which Marilyn has spent her life, but he has no habits for it.

The movie progresses with absences, breakdowns, crises. Olivier is close to collapse himself. The irony is that when one sees *The Prince and the Showgirl*, it is better than anyone has a right to expect from the history of its making, but that is because Monroe is superb—will wonders never cease?

Dame Sybil Thorndike, who plays the Dowager Queen, is even going to say after the film is done, "I thought, surely she won't come over, she's so small scale, but when I saw her on the screen, my goodness how it came over. She was a revelation. We theatre people tend to be so outgoing. She was the reverse. The perfect film actress, I thought. I have seen a lot of her films since then, and it's always there—that perfect quality."

She is also lovely. Milton H. Greene is indeed a genius with makeup. Never will Marilyn exhibit so marvelous a female palette, her colors living in the shades of an English garden. A hue cannot appear on her face without bearing the tone of a flower petal. Her lips are rose, her cheeks have every softened flush. Lavender shadows are lost in her hair. Once again she inhabits every frame of the film.

Of course, Olivier in his turn cannot fail to be excellent. He is too great an actor not to offer some final delineation of a Balkan Archduke. If there are a thousand virtuosities in his accent, it is because his virtuosities are always installed within other virtuosities—a consummate house of cards. It is just that he is out there playing by himself. So one can never get to believe he is attracted to Monroe. (Indeed, he is most believable when he snorts, "She has as much *comme il faut* as a rhinoceros!") Willy-nilly, he is therefore emphasizing the high level of contrivance in the plot.

A day arrives when Paula Strasberg strikes with "torrents of love and interest." She tells Olivier that his performance is artificial. It will not be long before she is banned from the set, then sent home from England. (Somehow, Olivier cannot grow accustomed to Monroe's habit of walking away from him to confer with Paula.) Mrs. Strasberg has been struck down, however, for loyalty on the right front. After this, Paula would be working with Marilyn for the rest of her life. And Milton Greene would catch the backed-up cess. From Marilyn's point of view, she was the producer of the film, but had no artistic control. Greene had given all that away to Olivier! One gets a glimpse of her rage, plus the mode in which Arthur and she have been talking about Milton, right after Greene announces to

the British press *on his own* that he is ready to set up a British subsidiary of Marilyn Monroe Productions in order to make films in England. How unaware Milton must have been of Marilyn's feelings. Obviously, she had given him too small a clue.

> Miller put in a call to Greene, but his anger was such that he was shouting into the instrument and all Greene could hear was an incoherent roar. He recalls his angry reply, "If you want to talk to me, talk to me. If you're going to yell, then I'm not going to listen." When the roar continued, he slammed down the receiver.

Doubtless, he could then measure the beginning of the end of his relation to Marilyn Monroe Productions. Implicated Greene! He was also forced to serve as Olivier's emissary to inform Paula Strasberg that she was exiled. Somewhere in these embattled weeks, Monroe summons her analyst from New York and delays production another week.

For a taste of mutual relations just before the banishment, then we must trust Zolotow. If this glimpse of a scene is not true, we know it ought to be.

> One day when Monroe was being insufferably slow about everything, Olivier said something about speeding things up a bit. Mrs. Strasberg said, "You shouldn't rush Marilyn. After all, Chaplin took eight months to make a movie."
> Olivier looked from Monroe to Mrs. Strasberg to Greene. He didn't say a word. But his expression indicated that the analogy between Monroe and Chaplin was possibly the most nauseating remark he had ever heard.

Olivier is wrong. British snobbery is once again building empires and buggering them. All parties concerned finish the film in a cloud of detestations and Marilyn makes a little speech to the cast. "I hope you will all forgive me. It wasn't my fault. I've been very, very sick all through the picture. Please—please don't hold it against me."

She is introduced to the Queen. It does no good. She has lost the British press. They sniff and snipe to a fare-thee-well. She did not have the common touch, she did not know *in the way Winston Churchill did* how to take fish and chips with Cockneys.

The Millers return to America. The dream that they were destined for a great and mighty marriage may already have foundered. One would like a picture of Olivier's face as he said goodbye.

They come back to the Greenes' apartment on Sutton Place, and divide their time between New York and Miller's farm in Connecticut. The racketing assembly line of daily publicity shuts down. They begin to have some of the married life Miller once envisaged. Later he will indicate that this fall, winter, and spring, plus the summer they had together in Amagansett, was their happiest time, and if this would clash with the Strasbergs' view that the marriage was already hurt in final fashion by the discovery of Miller's notebook in Egham, it is better to recognize that their marriage requires love to enter the service of medicine. So for a period he will be the most deeply devoted physician of her life, and she will love him back—in very much the way gentile girls are supposed to love Jewish doctors. There is so much concern for healing you! In all of Miller's early plays is one progressive theme: social evil derives from minds sickened by inhuman values. Those minds can best be cured by healing the heart. He loved her heart. It is significant that Paula Strasberg, interviewed in New York right after *The Prince and the Showgirl* (which is to say right after Egham), was sufficiently uninhibited to say, "I have never seen such tenderness and love as Arthur and Marilyn feel for each other. How he values her! I don't think any woman I've ever known has been so *valued* by a man." It seems Egham had not blown all the walls just yet.

Actually, they settle into good days and bad days. Which is the narrative line of marriage. In England he has been a failure to her. In *After the Fall*, Maggie cries, "You should've gone in there roaring! 'Stead of a polite liberal and affidavits. . . ." Greene remarked: "She wanted a fuehrer to deal with Olivier, and got a broker." No, Marilyn has not wanted Miller's insights into the complexity of the artist's working situation. So Arthur has been, yes, a failure in England, and at Egham a traitor. But the marriage can hardly be dead. She is in the deepest need of a cure. Her illness is made up of all that oncoming accumulation of ills she has postponed from the past, all that sexual congress with men she has not loved, and all those unfinished hours with men she has loved, all the lies she has told, all the lies told about her, all unavenged humiliations sleeping like unfed scorpions in the unsettled flesh. Worse! —all unfinished family insanity, plus her own abused nerves. Plus the need to come to rest in some final identity. (Even in her last *Life* interview with Meryman, she will say, "My work is the only ground I've ever had to stand on. . . .

To put it bluntly, I seem to have a whole superstructure with no foundation.") If she has known the best sexual athletes of Hollywood (that capital of sex) and Miller at his worst has to be an inhibited householder from Brooklyn, nonetheless she loves him. He is the first man she has met upon whom she can found an identity, be Marilyn Monroe, the wife of Arthur Miller. That alone may provide her such happiness that she is able for this period at least to grant him that indispensable fiction for the maintenance of marriage—you are the best lover I ever had. Of course, *best lover* is its own happy category. Many a man or woman has a sexual life with oncoming lovers who appear each in turn the *best*, one lover for each face of the sexual best; somehow there are twenty best faces. It would hardly be unnatural if, feeling some tenderness with him she has not necessarily known before, she would decide tenderness was, yes, best, tenderness was best, even as the number of certified sexual arrivals—call Dr. Kinsey!—may once have been best, or some high electric discharge into the stratosphere of the shaking sexual tree, some sweet taste of liberty (the freedom to fuck!), any category can be best: lips, smell, skin, *whatever*—there is no standard to keep us from deciding that our present sex is at the maximum. Of course, we all grow old—that little problem! Still, we can always carry our sexual past into the present (even as Miller suggested in *After the Fall*), but then we are able to succeed at making the present lover equal to the sum of all which has gone before only if we are also increasing, that is becoming wiser, wittier, or possessed of more psychic strength. We have to transcend what is past—in our emotions, at least, if not in our bodies. Emotion has to work through the

sorrow of the past without self-pity; so, one must find more wealth in the heart—no small requirement!

But there is small evidence that they were ever in such a state. Like everything else in Marilyn's life, she lived in the continuing condition of a half-lie, which she imposed upon everyone as an absolute truth—it was that Miller adored her out of measure. Like a *goddess*. Since Miller was also a man with such separate needs as the imperative to write well, as well as to profit from her talents as much as anyone else was prospering, yes, whenever he emerged as a *separate person*—fell phrase of romance!—this half-lie or half-truth that he adored her without limit had to collapse. Where she had claimed an absolute truth that was ill-founded, now there was an absolute denial, equally ill-founded. He did not love her at all. He wished only to use her.

A picture of just such emotional swings is revealed in her habits at Amagansett. The summer of 1957 is the period in which he works best as Young Doctor Miller, and often will get her off sleeping pills, or down to just one or two a night; sometimes she will even sleep. Restored by the least bit of rest, there are days when she will have endless energy and show exquisite sensitivity—at least to his lover's eye. She has only to study the petals of a flower to invoke the full appreciation of his adoring view—"she was able to look at a flower as if she had never seen one before," he would say in an interview—and we get a glimpse of what was most tender and attractive between them in a quotation Guiles selects for us from Miller's short story, "Please Don't Kill Anything."

> The waves were breaking into the net now, but they could not yet see any fish. She put her two hands up to her cheeks and said, "Oh, now they know they're caught!" She laughed. "Each one is wondering what happened!" He was glad she was making fun of herself even if her eyes were fixed in fear on the submerged net. She glanced up at her husband and said, "Oh, dear, they're going to be caught now."
>
> He started to explain, but she quickly went on, "I know it's all right as long as they're eaten. They're going to eat them, aren't they?"
>
> "They'll sell them to the fish stores," he said softly, so the old man at the winch wouldn't hear. "They'll feed people."
>
> "Yes," she said, like a child reassured. "I'll watch it. I'm watching it," she almost announced to him. But in her something was holding its breath.

We are finally dealing with the root of human comedy, and it is tragic. She is a girl who cannot bear the death of one little fish—she is thus genuinely sensitive to the expiration of life, to the *instant* when it stirs intimations, which go to the root of her divine nerves—yet she is ready to kill herself before she can allow his will to influence her will.

During years to come when her suicide attempts will be not infrequent, he will come to recognize that her desire to kill herself would kill him almost as effectively in the eyes of society. "I'm all the evil in the world, aren't I?" Quentin says to Maggie in the middle of just such an attempt. "A suicide kills two people, Maggie, that's what it's for!"

Of course, Miller is not without his own purchase on contradiction. He is a masterpiece of love and thrift, generosity and pinch. If he comes to her as a man bursting with the desire to offer his love to someone who has need of it, she must know all the pleasure of a thief who rips off a consummate miser. What a treasure in the hoard! For the first time in her life she can live in a milieu which adores her, adores her twice, first as a star, and then because she has chosen Arthur and so prefers intelligentsia and the theatre to capitalists, professional sports, or Hollywood. Moreover, there are the near to unlimited funds of his attention—it is such a special and loving attention. She has the most talented slave in the world. And she has full need to manipulate a slave after a life in which her nerves have been pulled by the imperatives of others.

That, however, is only one side of Miller. He is also ambitious, limited and small-minded, an intellectual who is often scorned by critics outside the theatre for his intellectual lacks. Nor has he developed to meet such criticisms. Rather, he has reinforced his old walls. He has virtually a terror of the kind of new experience that might open his ideas; so she is enough new experience to last him for a lifetime.

If these limitations have cut off his work even before he has come to live with her, the inability to do much writing in their first year together sets early patterns that will later hurt him. (Of course, the fact that he is still being harassed by congressional committees is no help to his work, either.) But from the beginning it is her money which they live on. From her work. In such a condition, it is natural to toady to her. Can anything be worse for him? He begins to develop the instincts of a servant. Since he is already full of the middle-class nose for petty increments of power, the vacuum in his own creative force has to be filled by becoming a species of business manager, valet, and in-residence hospital attendant. He manages too much. She, with her profound distrust of everyone about her, begins to suspect him. Has he married her because he can't write anymore? Is his secret ambition to

become a Hollywood producer? Or does he want to use her as a meal ticket? Such mean suspicions warm up the dynamos of all throttled insanity. Over and over, through the good months at Amagansett, she will plunge into sudden depressions. They are inexplicable to him. What he cannot recognize as he comes to grips with the full incalculable complexity of a woman is that he is just as much of an enigma to her, and unlike him she sickens before mysteries. They do not offer new literary lines of work, but are connotative of the pit.

In Amagansett they also discover she is pregnant. By the sixth week she is in such pain they rush to New York for an operation. It is announced that the pregnancy is tubular. But there is ambiguity even about this. The question remains whether her pregnancies were tubular or hysterical. Greene claims she once had a fearful abortion that made it impossible for her to be pregnant. Miller, in an interview, said she could not, but then later in the same interview thought she did have a tubular pregnancy. It is a confusion that she may even have disseminated herself and it persists. What may be the best explanation, from a friend who knew Marilyn well, is that she had had many abortions, perhaps so many as twelve! And in cheap places—for a number of these abortions came in the years she was modeling or a bit player on seven-year contracts—thus her gynecological insides were unspeakably scarred, and her propensity for tubular pregnancies was increased. Since her periods were unendurable—"the pain was so great she would writhe on the floor"—a doctor began to inhibit her menstruation with a drug that anticipated the Pill, and for such duration not able to become pregnant, she would "in hysterical compensation

think she was. Can you conceive what a frightful mess this had to make of her?"

"She never wore a diaphragm?"

"She hated them," said the woman friend. "What people don't understand is that Marilyn loved sex." (We are in *Rashomon* once more!) "I don't think she went a week in her life without having some man around. She took sex with men the way men used to take sex with women."

"Still, she needed sleeping pills."

"Nobody's perfect."

Now, with Miller, faithful to Miller, she will have an operation and then another to make a child possible, and will claim to have other pregnancies—what stays constant is the depth of depression each time the pregnancy, real, tubular or hysterical, is over. It is as if Zanuck's verdict upon her as a sexual freak is being confirmed. If few women are without depression after a miscarriage—they are dealing, finally, with a mystery, which for whatever reason, has chosen not to be born—then what an avalanche of depression for Marilyn. The unspoken logic of suicide insists that an early death is better for the soul than slow extinction through a misery of deteriorating years.

This depression lies so heavy upon her that Miller crosses his Rubicon. He has never written before with an actor or actress in mind. He derives from the high literary tradition that true theatre depends upon the play, and the script is inviolate. Great playwrights live with themes, not actors. But he will write a movie script for her. He will adapt his short story, "The Misfits," into her vehicle. It is, from Marilyn's point of view, either the highest offering of his love or the first aggressive calculation of a mean and ambitious brain. Her mood rises and she is gay for a

few days, but on their return from the hospital she slides back into depression and begins to increase her count of Nembutals. One day he sees her stumble into a chair and go immediately into a heavy doze. Her breathing is labored. Then for the first time he hears what will become the unmistakable sounds of a half-paralyzed diaphragm —her breath is coming with an eerie continuing sigh. The wind of death is in the winding sheet. He does not try to brew coffee or walk her around, slap her face, or pinch the back of her knees. Instead, he seeks "immediate medical help." It is in his character not to look for amateur solutions. Apparatus and technicians from a nearby clinic come *quickly*—can this be medical assistance with which any of us is familiar?— and they resuscitate her. He has saved her life. He will have to save it more than once again. In the days after this incident she will, according to Guiles, be endlessly affectionate to Miller, kiss his hands over and over.

What do we witness? Has she actually supposed (with her abominable facility for living in the unconscious of others) that he might let her die? Or has her hatred been put to rest by the look of relief in his eyes that she is still alive?

They begin to put down roots. He finds another farm in Connecticut, and they buy it. She is busy and happy with the details of alteration and studies the daily work of the carpenters, while he begins to work on *The Misfits*. It is a happy time, but will end he knows so soon as the alterations are finished. He is right. She is bored with the country, and begins to talk of their own apartment in New York. They move from the Greenes' apartment on Sutton Place to another at 444 East Fifty-seventh Street. Her love of Brooklyn is obviously not as intense now as it used to be. If there will be a view across the East River, it is from Manhattan that they will look at unhappy squats on the skyline of Queens. Now she picks up her classes with Strasberg again, and spends many an evening talking to other actors at the Strasberg home. Miller does not often accompany her, but he does not oppose her either. It is as if he senses that she must be forever engaged in feathering the nest of some future identity. Being among actors offers a culture she can finally acquire the way others pick up a foreign language—she is at least absorbing the milieu of the New York Method actor, his gossip, his prospects, his sophistication, his cynicism, and his sharp horizons. To live at last in a milieu must be the equivalent of oxygen to her. Yet, she is also most respectful of Miller during this time. When guests visit the New York apartment, she takes them on tiptoe past the important room of the house—it is the place where her husband writes. We must conceive of him sitting there, unable to put down a word for dint of listening to her caution the guests. Of course, during this time Milton Greene is also being sued for control of Marilyn Monroe Productions, a sordid episode. At Miller's urging, she even attempts through her lawyers to have Greene's name removed as executive producer of *The Prince and the Showgirl:* like Natasha Lytess, Milton has heard nothing from her in the interval. Since he has just turned down a $2,000,000 offer from television because "she isn't up to the strain of a series," he can feel he has legitimately been protecting her interests. Half of that $2,000,000 would after all have gone to him. While Greene threatens a lawsuit in which he will claim huge amounts, he feels small heart for the project and finally accepts $100,000, far less than Monroe's lawyers were prepared to pay. "My interest in Marilyn's career," he says with sad dignity, "was not for gain," and after three years of activity that has telescoped the focus of his life inside out, he goes back to his profession.

Whether this victory for Miller contributes a bit to the excellence of *The Misfits* is hardly knowable, but the script in any case proceeds well. He is out of his literary doldrums. Some time after a first draft of the movie is finished, he invites his old friend and neighbor, Frank Taylor, who has been a book editor *and* a Hollywood producer, to listen to the script. On an afternoon in July of 1958, Miller reads it to him, and Taylor is obviously impressed, for he suggests sending the work to John Huston in Paris, at once! and Huston wires back within the week that it is "magnificent." He will be happy to direct it. Clark Gable is given a copy and is also anxious to do it. Taylor agrees to take a leave from publishing and be the producer. United Artists is interested in financing. Now they have not only a major production, well launched, but a sudden sense of all-surrounding excitement. And promises at last of fulfillment. They seem to have emerged onto the good-working married ground that they have an exciting job they will do together. It is a long time since so much talent and celebrity have come together on a film.

et they cannot get free of entanglements. One may as well suppose a law: if the past is full of old complications, the future will grow new ones. They need money. So she is obliged to do another movie before *The Misfits*, and then complications in Gable's schedule force her to begin another. By the time she will finish *Some Like It Hot*, their marriage is in jeopardy; by the end of *Let's Make Love*, they are obliged to hang together like addicts.

What dismantling of hopes! She had believed he would open the life of the mind to her, and came to suspect that her own mind was more interesting than his. "You're like a little boy," says Maggie, "you don't see the knives people hide." Of course, if her unvoiced resentment of him is, after all this, secretly sexual, then who can not think she might have known better? At no time, certainly, will she live so much on sleeping pills as in her years with Miller, and an insight into the distance between their bodies comes from a story Miller tells of one miserable day when he discovers that the inside of her mouth is covered with open sores. Investigation of the medicine cabinet discloses another horror: she has several dozen bottles of sedatives of all variety; he introduces the cache to a chemist, who informs Miller that the reactions of some pills upon others can be literally poisonous. She is lucky to have gotten away with no more than a sore mouth. Poor pill-taking child. Her chemistry is on this occasion cleared up, that is, Miller succeeds in narrowing her addiction to a few compatible barbiturates, but what a misery of marriage is suggested if he "discovers" her mouth is sore. Is it a week, two weeks, or a month since they have shared a kiss? The episode takes place in Los Angeles and prob-ably occurs in the period just before *Let's Make Love*, when their marriage is again at its worst. But then they are never well suited for one another when she works. We have to attempt to penetrate into her condition at such times. As she begins *Some Like It Hot*, she appears as a monster of will. She is also a fragile shell. If we know her well enough to suspect fragility is her cruelest weapon, and she cannot possibly be as weak as she pretends, in fact we are witness to a debased portion of her strength, still she is in the unendurable position of protecting an exquisite sensitivity which has been pricked, tickled, twisted, squashed and tortured for nearly all of her life. The amount of animal rage in her by these years of her artistic prominence is almost impossible to control by human or chemical means. Yet she has to surmount such tension in order to present herself to the world as that figure of immaculate tenderness, utter bewilderment, and goofy dipsomaniacal sweetness which is Sugar Kane in *Some Like It Hot*. It will yet be her greatest creation and her greatest film. She will take an improbable farce and somehow offer some indefinable sense of promise to every absurd logic in the dumb scheme of things until the movie becomes that rarest of modern art objects, an *affirmation*—the audience is more attracted to the idea of life by the end of two hours. For all of Wilder's skill, and the director may never have been better, for all of first-rate performances by Tony Curtis and Jack Lemmon, and an exhibition of late-mastery by Joe E. Brown, it would have been no more than a very funny film, no more, and gone from the mind so soon as one stepped out of the lobby, if not for Monroe. She brought so good and rare an evocation it seemed to fit into the very disposition of things, much as if God—having put a

few just men on earth in order to hold the universe together—was now also binding the cosmos with a few dim-witted angels as well.

Talking about acting in her last *Life* interview, she says at one point, "You're trying to find the nailhead, not just strike a blow." But what a journey down each day, down to the nailhead. What old emotional mine fields to pass through as she navigates by stimulants out of her chemical stupor into her consciousness. And what bile she must dispense, what poison to her tricks. On the set of *Some Like It Hot* she will drive fellow actors into horrors of repetition. Through forty-two takes, Tony Curtis has to nibble on forty-two chicken legs because Monroe keeps blowing her lines. Repetition kills the soul—Curtis will not touch chicken for many a month. Jack Lemmon and he will stand around in high heels and breast padding, in silk stockings and false hips, for all of a long day's shooting all the while Marilyn is unable to say, "It's me, Sugar." "There were forty-seven takes," as Wilder describes it. "After take thirty, I had the line put on a blackboard. She would say things like, 'It's Sugar, me.' "

Maybe she is searching into nuances of identity. "It's Sugar—the name you know me by, which by my own reference is—*me*." Splendid. She is working out a problem in psychic knots worthy of R. D. Laing. But actors are going mad. When she cannot remember one line, "Where is the bourbon?" as she goes searching through a chest, Wilder finally pastes the line on the inside of the drawer: WHERE IS THE BOURBON? Soon he is pasting the line on every drawer. If she is trying to hit the nail on the head, and get down into that core of herself where the nail meets the nerve, she is also voiding her near to infinite anger at life, men, and the movie-working world.

How she exhausts the talents around her. "When I come to cut the film," Wilder says, "I look at the early takes. Curtis looks good on those and Monroe is weak. On the later takes, she is wonderful and he is weak. As a director, I must disregard his best takes . . . and go with Monroe . . . because when Monroe is on the screen, the audience cannot keep their eyes off her."

"Yes," Curtis will tell Paula Strasberg when she weeps after he has said kissing Marilyn is "like kissing Hitler," yes, he will say, "You try acting with her, Paula, and see how you feel." She will be hours late to the set. On a good day she is two hours late; on a bad day, six. The slightest suggestion by Wilder on how to do a scene puts her in a state. She must do it her own way, and once again we learn later that her instinct is right, but she chooses to do it her own way by walking off from him to consult with Paula Strasberg. Shades of Sir Laurence and Ms Monroe. She is ten years ahead of her time.

Of course, she knows what she protects, knows film is not life or the stage but exists somewhere else. In film, to quote from an essay on *Maidstone*, the actor can

disobey the director or appear incapable of reacting to his direction, leave the other actors isolated from him and with nothing to react to, he can even get his lines wrong, but if he has film technique, he will look sensational in the rushes, he will bring life to the scene even if he was death on the set. It is not surprising. There is something sinister about film. *Film is a phenomenon whose resemblance to death has been ignored too long.*

And we can wonder at the depth to which she must return each day to be again in contact with Sugar Kane; we can think again of grandmother

Della and the hour in which she may have tried to strangle the year-old child. With what, we can wonder, does Monroe finally make contact?

Is it with some last piece of her own exacerbated nerves, or some place she hovers not alive nor dead and spoiled forever for sleep? Now she spoils the air in which she works. Wilder completes the film in near to total agony. His back is in such misery of muscle spasms that he cannot go to bed at night but instead must try to sleep in a chair.

She will respond by failing to inquire about the state of his back. Since she has an interest in the film, she thinks it is a trick to make her fear the financial consequences if he cannot continue. But then she trusts no director alive. Even Logan in *Bus Stop* has cut out what she feels were her best moments. If she cannot forgive Logan, she will not be light on Wilder. Yet as if to demonstrate that any inability to remember lines is of her own choosing, she will also go through long scenes without an error. Weeks after it is over, Wilder will tell an interviewer he can eat again, sleep again, enjoy life, and finally be able to "look at my wife without wanting to hit her because she is a woman."

It is comic by then, but not very, for Marilyn will see the interview back in New York and excite Miller to send a telegram to inform the director that Marilyn Monroe "is the salt of the earth." Wilder sends his reply: "The salt of the earth told an assistant director to go fuck himself." Soon it is not at all comic. She has discovered she is "pregnant" during *Some Like It Hot*, and her time away from the set has been spent resting in bed. She even takes an ambulance from her hotel to the airport in order not to be jostled on the ride, but the fetus—tubular again? hysteri-

cal?—is lost, something in her body or mind is lost by her third month, lost around this time of exchange between Miller and Wilder, and the month of November passes in deep depression which lingers through the winter. Of course, it is her nature to rally. *Some Like It Hot* opens to her best reviews. She has never looked better at a premiere. Then she receives the David DiDonatello Award for *The Prince and the Showgirl*, and that is at least a small consolation to substitute for that Academy Award for which she has never even been nominated. In June of 1959, she goes into Lenox Hill Hospital for "corrective surgery." She is still trying to have a child. Guiles reports without substantiation that "a permanent strain had come between her and Miller before the summer advanced very far," but we can assume, since Guiles is careful in his statements, that Miller, or Frank Taylor (who commissioned Guiles' book) may have said as much, although not for quotation.

Then there is small record of activity in the fall of 1959. Presumably, Miller is polishing *The Misfits*. In February, they put up at the Beverly Hills Hotel while she gets ready to do *Let's Make Love* as another part of her four-film contract with Fox. The script is by Norman Krasna, who some eight years before first suggested to Jerry Wald that they expose her nude calendar in order to publicize *Clash by Night*. Small surprise if Wald is the producer of *Let's Make Love*.

Studying the script, there is trouble. She knows the film will not play as well as it reads. It is a fair expression of Twentieth Century-Fox's comprehension of her film art. Since the new contract was signed, she has made *Bus Stop*, *The Prince and the Showgirl*, and *Some Like It Hot*, and she could also have done *Nana*, *The Brothers Kar-*

With Simone Signoret and Yves Montand, 1960

amazov, *Anna Christie*, or *Rain* to much profit, but they give her *Let's Make Love*. Her role is as empty as the memory of an old Zanuck film. So she encourages Miller to build up the part. Once again her talented playwright goes into the lists, tries to add funny dialogue to a film that is not funny. Gregory Peck, supposed to play the male lead, discovers that his part diminishes as hers increases; he resigns the job. It is time for her to walk off as well, but it is possible she would rather work in anything at this point than spend time with Miller in Connecticut or New York. Besides, they still need the money. And then, Yves Montand and Simone Signoret are living across the hall at the Beverly Hills Hotel. Marilyn, who has been in profound depression for months and so deep on sleeping pills (which Miller doles out to her each night) that her eyes will now be incorrigibly bloodshot on color film, comes out of her most terrible moods whenever the Montands are with them. She loves Simone and announces to the press that Yves in his turn . . . but let us give the quote: "Next to my husband and along with Marlon Brando, I think Yves Montand is the most attractive man I've ever met." Miller is next in admiration for Yves. "He and Marilyn are both very vital people. They possess internal engines which emit indescribable rays of energy." Montand, in fact, is part of the perfect prescription for Miller's noble worker, since he comes from peasant stock in Italy, and his father has been a political activist who hated Mussolini enough to emigrate to Marseilles and work on the docks. Montand, who left school in the sixth grade, has worked in his turn since he was eleven. Such details have to rouse Miller. Besides, Montand has played in the Paris production of *The Crucible*. Now Arthur recommends him

to replace Gregory Peck.

The ante is up. Montand has been successful in French films. He is a theatrical star of respectable measure on Broadway, where he has done a one-man show—songs, monologues, dances. On the other hand, he is hardly an international household name, no Burton, Chevalier, and certainly no Sinatra, although we can assume he is as ambitious as any Italian peasant with strength and wit who has been working from the age of eleven and been transplanted twice.

Marilyn Monroe is his best ticket to notoriety since she has been famously faithful to Miller for the three-and-a-half-year run of their marriage. Of course, Miller has had to pay an increasing price—each year she speaks more rudely to him in public. In private we can take a fair idea of how she scourges him from *After the Fall*.

"All you care about is money! Don't shit me!" Maggie tells Quentin.

Two breaths later she will let him know his pants are too tight. "Fags wear pants like that. They attract each other with their asses."

"You calling me a fag now?"

"Just I've known fags and some of them didn't even know themselves . . ." Marilyn is beginning to sound like many another drunken blonde. She is also throwing herself at Montand.

Yet, Miller is grateful. He notes that Marilyn's temper seems to be kept in balance when Yves and Simone are about. "Anyone who could make her smile came as a blessing to me," he was to say later. It is the remark to etch the final lines of marital misery.

Any affair to come seems designed by the gods of purified plot. Signoret is abruptly called back to France for her next film. Worried about the security of her marriage, she induces a friend, Doris Vidor, to look after Montand while she is gone, but in her first conversation with Simone's mate, Mrs. Vidor is told by Yves in all anxiety that Miller is also leaving Los Angeles to see his children in the East. Montand will be left alone with Monroe. "What am I going to do?" he asks. "I'm a vulnerable man." Witness his feelings: "I can't alienate her because I'm dependent upon her good will, and I want to work with her. . . . I'm really in a spot." It is black market talk. Whether he knows it or not, he is trapped in a process not unlike the calendar nude. Publicity for *Let's Make Love* (which will need it) is going to be obliged to let the world in on the latest hottest name wave in Hollywood, Montand Monroe. Montand is *vulnerable*. He has been the first to declare it. He can be found open to stimulus. He can read reactions. Montand Monroe increases each day.

As if in revenge on Miller, Marilyn is docile with Yves. If they are asked to be on time at a party, Montand assures the host, "She'll be anywhere I say on time." He is right. To friends he brags, "She's got so she'll do whatever I ask her to do on the set. Everyone is amazed at her cooperation, and she's constantly looking to me for approval." That is also true. She has never made a movie where she is so agreeable to the director. She has also never made a movie where she is so ordinary. A sad truth is before us again. Art and sex are no more compatible than they care to be. She is wan in the film and dull. Hollywood looks at *Let's Make Love*. Hollywood offers the verdict: "Fucked-out." Ergo, Twentieth increases all publicity on Montand Monroe. If the film is flat, the love affair must show up at least in the final heats of the year.

All final heats come however to an abrupt ter-

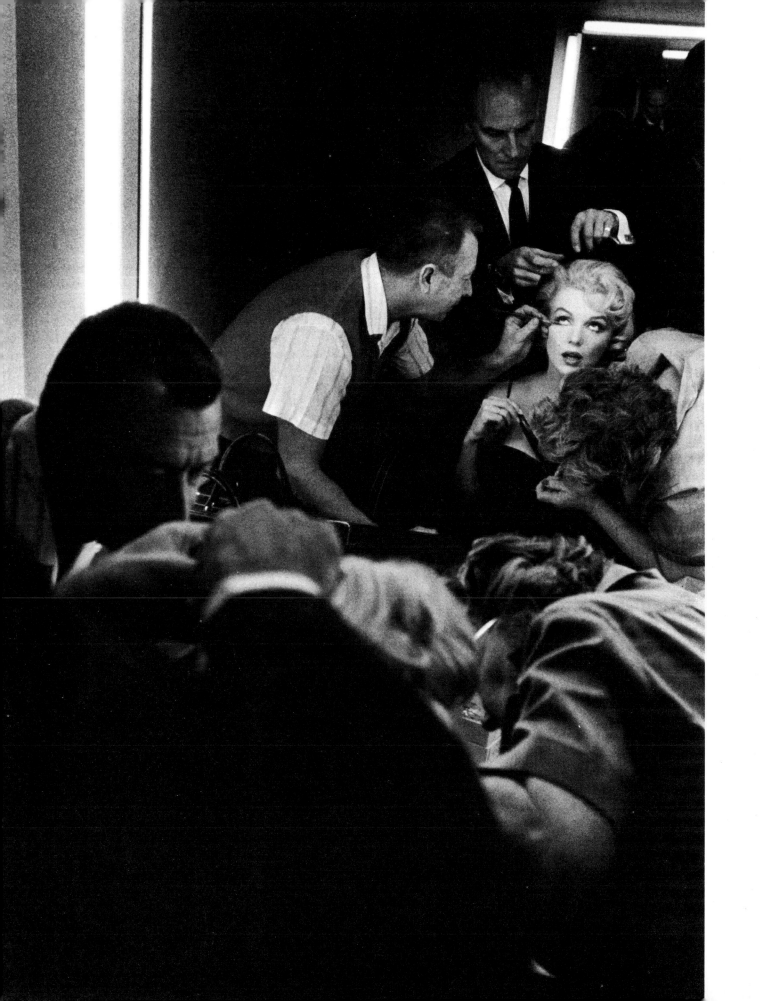

mination with the end of the film. The picture
has been delayed by an actors' strike and so she is
obliged to leave for New York and three days
of costume fitting for *The Misfits* without even
a day's rest.

In Reno, Miller is waiting for her. What horrors of the sleeping pill to take up again. Ejected
from a love affair of two months' duration (which
may or may not be the love of her life—not to
mention that she adores Signoret the wife) she
is now in the 110-degree July heat of Reno with
the remains of an ice-cold marriage: on hand is
that husband she will never forgive for giving her
away. They are there to stay together to make
the film, but she does not know by whom she
has been used the most, nor what is the curious
state of her womb, awakened again, then left to
molder. She is ill as she has never been ill before.
Her blessing is that the film will not be made in
color and so won't show every wash of bloodshot
in the lost white of her eyes.

The world comes to watch the filming. Before they are done, there will be hundreds
of press. The word is out. Frank Taylor,
the producer, has said to *Time:* "This is an
attempt at the ultimate motion picture. . . .
Not only the first original screenplay by a major
American writer but the best screenplay I have
ever read, and we have the best director, John
Huston, for it." In turn, Clark Gable thinks it
will be the best role he has ever had, and is right
if everything else he has done, including Rhett
Butler, has suggested a manner rather than a man.
It has been perhaps the most successful manner in

the history of cinema, but no one has ever seen the
actor. Since he has a bad heart and can die in any
season of any year, the film is no ordinary venture
to him. Nor can it be to Montgomery Clift, who
has often been considered the most talented actor
in Hollywood but has not had a picture in years to
measure this talent. As for Marilyn, she has never
had anything written directly for her before. The
picture, as we will see, must become nothing less
than her canonization. In his turn, Miller has committed everything. He has not had a new play
in half a decade, and has written only a few short
magazine pieces since their marriage, of which
one, published in *Life*, has been nothing more nor
less than tribute: "Her beauty shines because her
spirit is forever showing itself." *The Misfits* has
to be his justification. Five years of drought is
next to the loss of limb for a writer.

Only the actors Eli Wallach and Thelma Rit-
ter, ready as always to do their best work, and
the director John Huston, are principals who do
not find themselves laying their careers on the
line. Huston is, of course, the only celebrated
film artist to bear comparison to Hemingway.
His life celebrates a style more important to him
than film. His movies do not embody his life so
much as they seem to emerge out of a pocket of
his mind. He will take horses seriously and hunt-
ing, gambling, and serious drinking, he will be
famous for a few of the most elaborate practical
jokes in the well-documented Hollywood annals
—by implication he does his picture work with
disdain. It is as if film is an activity good men
must not take upon themselves too solemnly. Yet
he has made *The Maltese Falcon, The Treasure
of the Sierra Madre, The Asphalt Jungle, The
Red Badge of Courage, Moulin Rouge, Beat the
Devil,* and *The African Queen.* During the mak-

ing of *The Misfits*, it is possible he will have no hour of greater absorption than the day on which he wins a camel race against Billy Pearson, the ex-jockey, or an occasion where he will take more aesthetic pleasure than at the birthday party for Eddie Parone, age thirty-five, assistant to the producer. There, Huston reads a poem he has written in celebration. Who would bet his life that Hemingway, incorrect spelling and all, could not have written it?

> Eddie Perrone
> sits all alone
> Aug. 29 in sixty
> Yesterday's score
> was thirty four
> Tonight one more wound
> > licks he.
>
> Bind them up, Ed
> Take heart, arise
> lift up your bloody
> > head.
>
> "Farewell" say you to Fauntle-
> > roy tie
> And toy balloon & Esquimo Pie
> And hurl this challenge
> > to the sky
>
> "I Edward P
> Remindeth thee
> That I am infinately I"

Huston has been living in Saint Clerans, County Galway, Ireland, where Miller has visited him, and they have had a fund of talk about the script over Irish whisky and a fire. Since Huston has a social life that thinks a great deal of horses and very little about intimate movie gossip, he has not heard too much of Marilyn's problem of getting to the set on time; he has next to no idea of how sick she is. Miller will hardly tell him. Huston remembers Marilyn from *The Asphalt Jungle*, when she was somewhat unresponsive to direction, but then where is the film without an actor's quirks? On her first morning of shooting, however, which Huston has scheduled for ten o'clock rather than nine (out of deference to Miller's suggestion that she can use the sleep), he waits until eleven and there is no leading lady. His crew have their own relation to him. Incompetence is the hard stuff of mockery on a Huston set. As eleven o'clock strikes, so does the crew toll the hour. Miller, trying to camouflage the delay, looks to confer with Huston over the script.

It is a bad start, and in a few days word is out that Marilyn is taking a high count of Nembutals every night—the film promises to move as quickly as a wounded caterpillar. If Huston is furious, it is not in his style to give a sign. He has the contempt of a professional for the unprofessional. Since Miller and Monroe are obliged to make the film of their life in a state of nervous exhaustion, then that happens to be the way they have chosen to play their game and waste their psychic funds. He prefers to waste his substance in other fashion. (He will spend his nights losing a cumulative $50,000 at the crap tables.) There is the unmistakable possibility that Huston withdraws subtly from the film, which is certainly not to say that he does not work hard, but that he refuses to become involved in any hysteria about making a great film. No, he will do his best to do a good job under the dry hot circumstances of the Reno desert in summer, and the final film has all the tone of a dry distaste for any excess of effort, emotion, or sentiment, as if every pipe of com-

munication in the world was already coated with emotional glop and it was time to clean the pipes. If people were to be moved by *The Misfits* it would be out of a paucity of tricks. The story would deliver what it was good enough to deliver, no more. That is an aesthetic. It is perhaps the most classical of the film aesthetics. But it is not the easiest way to make a major film. If Huston had a problem as a director, it was precisely that he could not come to take his work seriously enough to create a full resonance of atmosphere. Finally, it was as if there was something obscene about moviemaking, some rip-off of emotion that might spoil a finer tissue of subleties not even to be described. Such as good horseflesh. Precisely because the script of *The Misfits* was so quiet in tone, it may have needed some commitment from the director to push the actors and crew beyond themselves. After one look, however, at Monroe's inability to give of herself in dependable fashion, Huston may have decided that all-out inspiration was going to be directly equal to a loss of face. Dignity for some artists has more worth than art. It is also possible Huston was bored by the miseries of Miller and Monroe. He had been through divorce, and could do without a good seat at this one.

The film settled upon a pattern. They shot with Monroe when available, shot away from her when not. With Miller, Huston worked closely. It was a script so delicate in the drift of its emotions and so taciturn in its story that the daily problem must have been to decide what motive they could offer the actors for a line. It was almost as if the story were too simple: a young divorcee, Roslyn Taber, begins to live in the desert outside Reno with a middle-aged cowboy, Gay Langland, played by Gable, while two other cowboys, Eli Wallach and Monty Clift, begin to find her attractive, flirt with her, and apparently wait for her relation to Langland to end. After a time, the men go out to hunt for mustangs to trap and sell. It is one of the few ways left to earn a living that is "better than wages." Roslyn accompanies them, but is horrified at the cruelty of the capture and the pointless misery of the purpose. If these mustangs were once sold as riding horses for children, now they are canned as dogmeat. "A dog-eat-horse society," Huston will say in comment. So Monroe has a war with Gable which is resolved (1) by his capture of the last mustang as a gesture to himself, plus (2) setting the horse free as a gesture to her. The film ends in such gestures. They drive off together to face a world in which there will be fewer and fewer ways to make a living better than wages. There has been a curious shift in Miller's powers. Values are now vague.

While more can obviously be said in summary, the point is that *The Misfits* is a film, particularly in its first half, that will move on no more powerful hydraulic of plot than the suggestion of one nuance laid like a feather over another—so it is going to be closer to the nature of most emotional relations than other films. But its virtue is also its vulnerability. We see Roslyn and Langland come together, sleep together, set up home together, we feel the other two cowboys perching themselves on the edge of this relation, but no emotional facts are given, no setting of category or foundation, for the plot is never bolted down. We do not know exactly how Roslyn comes to feel for each man, nor how much she feels. The film is even less precise than biography. Unlike other movies we have no blueprint to the emotional line of her heart. Instead she seems to shimmer on the screen with many possibilities of reality. When she holds Monty Clift's head on her lap after he has been wounded in the rodeo, we do not know whether she is maternal, or stirring for him, or both—nor is she likely to know what she feels. In life, how would she?

So they are making a movie which is different in *tone* from other films, and she is altogether different from other actresses, even different from her performances of the past. She has no longer anything in common with Lorelei Lee. She is not sensual here but *sensuous*, and by a meaning of the word which can go to the root—she seems to possess no clear outline on screen. She is not so much a woman as a mood, a cloud of drifting senses in the form of Marilyn Monroe—no, never has she been more luminous.

On the other hand, never has Gable been more real. He could be leaning on the fence next door. Finally we have an idea of what Gable is really like. He is not bad! So, scene for scene, as the first rushes are slowly stitched together, it must have been obvious to Huston and Miller that they had a set of cameos which were superb in their understated taste. It was as if some hollow had been created where one could listen for the echo. But would these separate scenes come together into a movie that might work? Speaking of ultimate films, no black and white movie has ever had so high a budget before. So they might also be striking a blow for the economic future of good films to come. But how to know if what they were accomplishing was really good? That was like trying to calculate the final grandeur of a palace from two or three rooms. The question of guiding actors through this plotless plot had therefore to put its full demand upon the playwright and director. In the day-to-day uncertainty of shooting, how were they to know whether an actor was ready with an emotion too rich or too poor, too strident or too vague? In turn, how could the actors know? The man who has become an actor to avoid that hungry hole of the mind which asks "Who am I?" now had to ask "Who are *you?*" of the role he was playing. It was even worse for Miller. In such a delicate shifting script, how could any scene be considered fixed, yet any change of dialogue in one scene might cause its uncalculated bend in another. Poor Miller! His head had to be overloaded with the most subtle literary equations while his life with Monroe was reduced to one livid state: hideous tension! If they had finally and most tragically arrived at the relation of cellmates who have learned over the years to detest each other into the pit of each intimate flaw, he was nonetheless obliged to work each day on scenes that extolled the beauty of her soul.

For Miller had written a lie in *The Misfits*. It was the half-lie that Marilyn was as lovely and vulnerable as Roslyn Taber, and that may have been all right in the beginning—a lie may be the only aesthetic structure available when working up a vehicle for a great movie star (because she can transmute the lie to magic), but Miller's problem was that he had to live in daily union with the lie, then refine it in his writing each night. Each night Monroe rubbed his nose in the other truth. If she had long been obliged when making a film to wrap herself in the psychic greatcoat of full hatred for some man, beginning with Don Murray in *Bus Stop*, then Olivier, then Wilder, and had discovered the cost of having no one to hate in *Let's Make Love*, Miller's suffering presence now became her real leading man. What must have doubled all hostility was that he was there to remind her she had not been superb enough to rise out of the bile of the past. So if Miller was the man who had loved her most, he would now become the man who had to pay the most, and was condemned to be with her in three rooms on the top floor of the Hotel Mapes while traveling down the clock through Reno night after sleepless night. And if the wound of her infidelities with Montand was still glowing, it could only measure the contempt she offered to his heart. Miller suffered. He had the psychology of poverty where the mark of a man is to suffer and endure. So he suffered. And fed her sleeping pills and held them back, and walked the floor, and listened to her abuse, which many another ear in the hotel would also hear—"You can project through steel walls, honey"—and in the pause between each squall, flopped down for a space, or stared at the script on his desk. Guiles gives a description of the morning after "one such all-night vigil with Marilyn finally asleep while others were getting ready for the day." May Reis, their secretary, and Nan Taylor, the wife of the producer, enter the suite.

> Miller was slumped in a heap on the sofa lapsing at moments into fits of trembling from nervous exhaustion. Nan Taylor . . . had heard that Marilyn had spent an especially bad night, but she was even more distressed to see what it had done to Miller. His hands half covering his face, Miller agonized over his situation. He confessed that he was obviously no help to Marilyn in seeing her through these terrible nights. He wondered if he shouldn't take a room in another hotel. "She needs care at night," he said, and then he seemed to defeat any hope of salvation by crying out, "But I care for her so much."

"I care for her so much." It is the bottomless cry of love. He is face to face with the most unendurable message of all: love by itself does not conquer hatred. Nor does it heal another heart. It can only climb the walls of its own misery. For love without courage is an insult to those who hate. So he is taken care of in his pain by the two women. "Perhaps we can't solve Marilyn's problem this morning," Nan Taylor will say, "but we can do something about you," and leaves the room, sees someone in the hotel management, and comes back with a key to a spare room on the same floor where he can work and conceivably sleep.

Each day the picture falls further behind schedule. With Miller a little more removed from her scene, Marilyn begins to firm up future guidelines—she will live with a chosen entourage of technician-friends and social helpers. Paula is always there, and Marilyn can also count on her publicity man, her hair stylist, her makeup man Whitey Snyder, her driver, and Ralph Roberts, an actor big as a professional football player who has been her masseur for many months and will yet be her confidant and come to know her as well as anyone in the remaining two years of her life. She will soon be very sick and go through a crisis that almost ends her participation in the film, but for a few weeks it is almost as if she manages to continue by deriving some strength out of her hatred of Miller. She actually slams a car door in his face one day on location in the desert and tells her driver to leave him behind. (Miller will not share a car with her again.) And then there is the record of an evening when she sat and drank with Roberts and Agnes Flanagan, her

hair stylist, while watching brush fires on the horizon of the desert. Power lines have come down in this blaze, and Reno is in blackout. Since Miller's room has a separate generator to provide him illumination by which to write, she asks Roberts to get a little ice from a portable refrigerator in that room, and when Roberts returns—as Guiles reports the dialogue—Marilyn speaks of Miller in the following manner: "I can tell by your face," she says to Roberts, "you saw old Grouchy Grumps. Did you speak to him? I mean did he say *hello?*"

He was lying on the sofa, Roberts tells her.

"He'll go that way until he's too exhausted to move," she remarks without compassion. "From the desk to the sofa and back again." She drops a cube in her glass. "Klunk!" she cries. "At least we got a little ice out of that room." Boom! Next!

Is it possible she is brooding over Montand? A few days later she is in complete collapse. Suffering agonies from a particularly bad menstrual period, she arrives on location at noon with the temperature over 110 degrees, has to be helped out of the car, and, unable to coordinate by herself, is led over to the set. Metty, the cameraman, tells Huston it is hopeless. "Her eyes won't focus."

Huston shuts down. They have to gamble. She is flown to Los Angeles and put in a clinic where it is hoped she will be able to go on with the picture after ten days (by doctor's estimate) of rest and "medication," which is to say a new poison will perhaps be found to overcome a few effects of the old poison. At her first opportunity, she gets up, sneaks out of the hospital, and looks for Montand at the Beverly Hills Hotel, but he is neither there when she calls nor does he phone back to answer her note. He merely tells friends in Hollywood that she has left a number where she can be reached. Soon a gossip columnist reports that Montand has told her how Marilyn has "a schoolgirl crush on him." It creates bad publicity for Montand and he is obliged to explain himself in more detail: "I think she is an enchanting child and I would like to see her to say goodbye, but I won't." Then he adds, "She has been so kind to me, but she is a simple girl without any guile. Perhaps I was too tender and thought that maybe she was as sophisticated as some of the other ladies I have known. . . ." *Mon Dieu!* "Perhaps she had a schoolgirl crush. If she did, I'm sorry. But nothing will break up my marriage."

Apparently she is not wounded crucially, for she will be in better condition when she comes back to the film. Perhaps she recognizes in the hospital that she can find a way to live without Miller and without marrying again. Perhaps she can even find a substitute for a mate by splicing the rope of her life with the short ends of lovers and friends. In any case, she returns to warm greetings, and for a busy week much is accomplished. Morale, for once, is good. (Huston has just won his camel race.) She does a five-minute non-stop scene with Monty Clift—the longest scene either actor or Huston has ever had to film, and is at her best in a number of crowded bar scenes at Dayton, Nevada. All this is accomplished in one productive week. Like most addicts, her energy is best when she is in transition from one state of drug-life to another, from addiction to abstention, or from abstention back to barbiturates again. It is only a constant state that seems certain to depress her.

In turn, Miller has apparently passed through his own kind of crisis. If their marriage is finally

197

severed, she, of course, will go out of her way to take a walk with him in Reno a night or two after she gets back. In the shooting that day he had delighted her by daring to show Monty Clift the kind of stiff-legged polka he wanted the actor to perform in a particular scene, Miller doing it with Marilyn before the crew. This species of artistic gallantry has touched her. They walk "like everyday people," as Marilyn will say to a reporter in all the bruised sorrow of an expiring marriage.

Of course, Miller is probably in better shape as a result of the separation. Isolation he can bear, and loss. It is the alternation of love and hate that wears him out. So as he withdraws from Marilyn his working relation to Huston intensifies. Miller may skirt the edge of a breakdown, but like some travailing ghost of an old prospector he manages to cross these desert lands of the West.

The film proceeds. It is weeks behind schedule and hundreds of thousands of dollars, more than a half million, over budget. (It will cost $4,000,000 before it is done.) But that reckoning is later. Now the company begins to move out each day to a dry lake perhaps fifty miles from Reno where they will film the climax, a trapping of the wild horses. Now the fundamental conflict of the script, the movie company, the marriage, and even the direction of the picture comes into focus across the years—it is precisely so banal and awe-inspiring as the war between the men and the women, which here becomes the war between Marilyn and her director, her male company of co-stars, and her scriptwriter once a husband. She is at war with each of them to become the center of the film, and if we will conceive of her competitive instincts as equal to a great prizefighter's, we may begin to perceive how so much of the film had to appear to her as a plot where she took on not one antagonist but many. ("You don't see the knives people hide.") Since her orgy of attention in *Gentlemen Prefer Blondes*, and her skill in stealing *How to Marry a Millionaire* from Betty Grable and Bacall, she has managed to get past *No Business Like Show Business* and *River of No Return* and gone on to be the center of every production since (except for *Let's Make Love*, which had no center), dominating directors and running away with each film. They have all, in varying degree, become *her* films. Few prizefighters could point to such a string of triumphs. But in *The Misfits* she is up against better opposition than she has ever faced, and it will affect her performance before the film is done. If she is more interesting and extraordinary in the first half of *The Misfits* than she has ever been before, she will yet find herself suffering many a new artistic uncertainty during the long weeks of shooting still to be done after that exciting week back from the hospital. With her suspiciousness of motive, how little can she trust Miller now that they are apart, or for that matter trust Huston with his lifelong absorption in male honor and male corruption. Huston's idea of a good woman is Hepburn in *The African Queen*. How unlimited must be his secret contempt for Marilyn, this converted Jewish princess. She is more spoiled than Marjorie Morningstar! The one time Huston and Marilyn play at a crap table in Reno, she wants to know, "What should I ask the dice for, John?"

"Don't think, honey," he replies, "just throw."

Inquiring about the disposition of the dice is the measure of her muddling with magic. No. Huston will have small traffic with such female mystique.

Besides, there is talent in this movie that for once is equal to hers. Clift gives what is possibly the best performance of his life. A recluse from the company, and attached to his thermos of grapefruit juice and vodka (which comes into his veins as regularly as a rubber tube and jar of hospital glucose), he nonetheless impresses Gable altogether with his rushes. "In that scene at the table when he said, 'What was that they put in my arm?' he had a wild look in his eye that could only have come," Gable says, "from morphine . . . *and* booze . . . *and* the steers."

Huston nods. "You can believe Perce has had it all."

When Marilyn, however, did a breakfast scene with Gable that pleased Huston sufficiently for him to embrace her spontaneously (and then hug her again for the photographers) she told one of her staff to save the picture. "I want to have it to show around," she said, "when he begins saying mean things about me." This is hardly uncharacteristic of her distrust of all directors, but there is a difference. Someone like Billy Wilder might hate her, but in that hatred was helpless adoration. She senses that she is not Huston's favorite, that he does not *react* to her. She has then no secret leverage upon the heart of the director. Pure perfidy of Miller, she begins to discover that the film can always go back to what it was from the beginning, a fine story about three good men whose way of living is almost ready to disappear. It was supposed to be her vehicle and yet she is in danger of being incidental to it. Finally she will have to act her utmost in order not to be left in the others' wake. Perhaps she even resorts to a trick. There had been a scene on which she counted much (indeed, she needed every one of her scenes to keep up with the men) and this was the moment when Gay Langland came back to the bed in the morning after their first night together and embraced her. In the script she must have seen it as some high moment of romance, an unforgettable fifty feet of film history—Gable Kisses Monroe. But Huston preferred to maintain his reserve with love scenes—why slide around in the muck after every other director had gone through the old town pipe? So he keeps their lovemaking dry. A middle-aged cowboy and a nice blonde offer a near-documentary style of hello, let's have some eggs, it's morning, wasn't last night fine?

Since she had succeeded, however, in playing the scene with only a sheet to cover her nakedness (which was also fair documentary—how else under such chaste circumstance could the audience know they had slept together?), and since there were two cameras on her, purposefully or inadvertently she let enough of the sheet slip to expose a breast on Take Seven to one of the two cameras, thereby creating a dilemma that would not be settled until the hour of distribution. Should they release the film with the shot of Monroe's nude breast? Monroe, no surprise, is for it. "I love to do the things the censors won't pass. After all, what are we all here for, just to stand around and let it pass us by?" Huston replies, "I've always known that girls have breasts." No, he will not want the aesthetic slant of his film to be nudged by her competitive tit. And the picture, when it finally comes out, has a clear view only of her back. The episode, however, offers its clue to her idea of cinematic balance. She would yet have to compete with Gable the King and Clift the Genius, plus Eli Wallach with his complete set of actor's skills, and she is even convinced that Wallach has formed a conspiracy

with Miller to build up his part by giving Roslyn an affair with him. Conspiracy between Miller and Wallach or no, it is true Miller wants to rewrite. Wallach is too good an actor to have nothing to do at the end of the film but rant at Gable and Monroe. If he has even a fair little scene of doing the lindy with Marilyn, she will accuse Wallach of trying to upstage her, since most of the dance takes place with her back to the camera, but then, sharpening the barb, will add, "The audience is going to find my ass more interesting than Eli's face." (She is reported to say "rear," but we know better.) She has been friends with Wallach for five years. Now it is as if in breaking with Miller she is moving from one land to another, for in private she even says to Eli, "You Jewish men don't understand anything."

Is she thinking of the Reform rabbi who told her there is no afterlife? Or of the duplicities in Miller's plot? The concept of this movie is by now three years old. For three years she has lived with the beautiful idea that some day she and Arthur would make a film that would bestow upon her public identity a soul. Her existence as a sex queen will be reincarnated in a woman. It is not that her sex will disappear so much as that the sex queen will become an angel of sex. While she had accomplished something like this already in *Some Like It Hot*, Sugar Kane was a flawed angel—she had no mind. Whereas Marilyn wanted to present herself at her best. Or at least as Miller's early and enraptured idea of her (which we can assume she must alternately have been delighted with and disbelieved), a woman so sensitive and alive, so nubile as flesh and so evanescent as a wisp of vapor, that to present herself in such a way to the world might wipe away all the old killing publicity of the past. It was as if she wanted to become the angel of American life; as if, beneath every remaining timidity and infirmity, she felt that she deserved it. Perhaps she did. Are there ten women's lives so Napoleonic as her own? So she had to hope (with the part of herself not without hope) that the final version of *The Misfits* would be her temple.

Of course, her power to comprehend the relation of the part to the whole was never superb. Actors rarely have such power. When they do, they become directors. Perhaps she never recognized how completely *The Misfits* was a narrative about men. In its original form, it was certainly one of the best short stories about men ever written in a Hemingway tradition. Indeed, much of the prose could pass for Hemingway writing in his quietest manner. It is possibly the best piece of prose Miller ever wrote, and since the subject was a departure for him—he had known next to nothing about cowboys—and he did it in that bold time when he was getting a divorce and embarking on the adventure of his life, a sense of male optimism lives better in that short story than in the film. Miller's strength had always been to write about men. It was just that in *The Misfits* the men were stronger than they had ever been before. And cleaner. (As he may have been in the weeks he wrote it.)

Difficulties were then implicit in bringing Marilyn into the film—not any actress, but Marilyn in a portrait of consummate loveliness. While Roslyn already existed in the short story, she was offstage and merely talked about, an agreeable and attractive middle-aged eastern woman living with Gay Langland (and supporting him). His friends, the other two cowboys, were also attracted to her, powerfully attracted, and Langland did not even know if she was faithful or not. Every movie possibility obviously existed for conflict and drama. But that was opposed to what Marilyn desired. She had no wish to be sleeping with two or three men in *her* film; she wanted respect! It was the cry of her life. Unhappily, she

had come to decide no audience would give that accolade to an actress who has carnal knowledge of two or more characters in one film. It is still 1960. So Miller's dramatic choices become limited. She can have a dalliance with Monty Clift and/or Eli Wallach, but only as in a mist. Marilyn wanted her film affair with Gable to be idyllic (exposed breast and all!), and Gable doubtless wanted no less. He was too old and too grand to be seen in some demeaning jealous state —his dignity had been the fuel of his own performances for the last fifteen years. How then is the script to move from celebration of its splendid stars to some obligatory minimum of conflict and plot? Miller is obliged to make the character of Roslyn so tender that the capture of a few wild horses is all of disaster for her, a dramatic bubble that cannot help but burst, since she also, as Miller himself points out in the short story, loves her dog, while neglecting to recognize that the meat in the can out of which she feeds that dog has come precisely from a wild horse. So Roslyn becomes a role that sits in the most hypocritical part of Monroe's nature— where she bleeds for the death of little fish and tries to kill her mate. It is also possible, however, that Marilyn does not begin to assess how unplayable will be her part by the end of *The Misfits* until she is deep into the film, or even done with it—then, too late, she will recognize that her share of the last reel is shrill—a liberal version of "we must stop the locomotive at the pass." So she has to stop Gable, Clift, and Wallach from bringing in the horses, but cinematically what we see is Gable, Clift, and Wallach taking chances, being knocked to the ground under rearing animals or dragged along by runaways, while she screams on the sidelines or dashes in hysteria from one to the

other until the movie audience is ready to yell, "Shut that bitch up!" Since her life is full of paradox, it is natural that the film by which she hopes to attain dignity will be the one that finally gives her the least.

At the end it is Gable who is canonized. Gay Langland has become the apotheosis of Gable. "Where are you going?" Wallach asks as Clark and Marilyn drive off in a truck at the end.

Miller put in no reply. Gable knew better. "Home," he answers Wallach in his guttiest voice, and the movie screen in every small-town theatre of America would give its little jump. He had finally found his role. Being Clark Gable had also been better than wages. As he drove along with Marilyn through the desert and the last of the film closed down on them, he said, "Just head for that big star. . . ." They were finally done with *The Misfits*. Perhaps it was his best moment since Rhett Butler smiled and said, "Frankly, my dear, I don't give a damn."

Of course, the film company had come down toward the end of their work in something like the bewildered ribald state of an army that has lived off the substance of a town for months and has forgotten the patriotic premise of its war. They had no idea if what they had done was good or ill. It was almost as if filming in Nevada was bound therefore to close with scenes of dust and strife while stuntmen were struck in the head by horses' hooves and Gable was dragged behind a truck on a rope, even as at night social lines were obliged to be drawn to a comic nicety: while Marilyn is losing the biggest bet of her life, Paula Strasberg is giving a party for Marilyn whose point seems to be that Miller and his intimates are not invited. Strasberg's Revenge —a Balkan *melodrame!* To which in turn Huston

gave a party for Miller and Clift to which everybody was invited. There the cameraman, Russell Metty, delivered a valedictory. Of course, only the Cameraman could speak in such a tongue, for he was the altar at which actors' prayers were laid. When the altar speaks, it is in good voice: "Arthur writes scripts," Metty said, "and John shoots ducks. First Arthur screwed up the script and now his wife is screwing it up. Why don't you wish him a happy birthday, Marilyn? Arthur doesn't know whether the horse should be up or down. Marilyn thinks we should keep the scene showing her half-naked in bed. Monty is buying into the Del Monte grapefruit business. . . . This is truly the biggest bunch of misfits I ever saw." Applause.

When the company left Nevada to work in Hollywood on final process shots, more small comedy continued. Looking at the rough cut, an executive from United Artists was unhappy, it did not seem a Huston film where "you put the ingredients in, and he builds up a terrific head of steam." The executive said if he didn't know, he wouldn't have had a clue to who the director might be. Miller agreed that he, too, was disappointed. Huston replied, "These things are missing in the script." Now they played again with the idea of writing new scenes for Wallach until Gable refused, and then over the next few weeks of editing and adding music, went through the other predictable drama, Huston and Miller, of coming to like each other's work again. They had aid. The film had become affecting after all. For Gable had a massive heart attack the day after shooting finished, and would die in the hospital eleven days later. Every scene in which he now appeared could bring to mind half the history of Hollywood's years.

VIII. LONELY LADY

The Misfits will be over on November 5, 1960. A half week later, Marilyn will be back in New York—to an empty apartment—and on the 11th, Armistice Day, will announce her separation from Miller to the press. Somewhere in the next week she will hear that Montand is flying from Los Angeles to Paris, and runs out to Idlewild to catch him for a few hours between planes. Drinking champagne, they sit in the back of her limousine, and she learns he is going back to Signoret. Simone, when her turn arrives to talk to the press, will make the wise and utterly oppressive French remark, "A man . . . doesn't feel he has to confuse an affair with eternal love and make it a crisis in his marriage" (to which Marilyn can only reply like a programmed analysand, "I think this is all some part of her problem, not mine").

After these separate blows, Gable dies. Reporters phone Marilyn at 2 A.M. with the news. She is hysterical. The circumstances of his end are unendurable; in the middle of filming, it had become known that Kay Gable was going to have his baby. Gable had been exceptionally proud of this late gift. Since he had a heart condition, he could never know when he might die, but he wanted to see his son. Just so confident was he of a son. But then each detail was more unhappy than the last. Kay Gable also had a heart condition. When Clark came down with his attack, Mrs. Gable was put in the hospital room next to his, so that she might rest her heart and protect the pregnancy. President Eisenhower even phoned to give Clark advice out of his own experience of heart attacks. Then word went out that Gable was better. Then, abruptly, he died. Kay Gable was not even with him. An hour before his death, she felt a small attack of her own coming on and retired to her room in order not to worry Clark. Then the doctors came to tell her. Was nothing in the situation free of pathos?

Where to calculate the measure of Marilyn's woe? She has met her surrogate father and embraced him on film, she has shown her breast, and now the surrogate is dead. Is it because of knowing her? She has to be in some new depth of insecurity. In the past, no matter what indignities might come to others because they worked with her, she had always one justification—she lived closer to death. Now, Gable had shown she was wrong.

If she had a hundred thoughts on the event, few could offer her life. She was on a slide into the longest depression of her existence. The days of dwindling are at hand. If she has held to a monumental ambition—she will be as great as Garbo—we can wonder if even the ambition is beginning to leave. How near she is to a burned-out case. She is living in her apartment in New York with Miller's goods and papers all gone. In his empty study he has left her portrait on the wall. It has been his favorite picture of her. Now in a couple of months they will get divorced. Carefully, she picks the day of Jack Kennedy's inauguration, January 20, 1961, and flies to Juárez. The date has been selected by Pat Newcomb, her new publicity woman and new intimate. Happily, Marilyn will receive less publicity on this day than on any other.

But then she will hardly want to make headlines about the shattering of the Hourglass and the Egghead. Quietly, she sits in a cocktail lounge at the airport in Dallas for a two-hour layover on the way to Juárez and carefully follows on television the first of Jack Kennedy's thousand days. Pale witch of the lonely American wind, there in Dallas she watches. In Dallas! Where else? The most electric of the nations must naturally provide the boldest circuits of coincidence. Indeed, if occult histories of the future wish to look for karma that leads from Napoleon to Monroe, let us recognize that she will die in a house on Fifth Helena Drive.

After the divorce, she puts herself together long enough to go up for a visit to the Roxbury farm, and collects her things from Miller, goes with her newfound half sister, Berneice Miracle, discovered to be living in Florida, a bona fide half sister by way of Gladys and the long-forgotten Baker, yes, the last search for identity proceeds along the lines of the flesh, and Marilyn drives up with her to a "difficult meeting," by Miller's description "trying to put a face on things and make me believe she was happy, carefree, the way she wanted to be." She leaves with some books, sculpture, a set of bone china and cocktail glasses, leaves behind some washed-out jelly glasses for Miller to drink out of. (Does she also leave her investment in the property?) She certainly deserts Hugo the basset hound, but mourns him when back in the city. Soon Sinatra will give her a white poodle which she calls "Maf," for she is forever teasing Sinatra about his connections. Somewhere in this time she also apparently has a small and reasonably friendly affair with him, for an intimate tells of driving her to the Waldorf where Sinatra is staying while she keeps taking nips of vodka, which "doesn't help much." Next day there is huge curiosity, but she indicates there was something wrong with the way the twin beds had been put together, some crack between the mattresses into which one or the other kept falling. (There is a flaw in the service at the Waldorf!)

"Was Sinatra good?" asks the intimate.

"He was no DiMaggio." Of course, she is wicked in most of her remarks about new lovers these days and will yet proceed to have a continuing affair with Sinatra. Perhaps her loyalties are confused, for she is back with DiMaggio again, although in no regular form. Still, they have had a resumption of romance. In late December, about a month before her divorce, there has been a phone call from Reno Barsocchini. "Can," he inquires, "a certain person call?" Tell your friend I'm waiting, is Marilyn's reply. On Christmas Day, DiMaggio arrives at her apartment with the largest poinsettia she has ever seen. So they recommence. Indeed, it may be the knowledge that she is unfaithful to DiMaggio which makes her nervous with Sinatra. In these days when she speaks of Joe to her closest friends it is in sentimental terms of the perfection of his body and unhappy accounts of the guilt of his mind once love is done.

Of course, she is not nearly this kind to others. Her tongue is probably never so sharp as now. Gone are the days when Amy Greene could remark to her, "Tell me, Goody Two-Shoes, is there anyone you don't like?" Marilyn now delights her friends with accounts of men and the advances they have made. The stories are scandalous and often improbable, but the characters are famous. Is it all too likely that she is making most of them up for the amusement of her friends? Often they seem to be aimed at those who have at some time in Hollywood or elsewhere been reported as being hardly flattering of her talents and her new mood brings with it a sharp word of retribution. It is all spice and sting, malice and new gaiety. Marilyn is conceivably

Carl Sandburg and Marilyn, 1962

trying out a few first readings on a future middle-aged role. Should she settle for successor to Tallulah?

She is sitting in the exhausted air of a career, and her sleeping pills are not far from cocktail party peanuts as she opens a capsule to speed up the effect and swallows it while speaking. She is like an invalid whose prospects of health do not quite equal the organs he has given to surgery—she draws up a will. It must be like returning on a midnight swim to pools of old depression. She assigns money to Berneice Miracle—the family comes first!—and then gives bequests to her secretary, May Reis, and to a few friends. Her personal belongings she leaves to Strasberg—he is the true curator of her art. For whatever reason, she does not mention Paula Strasberg. Of course, she has already lent her much money and given her stocks, and provided studio jobs for her at $3,000 a week. In January, just a little before Kennedy's inauguration, she has the will read aloud, and lawyers explain her finances. She is not nearly so rich as she hopes. In fact, she is living on a share of profits from *Some Like It Hot* and in the hopes of what *The Misfits* will do. But that film is off to a smudged start with mixed reviews.

In late winter, further depressed by her divorce and the lack of real excitement about *The Misfits*, she sinks into depression so severe her analyst is worried. Perhaps she makes a suicide attempt. We do not know, for her publicity agency now looks not to advertise but withdraw her life from examination. Still, she is admitted to Payne-Whitney, a hospital for mental disorders. The press descend, and do not get to see Marilyn. She has gone through one iron door after another, and the doors close behind her. Until now, she has not been told anything about the hospital. "What are you doing to me?" she cries out. The gate to the orphanage closes again. *"What kind of a place is this?"*

She spends three days in a room with barred windows and a glass door through which doctors can peer in. There is no partition to the john. Which nurse, intern, resident, visiting doctor, or hospital attendant will fail to take a good look? Soon gossip is blazing like brush fire. She has whipped off her clothes, goes the gossip, she has . . . one can fill in any obscene gesture if one wants to hear the gossip. The press keep vigil outside Payne-Whitney's walls.

Later, Marilyn will indicate to Pat Newcomb, her publicity woman, that she did offer a show. "If they were going to treat her like a nut," goes Guiles' description, then "she would behave like one."

Of course, the desire to take off clothes may even relieve the impulse that pushes one through an open window. She has always been working toward nudity. Certainly, she has not been a model for nothing, nor "wanted desperately to stand up naked for God and everyone else to see," nor had her nude calendar, nor the nude sessions she will still go through with a few photographers, nor a breast in *The Misfits*—not all for nothing. Perhaps as one drifts toward a state near-insane, there is some impulse to turn inside out, reverse habits, fling off clothes, morals, and one's relation to time. Does psychosis, like death, move back into the past?

Nonetheless, she is out of whatever state she is in quick enough to know she wants to be out of Payne-Whitney. They allow her one phone call. She makes it to DiMaggio, and he is up from Florida to New York by the evening plane and

With Carl Sandburg and hostess, Mrs. Irena Weinstein

on the phone to politicians and powers who would know how to open doors at this hospital. "Early the next morning, Marilyn emerged secretly from the Clinic clutching tenaciously to DiMaggio. . . . She went at once to a private room in the Neurological Institute of Columbia-Presbyterian," and so quickly was it done "that reporters overran the Payne-Whitney Clinic in confusion."

She has three weeks of rest, withdrawal from pills, and a hospital discharge. With Pat Newcomb at her side, she gets back to her apartment after running a gauntlet of reporters racing through traffic to catch her attention for one more comment. In such a quiet womb will the news of the day find gestation. Now she is back in her apartment, and as usual after such a bout, is restored for a little while. She makes plans to do *Rain* on television with Lee Strasberg directing her, and gets a letter from Somerset Maugham, who is delighted she will play the role. As Marilyn says to an interviewer about Sadie Thompson, "She was a girl who knew how to be gay even when she was sad. And that's important—you know?" Then *Rain* falls through. NBC will not do it with Strasberg because he has no TV experience. Nor will Marilyn do it with another director. "I only know what Lee's ideas are, and those are the ideas I want to put into the thing. I don't want to . . . find myself in something totally different from what I expected or what I hoped for." Yet, she is restless without work and nibbled at by the edge of financial concerns. The TV contract had been for more than $100,000, and that is now gone. She goes surf-fishing with DiMaggio in Florida and visits half sister Berneice. Then she gets "impatient" and flies back to New York.

She reaches her apartment in time to read in a newspaper column that Kay Gable believes Marilyn "had brought on Gable's fatal heart attack from tension and exhaustion." (If Gable never complained to Monroe—"when she's on the set," he had said to a reporter, "she's there to work!" —he had, however, told other reporters that in the old days of Harlow, "when stars were late, they were fired.") Marilyn opens her living room window and prepares to jump. As she describes it to a friend the next day, she knows that she must leap quickly. If she goes on the ledge and waits and is discovered up there by people down on the street, and then fails to jump, the resulting publicity will have to be worse than death or going on with life. So she stands in the room, and leans toward the window, eyes closed. Perhaps she passes through some migration of the soul before she returns to her life in that room. When next day she confesses how close she had come to jumping, her friends are certain she must move to Hollywood, and get a rented ranch house. With a single floor. She decides they are right. Lee Strasberg is all she has left in New York. Something vital seems to have left her. So she goes West still one more time, and lives in analysis again, is it for the third or fourth time— who can keep record of these arranged marriages of the mind? In the late spring of 1961, she is on little but a routine of diet and rest. She is to have a gall bladder operation (whose scar will yet show in the famous nude studies Bert Stern will take) and seems to respond well to the surgery— perhaps a knife in her belly pays part of the debt to Gable. (Can this be the birthday in June when André de Dienes sees her at the Beverly Hills Hotel after so many years?) She commutes between New York and Los Angeles over the months to come, her drug a life of no meaning.

A woman named Marjorie Stengel (who had previously been secretary to Monty Clift) has come to work for her now in New York, and through her eyes we get a portrait of these months in Marilyn's life. During the interview in which Miss Stengel is given the job, the house phone rings and Marilyn picks it up. Someone is asking for Miss Monroe. "She's not here," Marilyn says in a rough voice and hangs up. It is the last sign of life the new secretary will see. Days drift by.

Marilyn gets up late in the hot New York morning and wanders around in a blue baby-doll nightie. It is slightly soiled. After a while she chews on some lamb chops and eats cottage cheese, then takes a big glass of No-Cal black cherry drink. "That meal alone," says Marjorie Stengel, "might have been enough to kill you." Later in the day Marilyn talks on the phone for a very long time with her analyst in Los Angeles. No one else calls. Perhaps no one knows she is in town. Few letters arrive, yet when a particular piece of fan mail is obscene, she will take a look. On a bank application she carefully prints UN-KNOWN in the space for her father's name. But then the mood is not without its own blank space. In the kitchen, plaster is falling; the walls are a dirty New York kitchen-yellow. The bathroom has no glamour—no dressing table, no little lamps, no bright pattern for the shower curtains, just a bathroom. In the bedroom, her walls are a dark putty brown, and the furniture, French Provincial, is cheap and painted white. A satin quilt of putty color serves as a throw for the queen-sized bed. Overhead, on the ceiling, is a mirror. It is her major touch. For the second bedroom is almost bare. There a few pieces of odd carpet lie on the floor. In the reception room Marjorie works among file cabinets. The best decoration is a Toulouse-Lautrec in a frame; print and frame together must cost fifty dollars. In the living room a contrast: all is white. The walls are white and the rug, the white piano is there and a white couch. Even the Cecil Beaton photo of Marilyn in a white gown is there. White transparent leaves are in a vase. They are artificial. Plants are brought in from time to time, but they die. Only the artificial white leaves remain. And on the white shag rug is the old stain of a dog. While Stengel works for her, there is talk of cleaning the rug. It is finally picked up by Denihan's, who "charge her more than the rug can cost." It comes back clean except for the yellow spot: now chemists come from Denihan's to make tests. Doctors and pharmacists also appear, dressed in dapper dark clothes and in dark horn-rimmed glasses. They are waiting for Miss Monroe on the Spanish bench in her foyer with its black and white checked tiles, waiting to bring pills and prescriptions in Marilyn's name or in other names. Sometimes the pills will be ordered in Marjorie Stengel's name. On the end table, *The Nation* is sitting, and *I. F. Stone's Weekly*. On the night table in the bedroom is *The Carpetbaggers* and a volume of Edna St. Vincent Millay. In the dark den where Marilyn makes her calls, there is only a gray New York window on the court, yet here the plants stay alive. Perhaps it is because Marilyn sits there so often to share the undemanding gloomy light. And in the closet of the spare bedroom evening dresses are lined up on wire hangers. There is no padding to the hangers. Nor garment bags. In other closets are minks, and a row of furs in white, also on wire hangers. A host of Ferragamo pumps are on the floor. In another

closet, two dozen Jax slacks rest on wire hangers, with their price tags still attached. Yet when Marilyn goes out to shop she puts on no underwear. Salesladies gasp in their gossip over this. "She has a *smell*," they tell Marjorie Stengel over the phone. (Of course, they do not know that Marilyn, like many another artist, may not wish to wash if in the scent of the previous day some clue to experience can linger.)

One morning, going through the file, Marjorie encounters a diamond ring in the bottom of the drawer. How long it has been lying there, she does not know. Can it be a gift from DiMaggio? (Whom Marilyn now calls Mr. D.) One given morning Marjorie is told "a certain man" will call and she must do what he tells her. But when the phone rings, the voice is clear. "Marge, this is Joe DiMaggio"—he is obviously used to talking to people named *Stengel*—and he asks her to meet him at the Shelton where he will give her $5,000 to cover an overdraft in Marilyn's account at Irving Trust. Marjorie Stengel cannot comprehend Marilyn's secrecy. Many a morning she will get a glimpse of DiMaggio as he slips out of the apartment not long after she has arrived for work. Yet Marilyn will never indicate he has been there. It is as if no one must know DiMaggio sleeps over.

Marilyn is coming to the end of her years in New York. Each month she spends more time on the coast. Now, at her analyst's suggestion, she buys her house on Fifth Helena Drive in Brentwood. It is a house exactly like his! Somewhere in this period, she even phones New York in great excitement. She is having a gala evening out with Sinatra. Although she has bought two dresses at Magnin's, she needs a particular dress from New York. The maid, Lena Pepitone, flies out first class to bring the dress, but in the interim Marilyn has found another.

Now New York begins to dissolve. Marjorie Stengel is asked to move to Los Angeles and refuses, and will soon leave her employ. Marilyn has transferred to Los Angeles and the tedium of a life lived at low throttle. (Indeed, some hint of illness is almost visible in the midst of her attempt to project huge involvement in the pleasure of Carl Sandburg's company.)

She takes a trip to Mexico and comes back to Helena Drive with Mexican tin masks and lighting fixtures. It is April of 1962. She has four months to live, and work is ready to start on a film she will do at Twentieth for her contract. It will be called *Something's Got to Give*.

The script for the film has been rewritten from a story that is twenty years old. It is a Twentieth Century special! If the director is George Cukor, that is no splendid omen, for he directed her in *Let's Make Love*, but at least the co-star, Dean Martin, by way of Sinatra, is a friend. Peter Levathes, new head of the studio, is, however, furious at the waste Elizabeth Taylor has brought Twentieth on *Cleopatra*. He is not the best man to put up with Marilyn. She, on the other hand, can measure her salary of $100,000 against Elizabeth Taylor's $1,000,000.

She has lived in her own semi-retirement while Liz's photograph has been appearing on the covers of magazines. Naturally, Marilyn has also caught a virus. Since her time in Los Angeles usually consists of going from analyst to internist, it is as if the virus reflects some spiritual essence

of doctors' offices. She runs a small fever, small and chronic. Her temperature is usually over 100 degrees, if under 101, but she has an agreement that she can leave the set if it goes above 103. After three weeks of shooting, she has managed to show up for a sum of six days. Since they expect that, they have been prepared to shoot around her. They all seek to cooperate with her: even Levathes keeps away. But the script! It can hardly collaborate. Illness is eventually equal everywhere to illness, and so every false line of dialogue inhabits the metaphysical center of her virus. It is death to work on that set.

And she is not dead. Something of interest has been happening in her personal life at last. She would prefer to be free and pursue a good time. Since Sinatra is friends with Peter Lawford, she has met the Kennedys. She has, in fact . . . but there is more than a little to say. Suffice it that on a Friday morning in the middle of May, she does not appear at the set but gets instead on a plane to New York. Jack Kennedy is being given a birthday party at Madison Square Garden, and Lawford has invited her to sing "Happy Birthday" to the President before twenty thousand guests. She is not about to fail to appear. They have even prepared her entrance. Three times her name will be announced, and a spotlight thrown on an empty stage. Then she will finally be introduced as "the *late* Marilyn Monroe." It has been Peter Lawford's idea. He delights to play on tricky heights. Sometimes he wins, sometimes not. The *late* Marilyn Monroe comes out in all the champagne thermal of her evening gown, and sings "Happy Birthday, dear President" as it has never been sung before. The twenty thousand guests listen to a sexual electric of magnets and velvets. Her voice is every mischief. Every dead ear in

the house will stir. "She sounds like she knows him awful well!" Kennedy, with a fine grin, disengages himself from so supreme a throb of secret history by remarking in his speech, "I can now retire from politics after having 'Happy Birthday' sung to me by Miss Monroe."

In her good time, Miss Monroe, ready to retire from her present film, returns several days later to the movie set. Officials at Fox are on the edge of firing her, but she has a splurge of activity, as if the core of her delight is to shake male decision once it has firmed. She comes in on the day she has to do a swimming scene, and is in the pool for hours, virus and all, even pushes the premise further, as if some of the Kennedy family's competitiveness has gotten into her, and she will soon teach Hollywood who the center of female world publicity might be. There, with the photographers Larry Schiller and Billy Woodfield present for the magazines, and all of the camera crew, she takes off the flesh-colored bathing suit she has been wearing to simulate nudity, and is naked as she jumps in and out of the pool many times, photographed front and back, for all the world. The look in her eye as we study the stills is triumphant. These are "the first absolutely nude shots of Marilyn Monroe in fourteen years." She is all of a naked five-year-old having the time of her life, and yet is also become a part of the Kennedys—there is hardly a picture she will take after this day in which she does not bear a resemblance to the brothers and sisters of America's most well known Irish family, as if the Hogan in her has found identity in the balance between certainty and daring. Wit, competition, and victory are the alchemical elements of the psyche for which she has searched so long. Never does she look more in command of herself than

in the photograph by Larry Schiller that shows her with one leg hooked over the edge of the pool and the devil of the orphanage in her eye. She is about ready to come out of the water, but who can know what she will do next? The photographs of this swimming party are ready by Tuesday, a syndicated story by Joe Hyams is carefully broken on Wednesday. Every picture magazine in the world now tries to reach Schiller, who (with Marilyn's approval) controls the picture rights. Before he is done negotiating, the photos will appear in thirty countries. Marilyn has asked in her most charming manner for no more recompense than a slide projector by which to look at the color transparencies. She is, in effect, giving a gift of thousands of dollars to the photographers, but then she is once again our female Napoleon back from Elba to raise one last army for a march on Twentieth.

On Friday, June 1, she is given a birthday party on the set—cake, sparklers, candles, flashbulbs, and tears. She laughs at George Cukor for the camera as he is caught with a wedge of cake she has inserted in his mouth, and has a bottle of Dom Perignon with friends in her dressing room. But on Monday she does not come to work. She is under too much strain (as she easily convinces her doctors). On Tuesday she is not there either. That night the movie is suspended; Wednesday the producer is quoted as saying, "There has to be an agonizing reappraisal of the situation." (John Foster Dulles has not used his command of language in vain.) On Thursday night she is fired from the film, and spends the next day locked in her room weeping, while Pat Newcomb sends a statement to *Variety:* "Miss Monroe is ready and eager to go to work on Monday." Later, on Friday, Levathes will announce that she is discharged for "willful violation of contract," and Fox is ready to file suit against her production company "for half a million dollars. We may have to increase that figure to a million."

She is triumphant and crushed. She is a female Napoleon, but only for one pride. The other soul, more timid than ever, is a virus-ridden orphanage mouse. It is as if she has spent her life installing victories in all the psychic furnishings of one personality, while assigning all defeats to the other. So we are at the seat of complexity in such a view of her person. For if she is living with the full equivalent of two people within her, it is equal to saying that she will undertake many an action that benefits one at the cost of the other, and in turn like a frustrated general must retire from the action while her *other* mends. It is why so much of her life consists of stops and starts, and why so many of her affections are replaced by hate. Few are the activities she can perform where both of her selves can participate: it is the harshest irony of her life that this collaboration works best every time she disrupts a movie set, for then everything in her of raw and buried force can enjoy the discomfiture of the company —she is forever marching through Hollywood— yet these massive disruptions, all to the tuneless flute of a lingering virus and a slight fever, are precisely able to employ that other part of herself which is sick, weak, wounded, miserable, stunned, and near to used up. At last such weakness and void is finally employable! It is a method that has worked for years. Now, however, she is in the psychological midnight of being unable to know if she really wished to end the filming, or simply miscalculated what stress the studio could bear. In the weeks ahead, one more of the loveless comedies of her life is played out as studio heads on their side react to the displeasure of stockholders in New York at her irreplaceable loss, while she, swallowing her detestations of the script, is brought by her lawyers to agree that she must go back to the picture in September, when Dean Martin's nightclub tour is over, "in order to reinstate herself as an insurable property for films." What an eternity to contemplate, but she does not have the finances or the desire to go off into litigation.

Commiseration pours in, of course. She is welcomed back to New York by the Strasbergs. She says, "I've got to start thinking about the stage." Quickly they give her an opportunity to do Blanche Du Bois in *Streetcar* for Strasberg's class, and she turns in an electrifying piece of work, so nervous her body is trembling from the effort. When she is done, the seat of her dress is wet. She has urinated upon herself in some whole anguish of the part. It is an incredible and unforgettable performance, but her farewell to theatre. How could she ever do this every night? No, she is not in New York for long before she must rush back to the coast, as if in panic for being away too long from her analyst, back to the walled-in hacienda and swimming pool with one acre on Helena Drive, back to her half-furnished house with its paucity of closets and piles of records sitting in the corners with bales of magazines, cartons of books, all the unshelved collection of a life sitting in the corners. She is back to her analyst, Dr. Greenson, approaching the last couple of weeks of her life, and yet it is as if the ambiguity of her presence will travel with her even into the last romances of her life, the debatable condition of her health, and the mystery of her death. For there were many who thought she was even getting better. She has told her masseur,

Ralph Roberts, that she is finally taking nothing more than a little chloral hydrate: "They've got me back," she says proudly, "to World War I stuff." (Of course, chloral hydrate is just as powerful as any other sleeping pill.) Nonetheless, it is Roberts' impression that she is in better health this last summer than she has been in several years, and her muscle tone is no longer flabby.

The photographs taken by George Barris almost a month after she has been fired by Twentieth are hardly portraits to reveal an abyss. No suicide is contemplated in her eye. Just a sensitive and not unsturdy young woman sits in a sweater at the beach and looks wistful and tough. But then the point to make is that she hardly seems finished. The nude pictures of her swimming have come out on the covers of the world's magazines—she has finally and triumphantly overtaken Elizabeth Taylor's publicity on *Cleopatra!* —and in a spurt of activity over this, will have her *Life* interview with Richard Meryman and a personal meeting with studio heads at Twentieth where they will indicate how much they want her back, and will also sit for a series of photographs with *Vogue*, *Life*, and *Cosmopolitan*, will indeed have her famous nude studies with Bert Stern. As if anticipating the big dinner at Peter Lawford's to honor the Attorney General, she has never looked more like a Kennedy than in Stern's pictures of her drinking champagne.

No, she does not seem ready to kill herself. An underground of Hollywood gossip will wash over the end, and accounts of the witnesses to her last day will not agree. Just as the trail of Jack Kennedy's assassination in Dallas may be lost forever in the tracks of a thousand terrified moves by people who crossed over that trail in fear others were implicated, so too will her death be confused by every current of rumor until it is not possible to decide if she was dead of a suicide by barbiturates (after all the ones that failed), or by the accident of taking, as she had on many another night, more barbiturates than she could carefully count, or whether she was even—thirty-five years late—murdered, murdered again, and if that is the wildest of suppositions, with the feeblest of evidence to support it, there was motive nonetheless for murder and no weak motive.

So one could not dispense altogether with such a thought. Let us try to find our way into the final confusion of her death.

Her time, this last summer, is spent at home around a pool in which she will not swim, although characteristically she is offended if her friends won't go in. There is a guest cottage beyond that pool musty with dog smell. Old friends like Norman Rosten come and visit, and once she goes out with him to a gallery and buys a copy of a Rodin statue of a man and woman in embrace. The man is fierce and the woman compliant. It costs over a thousand dollars, which she cannot necessarily afford, but she buys it in half a minute, pays by check, and takes it with her. Of course that is less common than daily visits to her analyst or staying at home. It is close to an ordered existence. She has other old friends who visit, and takes a host of phone calls in this place. Often she speaks to DiMaggio, and often Pat Newcomb will spend the day with her. At night when she

cannot sleep, Ralph Roberts comes over to give her a massage. Over the years they have become close, as close perhaps as orphans who have come to love one another. Roberts is from a large and poor family in North Carolina and was not able to speak until the age of eleven—how moving must such a detail be to Marilyn. Then an operation freed his tongue from his palate. That childhood infirmity could account for some of his size and physical strength and certainly for his sense of touch as a masseur. It could also account for his sensitivity to Marilyn's thoughts, as well as his earlier determination to be an actor. Yet for two and a half years he has been submerging his own career in order to be on call—Marilyn has such need of him. Often she will phone at 2 A.M. when the pills she is using have failed to work. "I feel terrible, Rafe," she will say, "I'm about to jump out of my skin." He will come therefore in the middle of the night and proceed directly to her bedroom, which is kept absolutely dark. The heavy drapes are always drawn since she cannot sleep with the faintest crack of light, indeed, the drapes are even stapled to the frame. In the blackness of that room, he will locate his bottle of rubbing oil, undo her brassiere (which she puts on every night in compensation for not wearing anything during the day!) and massages her until she is ready for sleep. Sometimes it will take an hour. Then he hooks the brassiere and steals out. They have a psychic communion that is obviously not ordinary. On the first occasion he gave her a massage, back with Miller when she was getting ready for *Let's Make Love,* Roberts, after a half-hour of such work, was off in silent thoughts of Willa Cather. Then Marilyn asked, "Have you ever read *A Lost Lady?*" He was not likely to recover from such connection

between book and author. Since her skin may have been the most delightful he had ever touched, with a rare underskin beneath the skin, or so he would describe it, suspicion of an affair naturally has to arise, and in a hurry, given a man as powerful in appearance as Roberts in a treatment so sensuous as massage. While Miller had civilized faith in the separation of sex and therapy, and was never overtly uneasy, DiMaggio would prove jealous more than once, as if, final physical connection or not, Roberts was still too close to his woman, feeling too much of what might come off her body as love. DiMaggio had an Italian sense of the whole when all is said—if it is mine, it must be all mine! I do not need another man to fix the edges of my work.

By now, we should be able to suspect, however, that Marilyn enjoyed looking on with detachment while her body was manipulated by professionals. Perhaps she was even at her best when her relations were not sexual. No woman could be more charming than she will prove to be with Norman Rosten, and no woman more honest than she is with Roberts, as over the years —they are, after all, but a step away from Reichian analysis—she tells him, as she will tell few others, of what is happening in her life.

If we enter her relation to Ralph Roberts now, two and a half years after it is begun, it is because she asked him one night out of a silence while he was massaging her, "Have you heard the rumors about Bobby and me?"

"Heard them? Why, all Hollywood," Roberts told her, "is talking of nothing else."

"Well, it's not true. I like him, but not physically." Since she has begun to talk, she goes on to say that she loves his mind, yet does not find him as attractive as his brother.

She could, of course, have been lying to Roberts—there is many a rumor to claim her affair with Bobby began in the back seat of a car after they have both stolen out from a party. Still, one has reason to believe her story. If the thousand days of Jack Kennedy might yet be equally famous for its nights, the same cannot be said of Bobby. He was devout, well married, and prudent. If he was also a hard-working young man who might wonder about sexual worlds he had never entered, such wonder was hardly going to weigh in balance against his ambition. His brother had managed miracles of indiscretion, but Bobby had a hard enough attorney's head to recognize that he was vulnerable to scandal. Those who would not dare to attack the presidency could fix upon the younger brother. Besides, his relation to his family seems to be as deep as any public figure's of our time. It may be more comfortable then to assume that merry he might be, and as wistful about Marilyn as a high school boy with forty cents for a fifty-cent sundae split, cherries and banana! but finally his hard Irish nose for the real was going to keep him as celibate as the happiest priest of the county holding hands with five pretty widows.

Still, what a flirtation! He would call her when he came to stay at Peter Lawford's house. She would come to see him. Given the species of house arrest in which she lived, how superb to see him, how absolutely indispensable to her need for a fantasy in which she could begin to believe. ("Don't meet Gertrude Nissen," she would say to Roberts as a standing joke, for he had a crush on Gertrude Nissen.) Now, here at last was a fantasy where the company was sensational. Bobby had a mind she may even have seen as similar to her own mind—no matter his education,

he had, like herself, learned on the job. By getting the biggest jobs.

Of course, she was not only living in the future, but in what she could retain of the past. Guiles, who believes she did have an affair with Bobby, and therefore favors him with an alias, has this interesting passage:

> In late July, when word reached DiMaggio of her interest in the Easterner, they had a bad row. . . . Possibly afraid of permanently losing DiMaggio as her most valued friend, she sat down and wrote him that if she could only succeed in making him happy, she would have succeeded in the biggest and most difficult thing she could ever imagine—that of making *one person completely happy*. She concluded by informing him that his happiness meant her happiness.

The letter, however, was never sent. Discovered in her desk, it was unsigned. The impulse that brought her this close to DiMaggio consumed itself in its own literary expression.

But, then, her life is so quiet at this point. In comparison to the past, it is quiet.

> During the final summer, Marilyn confided to a friend that Dr. Greenson was attempting to make her more independent and less insecure in her opinions. She volunteered this information when asked why she was cutting herself off from several old and trusted friends. Clearly Dr. Greenson was concerned by her reliance upon the judgment of her hirelings. During that summer, the regulars who had been in her employ, along with a few others, found themselves outside Marilyn's inner circle. . . . Ralph Roberts was to feel Mrs. Murray's role in this very keenly, for when he came in the evening to give Marilyn her massage, he found after his services were over that his presence was no longer appreciated. Once, as he was lingering by Marilyn's bedroom door exchanging a word or two as in the old days, Mrs. Murray gave him a look that clearly implied, "I thought we'd gotten rid of them."

The lady is not an insignificant presence:

Mrs. Murray was a family friend of the Greensons, had retired from part-time interior decorating work, and though she had never been a housekeeper before, she was available. Mrs. Murray, who spoke in careful accents, was to keep in constant touch with Dr. Greenson. Marilyn knew of this arrangement, but she was so deeply involved with her attempt at emotional recovery she did not protest.

If we feel uneasy before this whole and jealous appropriation of her life, still we are dealing not even with the essential logic of psychoanalysis: she is so changeable that she is scientifically intolerable. No doctor can follow the results of his prescription. Not with her. So there is a natural tendency to circumscribe her life to that point where fewer people are able to affect the incommensurately sensitive needle of her inner deflection. Fair hope! She may as well be quartered by horses. Her strongest emotions become her most isolated. That she has love for DiMaggio we can hardly doubt by now. Finally, he is the man who wants the least from her—he is without calculation about her talent! He only wants the rest of her. She will do well to discover the rest of her! Perhaps she has never been so divided. Her ambition to make films—that ambition which has beat like an animal heart beneath every weakness since she first came to Fox sixteen years ago—is an ambition now cautioned by a council of lawyers. Installed upon an analyst's couch, she has been reduced to the smallest pieces of her person, and yet may be on the edge of the most important affair of her life. It is as if the ambition which is dying on one stage has sprung to life on another. In some part of herself she has to be calculating a new life that will be grander than she has known. Where that might offer hope, it will also

accelerate her terror. She will be further away from any comfortable sense of a modest identity on which to attach a few self-protecting habits. No, that modest identity, that sense of a comfortable middle in her own body, can only come now from the bitter taste of barbiturate. The recognition of defeat in the bite of the capsule becomes her middle.

If the law of passion is that we cannot begin to love again until we find a love greater than the last, the law of narcissism must be that we cannot continue to adore ourselves unless our display is more extraordinary than before. So, even as she clings to DiMaggio on one flank, she is dreaming of historical eminence on the other. Yet she is still interested in adventures up the center. A clue to the unfinished state of everything about her is that even on the last day of her life she discusses the *Playboy* contract she is supposed to sign when Larry Schiller comes by to visit. It has been arranged for her to do a camera session with Schiller to provide the necessary pictures. She will appear on the front cover of *Playboy*, respectably dressed in a white fur stole. On the back cover, however, will be seen a shot taken at the same instant from the rear. With the exception of the fur stole (which only passes around the nape of her neck), she will have, from this second angle, nothing on. She will finally show that famous set of cheeks which, as Philippe Halsman once remarked, "seemed to wink at the onlooker." Of course he had also said, "to capture this wink with a [still] camera . . . is not so easy." Perhaps she has had similar thoughts; perhaps Dr. Greenson has dissuaded her (if we are to assume she has told him). In any case, Pat Newcomb has already phoned Hugh Hefner to cancel the sitting, but since Schiller has not yet heard, Marilyn does not bring herself to confess this publicity dream has been filed, and instead squanders a good amount of her morning's energy being animated. It is typical of one more minor episode in her day that will cost her as much as a major transaction, but otherwise it is like many another noon in that quiet almost humdrum summer (if not for the occasional evening at Lawford's) in the weeks after *Something's Got to Give*.

The shock is that she will be dead in hardly more than twelve hours. Or will it be in less? The autopsy will prove casual, and never determines the hour of her death. It could be as early as nine o'clock that night or as late as three in the morning, and the bottle from which she takes her final pills is never determined, since the specific drug is never analyzed in her autopsy. Still, enough barbiturates will be discovered in her blood to kill her several times over if she took the pills on an empty stomach. On the other hand, if she ate that night, the dose could not prove fatal until she digested the food, for the autopsy showed her stomach and intestines are completely empty. The hour of her death is therefore not insignificant. If she was no longer alive by midnight, every account which has her going to dinner is obviously a lie. Her intestines could not have digested the first part of her food so quickly, even if she had regurgitated most of the meal. Only a stomach pump could have left her so empty. But then only a doctor could have administered the pump, an act which no doctor reports. The possibility that she was dead for hours while attempts were made to resuscitate her has to be prominent.

Besides, there are several versions of her dinner. One, given by a reporter who would not allow his name to be used, offers a quiet party at Marilyn's house which is attended by Peter Lawford, Bobby, Pat Newcomb, and Mrs. Murray. After dinner, the others want to go on to Lawford's place on the beach, but Marilyn wishes to stay where she is and then wants Bobby to stay with her. He refuses and leaves. A little later Marilyn begins to call, and keeps phoning him.

Another version places Natalie Wood and Warren Beatty in a party at Lawford's house in Malibu which Marilyn proceeds to leave. What is common to both stories is that nothing remarkable is happening. If she had been alive in the morning, there would be little interest in the night. One way or another, she seems to have had some disagreement with Kennedy. Whatever was the dimension of her quarrel, it was apparently sufficient to start taking pills. If she then calls Lawford's house several times, we do not begin to guess what abuse or importunings took place. It is after all just as likely she made every effort to be gay, at least until the last call.

In its turn, Guiles' version, which may be here no more than a compendium of the lies he was told, has Marilyn alone that night, and agitated by a phone call from Malibu, where she is invited to join Lawford, Kennedy, and, by Marilyn's description, "a couple of hookers." Much offended, she goes early to her bedroom, where Mrs. Murray reports her resting for a period and trying to sleep while a stack of Sinatra records are played. Then comes a time when she must have felt a warning she had taken too many pills. She begins to make calls. It is almost certain she tried to reach Ralph Roberts, for his answering service would later report that a call came in "from a woman who sounded fuzzy-voiced

and troubled." Guiles has it that "she did get through to" the Easterner or his friend,

and she told one of the men that she had just taken the last of her Nembutals and she was about to slip over the line. One of them attempted to phone Mickey Rudin, Marilyn's Hollywood attorney, but he was out for the evening. Why such indirect means of summoning help were chosen will never be known.

Of course, the means is not so indirect. Mickey Rudin, who is also Sinatra's lawyer, is as well Dr. Greenson's brother-in-law, and it is possible they are looking to discover Greenson's number. What seems to agree in all accounts is that they are far from complacent at this point. If they have been laughing at Marilyn earlier in the evening, or been made uneasy by a hint of desperation or threat in the manner, her last phone call has been to say goodbye. Whoever was on the phone with her has now heard the unmistakable entropy of a sleeping pill stupor, that thickening whistle of death around each lurch of the voice, that moronic halting urgency which is shocking to whoever will hear it. What the two men did in response (since it is almost certainly too late) may be less interesting than what they were to do in the next few days. If Marilyn was a suicide, however, it is possible that the doctors were reached earlier than they declared and were working on her with that stomach pump. In any case, whether in contact with Marilyn's house or not, this won't prove the Easterner's most shining hour. He will next appear in San Francisco with his family after a Marine helicopter puts down at the pad next to Lawford's house on Sunday morning. Of course, what other high government official would not have done precisely the same? What we can expect from all the stories is that if efforts were being made to protect Bobby Kennedy, none of the versions can afford to be accurate. Some were obviously shaped in isolation from others. It is unlikely Dr. Greenson and Pat Newcomb, for example, had an opportunity to exchange notes, since each places himself alone with Marilyn in the early evening. It is probably such discrepancies that would later feed rumors of murder. For example, Mrs. Murray reported that when Marilyn's door was found locked at three in the morning (although Marilyn's door was always locked), she went outside to the garden after hearing no reply to her knocks and peered through the drapes of Marilyn's bedroom window. From there she claimed to have seen Marilyn lying across the bed in a "peculiar" position, and proceeded to call Dr. Greenson to come over. One wonders why a psychiatric assistant did not proceed to break the window herself, but instead was content to wait for the doctor. Then there is a discrepancy whether Dr. Greenson arrived first, which is Mrs. Murray's version, or whether it was Dr. Engelberg, the internist, who had at Marilyn's request changed her prescription from chloral hydrate to Nembutal just the day before. The police report has Dr. Engelberg using a fireplace poker on the window to "gain admittance." Finally, we are asked to suppose Marilyn's drapes were sufficiently open for Mrs. Murray to look in, when they were stapled down ever since Marilyn occupied the house. An assumption has to arise that Mrs. Murray discovered the death in other fashion. Since Marilyn was found in the nude and yet without a brassiere, it is also not impossible she was in bed with a lover when she died, a most

unhappy thought. Equally, she could have gone into some final coma while trying to get dressed to go out, and later have been undressed by others on the assumption it would look more natural. Nor are one's questions reduced by the fact that Mrs. Murray will go off on a six-month tour of Europe in the next few days, and Pat Newcomb, who is naturally hysterical in the aftermath, will be flown to Hyannisport. Then the FBI—we are face to face once again with a story whose author does not choose to give his name—is reported to go into the Santa Monica phone company's office in the next day and remove the paper tape that lists Marilyn's toll calls for the night. Perhaps that is why for many a year rumor will have Marilyn dialing the White House on her last night. Brood long enough on the terror of such an end in vertigo and frustration, and one can believe she left with a curse and lives near us still—First Lady of American ghosts. Why then not also see her in these endlessly facile connections of the occult as giving a witch's turn to the wheel at Chappaquiddick? Yes, it is easy in the echo of her poor death across that bed in the cement-brick room of a Brentwood hacienda to see the beginning of many a vow and many a career. For if it is true of Bobby Kennedy that his presence developed with every year, and he was not without greatness by his last night, why not also assume that part of so fine and mysterious a process was not only commenced in the hour of his brother's death but in the reckoning he took of himself on the escape from Los Angeles in the dead morning hours after Marilyn was gone.

Yet if we are to grant her this much effect upon the development of one American hero, why not assume even more and see her death as the seed of assassinations to follow. For who is the first to be certain it was of no interest to the CIA, or to the FBI, or to the Mafia, and half the secret police of the world, that the brother of the President was reputed to be having an affair with a movie star who had once been married to a playwright denied a passport for "supporting Communist movements." While even the FBI would hardly be so imaginative as to cast Marilyn in the mold from which Mata Hari is made, they did not need to keep a tight surveillance upon her for any better reason than to keep surveillance upon the Kennedys. The question to propose, if we are ready to think the FBI did remove the Santa Monica telephone company's tape, is, *which* wing of the FBI? Are they protecting the reputation of the Kennedys, or amassing evidence against them? And is there some fear in the summits of the CIA that the President himself—it is not long after the Bay of Pigs—is the willing or unwitting leader of a movement from the left that will wash at the roots of America? If such a suspicion is much too grand, one can still suppose that the head of the FBI was interested in obtaining a few more pieces of information to trade against the time he might be asked to reduce his power. Do we have to decide it is altogether impossible that in years to come Bobby Kennedy might feel his power to criticize the official investigations of his brother's death would have to wait until the hour he was back in the White House? If Marilyn was the spirit of mischief—"Happy Birthday, dear President"—that spirit may have reached into the machines of history. By the end, political stakes were riding on her life, and even more on her death. If she could be murdered in such a way as to appear a suicide in despair at the turn of

her love, what a point of pressure could be maintained afterward against the Kennedys. So one may be entitled to speak of a motive for murder. Of course, it is another matter to find that evidence exists.

There seems next to nothing of such evidence, and we have all the counterproof of Marilyn's instability, and all the real likelihood that she had taken too many barbiturates and was labored over for hours by frantic medicos trying to save her life, which certainly accounts more simply for many of the curious discrepancies. (They might well, for instance, have removed her brassiere in order to give artificial respiration. As simply, to hide the gap in time, Mrs. Murray could have indulged in window-breaking and drape-pulling.) Of course, it is also possible a stomach pump was used to remove evidence of what did kill her. Yet to press further upon the small likelihood of murder is to stand in danger of a worse loss. In all this discussion of the details of her dying, we have lost the pain of her death. Marilyn is gone. She has slipped away from us over the edge of the horizon of the last pill. No force from outside, nor any pain, has finally proved stronger than her power to weigh down upon herself. If she has possibly been strangled once, then suffocated again in the life of the orphanage, and lived to be stifled by the studio and choked by the rages of marriage, she has kept in reaction a total control over her life, which is perhaps to say that she chooses to be in control of her death, and out there somewhere in the attractions of that eternity she has heard singing in her ears from childhood, she takes the leap to leave the pain of one deadened soul for the hope of life in another, she says goodbye to that world she conquered and could not use.

We will never know if that is how she went. She could as easily have blundered past the last border, blubbering in the last corner of her heart, and no voice she knew to reply. She came to us in all her mother's doubt, and leaves in mystery.

The police will soon arrive. One of the cops knows Jim Dougherty and phones to give the news. Dougherty looks at his wife—it is four in the morning, they have been married for sixteen years, and Marilyn as a subject of conversation is altogether taboo. Now Dougherty says, "Say a prayer for Norma Jean. She's dead."

Across Los Angeles, Ralph Roberts wakes up at 3 A.M. with the unendurable impression that Marilyn is gone. A girl is sleeping beside him. Roberts has attempted to speak to Marilyn that afternoon, and Greenson has answered the phone. Trying to quiet himself out of the intolerable sense of displacement Greenson has given to his relation with Marilyn, Roberts has gone out drinking that night, has picked up the girl, taken her home, and finally gone to sleep beside her. Now he is in the unbearable condition of finding himself obsessed by the presence of one woman while lying next to another, and the pain of this hour may be engraved forever on his psyche since there is almost never a night that passes in the next ten years when he does not awaken again at three in the morning.

DiMaggio will take care of the funeral, and invites no Sinatras, no Lawfords, no Kennedys. Lee Strasberg will give the eulogy:

Others were as physically beautiful as she was, but there was obviously something more in her, something that people saw and recognized in her performances and with which they identified. She had a luminous quality—a combination of wistfulness, radiance, yearning—that set her apart and yet made everyone wish to be part of it, to share in the childish naïveté which was at once so shy and yet so vibrant.

Arthur Miller will not come. He will give his eulogy in *After the Fall*. It will prove one more misery to Miller, for he will be accused of cheapening her image. Miller's only crime is to have failed to have foreseen that no production can offer the presence of Marilyn. If she had been alive, it might have been her greatest role and Miller's greatest play, for in the pain of that relation, he had come his own distance from the man who puffed on his pipe while looking as monumental as the master of all Meerschaum.

Now she is dead, and how do we say goodbye?

In that happy summer of 1955, when she was first going with Miller and the future might even be sweet, she was sitting once on the beach with Norman Rosten when teen-agers in premature appreciation of films by Bergman not yet made came up to surround her,

first in wide circles around our party, then moving in closer, and finally about fifty worshipers converged on the umbrella under which she demurely sat.

"Hey, Marilyn, I saw all your movies!"

"You're my favorite!"

245

"You look terrific!"

"Marilyn, let me kiss you!"

She shook their hands. They brought stones for her to autograph. The boys circled her tightly, the girls screamed, and a kind of panic set in. They reached for her with wild little cries, touching her, uttering pleas, begging favors while she laughed, fended them off. . . . Finally, the only escape was the water, and with an apprehensive wave, she started swimming. With a barrage of cheers, fifty tanned young bodies plunged in after her and gave chase. . . .

"Hey," she called to me faintly, "get me out of here!"

I managed to plow through to her side, shouting at the kids, "Beat it, get moving, go on home!" I struck at them blindly, furiously, and seizing her by the arm, started swimming out into deeper water. I threatened the hardier ones who followed. They watched, grinning, as we plodded on.

Suddenly Marilyn stopped. "I can't swim any more," she pleaded.

"What do you mean, you can't?"

"I'm not a good swimmer even when I'm good," she said. . . .

She was breathing hard, her chin just above water. "Listen," I said. "Can you float? Try it. Take a deep breath, and lean back."

She tried, but swallowed water and began to cough. I circled her, puffing a bit, and attempted to get her to lie back on the water. "Boy, what a way to go!" she gasped, clutching me. . . .

How else would we be saved if not by a Hollywood ending? The roar of a motorboat on the sound track. Real boat on wide-screen water. This crew-cut kid snaked up alongside, idled the motor. We both grabbed the side. I climbed into the boat, and there was the problem of hauling M. over the side. She . . . was not then or had she ever been a thin slip of a girl. I finally pulled her up, and she fell heavily into the boat.

I looked at her as she lay exhausted, her legs curled up, her pink toes gleaming in the sun. The boy pilot also regarded her . . . forgetting the wheel and executing two tight circles before I realized what was happening. I shouted at him, and she said, "Don't be nervous. It's a wonderful weekend!"

Yes. Maybe it was more wonderful than Rosten knew. For if she had begun to find a little happiness with Miller, she must with her natural fear of happiness have also been living in fear of some unnamed disaster to come. Now it seemed to have come, and she was still alive. She was going to remain alive and happy until Mr. Dread was at the door again. Once, across the years, she sent Rosten a postcard with a color photograph of an American Airlines jet in the sky, and on the back, in the space for message, she put down, "Guess where I am? Love, Marilyn."

Rosten wrote: "I have my own idea but am keeping quiet about it." Let us not hope for heaven so quickly. Let her be rather in one place and not scattered in pieces across the firmament; let us hope her mighty soul and the mouse of her little one are both recovering their proportions in some fair and gracious home, and she will soon return to us from retirement. It is the devil of her humor and the curse of our land that she will come back speaking Chinese. Goodbye Norma Jean. Au revoir Marilyn. When you happen on Bobby and Jack, give the wink. And if there's a wish, pay your visit to Mr. Dickens. For he, like many another literary man, is bound to adore you, fatherless child.

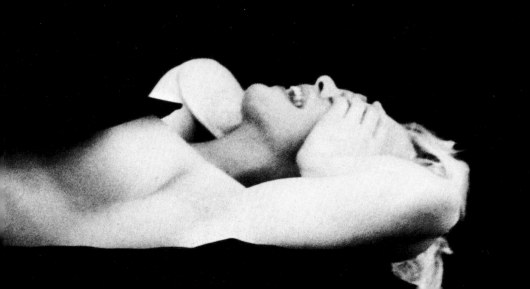

AN ACKNOWLEDGMENT

The writer contracted for a preface and discovered after reading Fred Lawrence Guiles' book *Norma Jean* that he wished to do a biography. The wish came, however, almost too late. In a polluted and nihilistic world, one clings to professionalism, so the work was done with the private injunction to finish a text in the allotted time, even though the preface crept up to forty thousand, fifty-five thousand, seventy, and finally ninety thousand words. It is a biography now, a *novel* biography as described, indeed a species of novel, for a formal biography can probably not be written in less than two years since it can take that long to collect the facts—princes have to be wooed, and close friends of the subject disabused of paranoia. For a work done in greater haste, one does better to claim that no new errors of fact have been willingly introduced, and that other than recapitulating the errors of former writers, one has also brought along a few of their investigations. So, once again, it is right to make acknowledgment to Maurice Zolotow for the bright pictures he paints in *Marilyn Monroe* (Harcourt Brace, 1960) when he is at his best, and to Fred Lawrence Guiles for the thousands of details his work, *Norma Jean* (McGraw-Hill, 1969) provides. Indeed, the facts of this book have been based in the main on his book. Obviously, one must think Guiles is accurate for the most part (a few small errors have been discovered), but indeed one has to hope so—our own chronology rests on his. Acknowledgment of a greater order is, however, certainly due. For one could never have undertaken this biography if *Norma Jean* did not exist, and any reader who has become interested in Monroe's life on the basis of reading my book is well advised to go next, and with considerable reward, to Guiles' devoted study. Hundreds of episodes and interesting details await him.

Some other books need hardly be mentioned. Ben Hecht's opus printed weekly in the *Empire News* of London from May 9 to August 1, 1954, caters to British journalism at its worst, and that is equal to making sauce flambé for decayed fish. Yet these pieces offer insight to future students of Monroe, since she has had to provide Hecht with some of the flavor of those flaming factoids, and so gives us an insight into herself at her worst. (A warden of spiritual economy could even claim that the intake of her sleeping pills may have been a material counterweight to the poisons of publicity she had helped to promote.)

Books by Sidney Skolsky, *Marilyn* (New York, 1954), by Pete Martin, *Will Acting Spoil Marilyn Monroe* (New York, 1956), and by Joe Franklin and Laurie Palmer, *The Marilyn Monroe Story* (New York, 1953), were out of print or not available, and therefore never used. *The Story of The Misfits* by James Goode (Bobbs-Merrill, 1963) had exhaustive minutiae on details of making the film, but a paucity of insight. Edward Charles Wagenknecht's anthology, *Marilyn, A Composite View* (Chilton Book Co., 1969) proved a uxorious selection perhaps too much devoted to her image to serve it (although the quotation from Diana Trilling was found in those pages). A comprehensive listing of all of Marilyn's films with photographs, cast lists, credits, reviews, and an introduction by Mark Harris is found in *The Films of Marilyn Monroe*, edited by Michael Conway and Mark Ricci with a tribute by Lee Strasberg (Citadel Press, 1964). It is a useful and amusing book. Then *Marilyn, The Tragic Venus*, by Edwin P. Hoyt (Duell, Sloan & Pearce, 1965) was discovered only after this text was locked in page proofs. That work would have provided a few interesting lights on what proves to be, according to Hoyt, a bona fide affair with Joe Schenck. (This is lately and obliquely confirmed by a story an agent told Larry Schiller. George Seaton, then a young producer wishing to interview Marilyn for a possible bit in a film—the year is 1947—asked her to come see him at three o'clock. Marilyn said, "I can't come to your office at three o'clock because every day at three o'clock I go to Mr. Schenck's office. But don't worry, I'm always done with Mr. Schenck by three twenty. I'll be at your office at three twenty.") Since Hoyt interviewed many publicity people in the middle echelons of several studios, *The*

Tragic Venus also offers considerable, if insubstantial, material on her long affair with Frank Sinatra, which was given little emphasis in my work, but would certainly have been developed further if the material had been then available. (Indeed, gossip in favor of Sinatra went so far as to suggest Marilyn played at having an affair with Bobby Kennedy in order to make Sinatra jealous—for he was then engaged to Juliet Prowse.) Other gossip, however, would suggest that Marilyn and Sinatra merely found each other useful, even helpful, for each other's careers, and so delighted in going out together, and receiving publicity together.

Finally, there is a book *Marilyn—An Untold Story* by Norman Rosten, which will be published by New American Library about the time this work appears, and one awaits it with real interest. The fine and intimate accounts of Marilyn as a house guest, and Marilyn near drowning, have been taken from a few pages of *An Untold Story* which were seen in manuscript.

Another source, offered through the generosity of Pat Newcomb, was the opportunity to hear Marilyn talking casually on tape, no small bonus.

There were interviews in modest depth with Miss Newcomb, Elia Kazan, Eli Wallach, Lee Strasberg, Arthur Miller, Milton and Amy Greene, André de Dienes, Hedda and Norman Rosten, Marjorie Stengel, Ralph Roberts, Gardner Cowles, and a phone conversation with Jim Dougherty to verify the accuracy of Guiles' account of his marriage to Marilyn. (Dougherty was much impressed with that accuracy.) There were also conversations with people who wished to remain anonymous. That another fifty interviews could have been undertaken in Hollywood with profit is indisputable, but the pressure of time made such a trip impossible. Besides, it was the author's prejudice that a study of Marilyn's movies might offer more penetration into her early working years in film than a series of interviews with movie people who had considered her something of a joke while alive and now in compensation

August, 1962

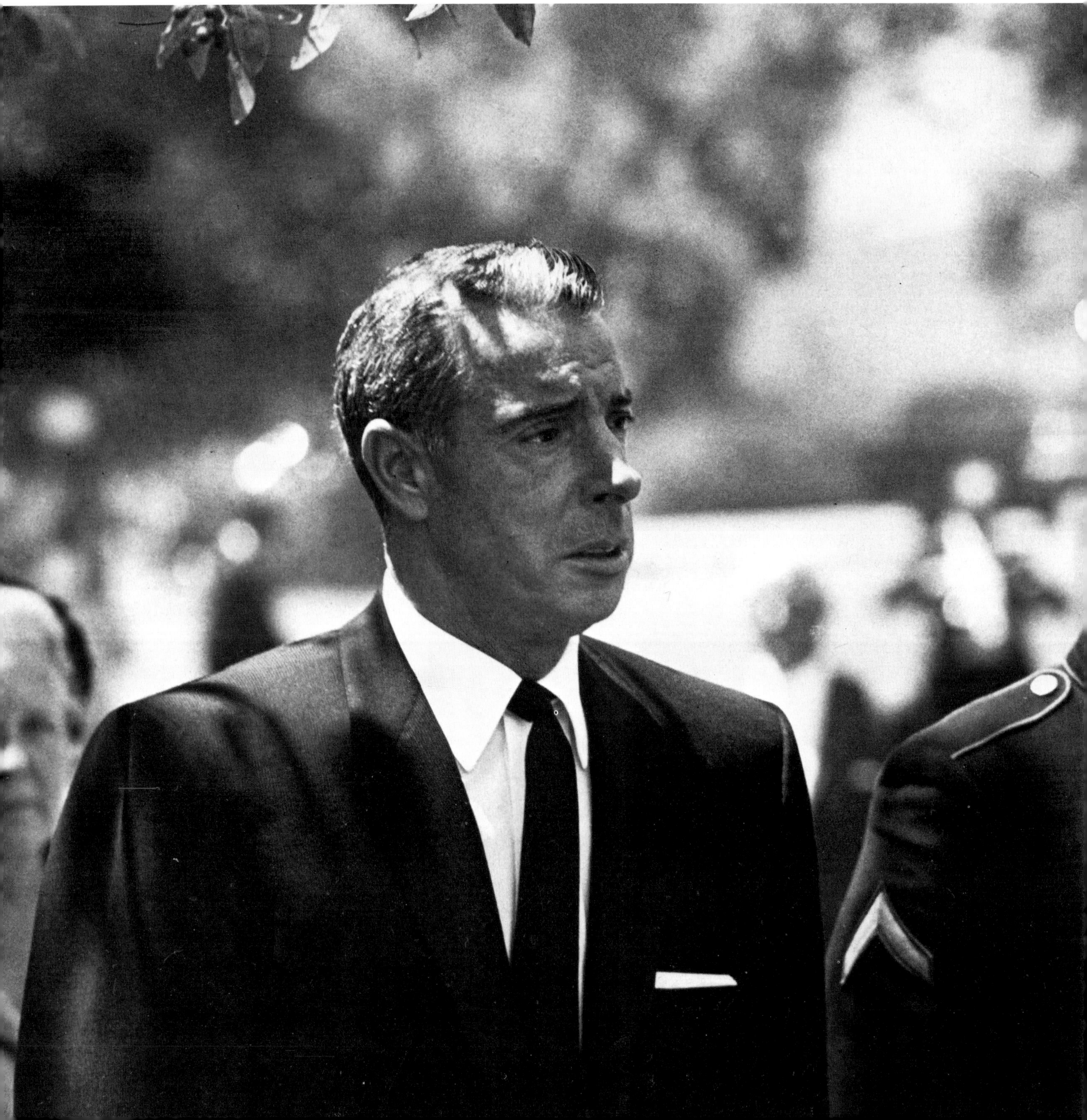

might be pious. So thanks may be offered instead to Harold Lager of Twentieth Century-Fox, Elizabeth Marchese of Metro-Goldwyn-Mayer, Michael Mindlin of Warner Brothers, Jason Squire and David Chasman of United Artists, Stanley Schneider of Columbia Pictures, Douglas Patterson of Films, Inc., and Judith Riven of Grosset & Dunlap for their cooperation in making available twenty-four of her thirty films. It is the author's hope that under these chosen circumstances he has been able to give a portrait of Marilyn which is reasonable in its proportions, and interesting in its estimations, even if it can hardly be depended upon to have contributed much original material to the facts.

One would also acknowledge the pleasure of working editorially with Robert Markel, Nancy Brooks, and Larry Schiller.

Still another work, brought to my attention by Gary Null, must certainly be described. It is *The Strange Death of Marilyn Monroe*, by Frank A. Capell, and was published in 1964 by the Herald of Freedom, a right-wing press. Its thesis is that Marilyn was murdered. Once again, this book was discovered after one's own was finished. It is interesting that its thesis on murder proved to be the opposite of the one presented here, for *The Strange Death* proceeds to suggest that Marilyn was killed by a Communist conspiracy of agents expressly because she had threatened Bobby Kennedy with exposure. The corollary is that the Attorney General was secretly, even publicly, sympathetic (in 1962!) to left-wing groups. According to Capell, Dr. Greenson and Mrs. Murray were fellow travelers, and Dr. Engelberg had been a member of the Party. It is, of course, a considerable metamorphosis to go from being a man or a woman with left-wing attachments to an agent capable of a job of murder for the more advanced echelons of the Soviet secret police—which is exactly the surrealistic apocalypse to which Capell's thesis leads—but his short book is nonetheless valuable on two counts. He traces most of the discrepancies of the discovery of Marilyn's body to a point where further investigation can continue, and also gives a full if unconscious

261

portrait of how sinister a figure Bobby Kennedy must have appeared to ultra-conservative groups. On reflection, that may serve to bolster one's own argument that there was much motive for the right wing of the FBI or the CIA to implicate Bobby Kennedy in a scandal. And if one is looking for a tool in such a right-wing conspiracy, who indeed could be more vulnerable, and therefore more subject to severe pressure, than a Communist or former Communist who has been under an investigative eye for years. The execution of the Rosenbergs still weighed in full horror over any American Communist who had cause to wonder whether some errands he had done for the Party in the past were altogether free of implication. But, then, if we are not careful, a new round of speculation can begin—and this is merely an acknowledgment. Perhaps one must finally acknowledge that all of this work has brought us to the point where we can recognize that a corner of biography is no more simple to put into perspective than a warp in the matrix of lost space–time. If every human is a mystery, then perhaps we can obtain our only gleam of the truth in the relations we find between mysteries. Let us then take our estimate of her worth by the grief on Joe DiMaggio's face the day of that dread funeral in Westwood west of Hollywood.

Index to the Photographs

The photographers wish to thank the following individuals and organizations for their help in contributing to this work:

Mr. Mike Lorimer of Loeb & Loeb for his continued help throughout this project.

Mr. David Stuart of the David Stuart Gallery for first showing the photographs with the aid of Mr. John Bryson and Mr. Jet Fore.

Hecht Custom Lab of Los Angeles for producing the black and white prints.

Robert Crandall & Associates of New York City for fine duplication of the original color photographs.

The printers Case-Hoyt of Rochester, New York.

Special appreciation is given to Mr. Allen Hurlburt's assistant, Mr. William Rosivach, for his art production assistance.

Mr. Bruce Crabb for his personal care in handling the negatives of each of the photographer's work.

Mr. Gerald Rosencrantz and Mr. Will Hopkins for their assistance on the project not directly related to the book.

A personal thanks to Susan Rubenstein, who coordinated so much so well.

Mr. Irving Ross of Grosset & Dunlap for so faithfully supervising the production of the book.

ATOLSON
50 W. North
Tom 3:11
$5.25
Gicus